W9-ABF-866

Thunder Rumbling at My Heels
Tracing Ingeborg Bachmann

Studies in Austrian Literature, Culture, and Thought

Thunder Rumbling at My Heels
Tracing Ingeborg Bachmann

Edited and with an Introduction

by

Gudrun Brokoph-Mauch

ARIADNE PRESS
Riverside, California

Ariadne Press would like to express its appreciation to the Austrian Cultural Institute, New York for assistance in publishing this book.

Library of Congress Cataloging-in-Publication Data

Thunder rumbling at my heels : tracing Ingeborg Bachmann / edited and w
an introduction by Gudrun Brokoph-Mauch.
        p.   cm. -- (Studies in Austrian literature, culture, a
thought)
    Includes bibliographical references and index.
    ISBN 1-57241-043-4
1. Bachmann, Ingeborg (1926-1973)--Criticism and interpretation.
I. Brokoph-Mauch, Gudrun. II. Series
PT2603.A147Z925   1998
838'.91409--dc21
                                 97-13187
                                 CIP

Cover design:
Art Director and Designer: George McGinnis
Photograph: Courtesy Barbara Klemm

Copyright ©1998
by Ariadne Press
270 Goins Court
Riverside, CA 92507

CONTENTS

Gudrun Brokoph-Mauch 1
Introduction

Gerhard Austin 3
Malina
Ingeborg Bachmann's Text, Elfriede Jelinek's Filmbook,
and Werner Schroeter's Film

Robert von Dassanowsky 24
The Role of Austria Will Be Played by...
Ingeborg Bachmann's *Requiem for Fanny Goldmann*
as Sociopolitical Allegory

Sabine I. Gölz 42
The Ruins of an Illusion. Intertextuality and
the Limits of Friendship in Bachmann's
Die Zikaden (The Cicadas)

Geoffrey C. Howes 60
"Flying Blind": A Neglected Early Essay by Bachmann

Linda C. Hsu. 76
"A Favorite Selection at the Beauty Parlor?"
Re-reading Ingeborg Bachmann's *Oh Happy Eyes*

Manfred Jurgensen 91
The Intellect of Love: Female Thought and Presence
in the Poetry of Ingeborg Bachmann

Kirsten A. Krick 105
Ingeborg Bachmann's *Death Styles*:
A Narrative Historiography of Fascism and the Holocaust

Gudrun Brokoph-Mauch 123
Ingeborg Bachmann's Flight from Song:
The Radio Play *Die Zikaden* (The Cicadas)

Reingard Nethersole 139
Ingeborg Bachmann's Poetry: A Sense of Passing.

Ingrid Stipa 161
Female Subjectivity and the Repression of the
Feminine in Ingeborg Bachmann's *Malina*.

Amy Kepple Strawser 179
The Development and Ultimate Cessation of Ingeborg
Bachmann's Lyric Voice

Kathleen Thorpe 188
"Monuments looking out upon Utopia":
The Thirtieth Year by Ingeborg Bachmann —
a Reading.

Bibliography of Cited Works 207

Index 217

Introduction

With the recent translation of Ingeborg Bachmann's work into the English language her writing has become accessible to readers of limited or no German-speaking ability. Thus it is now possible to introduce the literary work of this important Austrian writer to the classrooms and reading lists of English and Comparative Literature departments at universities in English-speaking countries. This volume of essays written in English by scholars residing in English-speaking countries has been originated in the spirit of supporting and expediting this expansion of her works out of the confines of German Literature departments of these countries into a larger readership. Since it has been the philosophy of Ariadne Press from the beginning to act as the intermediary between Austrian literature and the American reader, student and scholar, it appeared to be the most appropriate publisher for this project.

The voices in this volume analyzing Bachmann's work are from the USA, Australia and South Africa. For the regrettable absence of the UK I have to refer you to the recent publication of the London Symposium, *Kritische Wege der Landnahme*, unfortunately written in German. Pioneering in the area of bringing scholarship into the English-speaking classroom is only one mission of this book. The other is the continuation of the work of the Symposium at Saranac Lake, New York, 1991, published in the volume *Ingeborg Bachmann, Neue Richtungen in der Forschung.* It is a continuation as well of the aforementioned London Symposium, namely in pursuing new directions in Bachmann research for the nineteen-nineties.

It is therefore appropriate to present a volume that covers a wide range of elements and aspects of her work. Two essays present fresh insights into her short prose writing from the volumes *Simultan* and *The Thirtieth Year*, two others are devoted to much neglected works, the radio play *The Cicadas* (coming out in

English soon at Ariadne Press) and her early essays. Two contributions examine Bachmann's cycle *Death Styles* from the perspective of a socio-political allegory or metaphor. The novel *Malina* receives attention from two aspects. One relates to Bachmann's theoretical writings in the *Frankfurter Vorlesungen*, while the other explores once more the relationship between text and film, but offering a different perspective from previous research on this topic. Not surprisingly and very appropriately after the recent translation and collection of Bachmann's poetry in the volume *Songs of Flight*, the essays on her lyrics make up the lion's share in this volume. The essays examine the development of her lyrical voice, the recurring and persistent topic of passage, as well as the feminine presence and voice.

Ingeborg Bachmann has finally been accepted in her homeland, twenty-three years after her death. During my recent visit to Vienna I could attend three different performances of her work within one week: The *Literaturhaus* showed the film version of her novel *Malina* as well as a sound/picture collage production of Bachmann interviews and readings from *Three Paths to the Lake* at the occasion of Robert Pichl's presentation of the *Todesarten* project (*Death Styles*), the Burgtheater performed a composite collage of *Malina* and her poetry, and the WUK staged the prose fragment *Gier* in a provocative multimedia production. It is unlikely that Bachmannn's writing will ever achieve this kind of popularity in other countries, just as the work of the recently deceased and much performed Austrian writer Thomas Bernhard will never achieve the same recognition in a foreign language and culture, regardless of how much attention and praise the respective authors receive from scholarly enclaves. This realization, however, should not discourage our efforts to carry Bachmann's voice to a wider audience in our host countries, a mission often neglected by scholars of German literature. This volume intends to support such an undertaking.

I would like to thank St. Lawrence University for its grant in support of the project and give special thanks to Dale Lally, Director of the Carnegie Language Center at SLU, for his patient and dedicated work on the technical aspects of the publication of this book.

Gudrun Brokoph-Mauch

Malina
Ingeborg Bachmann's Text, Elfriede Jelinek's Filmbook, and Werner Schroeter's Film

Gerhard Austin

When it appeared in 1971, Bachmann's book achieved a re-markable success among discriminating readers in the German-speaking countries in spite of the uncompromising nature of its composition. It demanded an unusual devotion from its readers, who would be hard-pressed to understand the ramifications of the narrative. Trying to visualize how, in the end, the main character simply disappears in a crack in the wall of her own apartment did not lead to unequivocal answers about the nature of the characters. The basic emotional response based on an identification with the *I (Ich)*, the nameless Frau, was, however, not diminished by the intellectual disappointment experienced by those readers who would remain mystified by the author's intentional disorientation of the reader.

Werner Schroeter's film enjoyed a comparable success, although the cinema audience would be even more disoriented, especially those who had not read the book. Again, the emotional response overcame any disappointment about a director who refused to allow an easy access to the events represented in his film. To be sure, the audience was divided in its response. Ute

Seiderer, who has granted us a most precious tool for our scholarly discussions, a second-by-second account of film sequences and the actual film dialogue, a post-shooting-script, attended public performances ten times. She observed that a large part of the audience viewed the film with growing resentment, with some visitors leaving indignantly, whereas others allowed themselves to be emotionally overwhelmed by the events. Primarily women would leave the cinema with tears in their eyes, admitting that they had not understood everything but that they had been deeply moved.[1]

Notwithstanding the controversial reviews of the film critics, the public approval of judges on film panels yielded one award after another in 1991, immediately after the release of the film: The Bavarian Film Award as best film; the German Film Award; Film Ribbon in Gold for the best film, Film Ribbon in Gold for Isabelle Huppert as best actress, and for a third time Film Ribbon in Gold for Werner Schroeter as best film director.

What kind of a film is capable of winning all these awards? The cover of the videocassette, which was produced in a limited edition of 5000, explains to the potential viewer:

> In this unusual triangular story, a woman in Vienna lives together with a man called Malina. The woman meets Ivan and surrenders herself to him. He will be her last great passion. The exclusiveness of this woman's love is so great that it cannot be understood or answered. The film is about nothing else but love. It shows the loneliness of the one who loves.

In addition to this embarrassingly misleading abstract, the German original uses the phrase "the loneliness of one who loves" (die Einsamkeit dessen, der liebt), nonchalantly ignoring the sex of the woman. Only a direct quote reminds us of the woman's essential experience: "I lived in Ivan and I die in Malina."[2]

Reclams Filmführer, the German standard handbook on international film, does not attempt more seriously to do justice to the events in the film. Again we encounter the catch phrase of a triangular story, and the woman is reduced to a "helpless" person.

Supposedly, she is "helpless because dreadful experiences (or delusions?) separate her from her childhood, because the affection of two men is not enough to support her."[3]

Perhaps the two preceding statements only demonstrate the hesitation of editors and critics to deal with Bachmann's approach, whose essence, as he understands it, Schroeter transports into visual images. Maybe they show the negligence of people who have many other things to do and who will not take the time necessary for an understanding of Bachmann which takes into account the evidence of the text and of her personal statements. What is amazing, however, is the outright sloppiness reflected by the author, whose film book was to mediate between Bachmann and Schroeter when she writes about Bachmann and *Malina*. Although we cannot expect too many kind words spoken about men by Elfriede Jelinek, it seems fair to expect that she would honor and respect Ingeborg Bachmann enough to refrain from using *Malina* and other works as a quarry from which to extract certain excerpts that can be used for an anti-male diatribe under the title "War with other means." We wonder whether Jelinek realizes to what extent she diminishes Bachmann's achievement in *Malina* when she characterizes the two male figures in this way: "The two men, Ivan and Malina . . . two master-stags *[Platzhirsche],* each in his preserve, need not even perceive one another while they are crushing the woman between them."[4]

Do I have to apologize to Frau Jelinek for criticizing her? I do not think so. Having seen her respond to questions and (cautious) criticism in televised interviews, I rather tend to imagine (if we had a chance to meet) a joking sarcastic reaction, intimating that she does not need to take into account whatever else the literary scholars know about Ingeborg Bachmann. Would I try to insist (like Galilei in Brecht's famous scene with the astronomers) that she look through our telescopes? I believe not, because she is protected by the privilege of the ingenious author whom we will rarely blame for being carried away by a metaphor such as, in this case, *Platzhirsche.*

We, the more pedestrian investigators, are held responsible and so we cannot but observe that, at least for Malina, the term *Platz-hirsch* simply does not make sense. The sexual implications do not exist in Bachmann's text as far as Malina is concerned. Jelinek uses Bachmann for the purpose of condemning men and the male-dominated world once again. When a line of thought develops its own dynamics, she does not ask what speaks against her theses in Bachmann's work. The male character Trotta in *Drei Wege zum See (Three Paths to the Lake)*[5] is mentioned,[6] but Jelinek disregards his fate: Although a growing loss of confidence in his own existence leads to his suicide, one of the contributing causes lies in the attitude of the female character Elisabeth towards him. It is an attitude vaguely comparable to Ivan's attitude toward the Frau in *Malina*: a constant gesture of rejection which keeps the partner at a distance in spite of moments of surface harmony. Jelinek is certainly not the only one who utilizes Bachmann for feminist purposes.

> With disbelief and amazement I responded whenever, in recent years, Ingeborg Bachmann's works were seen, again and again, as testimony of a specifically female behavior towards the world and life – even with more amazement and disbelief when it was even called the beginning of a feminist attitude.

Barbara Völker-Hezel wrote this a short time before her death in 1982 in her article "Neither the Realm of the Men nor the Realm of the Women. Ingeborg Bachmann's View of the Whole Disaster:[7] "

> Quoting Bachmann's most significant statements on men and women and referring to male and female characters in her prose works, she observes that we can once and again recognize "those dimensions which transcend the realm of the men and the realm of the women."[8]

The misleading term "triangular story" may be acceptable to viewers of the film who do not notice the numerous signals that Schroeter has included hinting at a different status of Malina's existence as compared to Ivan's. One of the most obvious ones is the manner of Malina's appearance and disappearance. Whereas Ivan's comings and goings can be explained in terms of daily life, Malina emerges and vanishes suddenly, sometimes from and into a smooth black background, lacking any indication of belonging to our visually perceivable world.

In Sq 2 (0:05:36)[9] Malina and the Frau stand in front of an (almost) black and white background divided vertically in the middle. Malina leafs through the newspaper while talking with her. A passing car covers the whole screen for about one second and Malina is gone. In real time he would not even have had the time to fold up the newspaper. The dialogue, which is a key to their relationship, continues uninterrupted, however, while she is already entering her apartment alone. She says to Malina: "You have always existed in my life, at least your space in myself. On the other hand, I am always absent. When I sit down and want to write something, I become painfully conscious that I am absent. It is as if I am not there." The dialogue ends with two Slovenian sentences spoken so fast and with so little emphasis that even a Slovenian viewer might miss them: After she has entered the hall of her apartment, she says, her mouth not moving: "Jaz inti!" ("I am you!") and, in the same matter-of-fact tone, his voice responds: "In ti in jaz." ("You are I.")[10]

In Elfriede Jelinek's filmbook, this dialogue (Scene 2) is spoken while they saunter "affectionately" through the Beatrixgasse. It does not end with the visual message that the dialogue takes place in the mind of the Frau but with one of the repeated scenes in which she almost runs into a car. This time Malina holds her back "affectionately."[11] This "affectionately", which occurs here in reference to Malina for the third time on the last four pages, indicates (as her *Platzhirsch* characterization) that Jelinek sees Malina as a separate person who has psychologically definable feelings for the Frau.

Schroeter reaches out beyond Jelinek and appears to take his cue directly from Bachmann. In an interview of April 9, 1971, she said: "As far as I am concerned, it is not necessary for the reader to understand immediately what Malina and I [the Frau] are, that they are basically the same person."[12] Five days later, she speaks about Malina as the Frau's *"Doppelgänger,"* her "Alter ego": "The book is, of course, much more complicated [than the love-story advertisement of the publisher], first of all because of the I-person who narrates . . . who is a woman and simultaneously a man." She finds it quite acceptable that the reader is mystified in the beginning about the relationship between the two. "In any case it becomes more and more obvious that he is the objective, and thus the thinking, male part, and she the female part of this *Doppelgänger.*"[13]

Even if Bachmann's unequivocal statement had not been published, the text alone makes it abundantly clear that we are not dealing with two separate persons. Defending the two-person thesis would mean ignoring all utterances such as the I-am-you/You-are-I exchange of words between the Frau and Malina. On the very first page the characterization of Malina makes little sense if we interpret the statement, "As a disguise he has assumed the status of a Class A Civil Servant employed in the Austrian Army Museum,"[14] as having something to do with the secret service. Instead, his presence in the museum is related to the Malina/Frau person's interest in the phenomenon of war, be it the declared war whose artifacts are exhibited in the Army Museum or the hidden war among people who cover up their aggression under a blanket of publicly acceptable behavior.

The disguise becomes comprehensible if we understand that Malina's bourgeois existence covers up the essence of his being: He is the embodiment of what causes rational thinking in a person, and since rational thinking has, traditionally and in Bachmann's personal experience, been associated with men, she assigns a male body to him, a body that, because of its cognitive origin discloses no sexual desires. From the creation of mythological personifications to the personifications of the powers of Good and Evil in science fiction stories, it has always been considered legitimate for poets and writers to transfer into the realm of our senses those invisible entities we may otherwise refer to abstractly. Dialogues that make little sense if we read them as communication between separate people become accessible if they are seen as interior monologues in which one person evaluates her experiences from two opposing viewpoints.

This was recognized in the very first reviews of 1971.[15] Hans Mayer, who wrote one of the many positive reviews of *Malina*, talks about Malina as the *Doppelgänger*, just as Bachman herself did, and of a "double ego" with a female and a male part. He connects Malina's existence directly with the author:

> Ingeborg Bachman has not given up her basic substance. Cautiously but in pursuit of a plan, she widens her circles. First, there was the form of the poem, however, even at that time Malina had appeared; he wrote the philosophical essays of Ingeborg Bachmann.[16]

In spite of a large number of positive reviews such as Mayer's, the myth of a *Malina* rejection by the critics refuses to die. There is, of course, Reich-Ranicki's notorious, frequently quoted "evil verdict" but is it really "typical for the attitude of the male reviewers" as Sigrid Löffler reiterates as late as 1995 in her review of Bachmann's *"Todesarten"-Projekt*?[17] If we consult the fifty-eight pages of *Malina* reviews in Schardt's anthology (cf. endnote 15), we find that clearly more than fifty percent are appreciative of Bachmann's achievement. The negative reviews are at times rather pathetic, especially when the criticism is reduced to a complaint about the difficulty of Bachmann's text. In no way does the gender of a reviewer allow us to predict his/her verdict. As a matter of fact, the most scathing and sarcastic review was written by Sibylle Wirsing for *Neue Deutsche Hefte*, whereas Karl Krolow's carefully phrased praise has nothing in common with Reich-Ranicki's condemnation. Interestingly enough, neither Koschel/Weidenbaum nor Schardt were permitted to reprint Reich-Ranicki's review.

Such an approach as Bachmann's projection of the forces of emotion and reason in a woman's mind into two discernible entities is reminiscent of Hofmannsthal's. In his dramas, libretti and prose works, he tends to project complicated phenomena into rather simple structures as, for instance, in the libretto *Die Frau ohne Schatten*. In his novel fragment, *Andreas oder die Vereinigten*, his procedure is strikingly similar to that of Bachmann's. In this novel Andreas is fascinated by two beautiful women of whom one, Maria, attracts him primarily through the beauty of her spirit and her knowledge, whereas the other one, Mariquita, enchants him through her body and her emotional appeal. The readers will soon discover that Maria and Mariquita are two personae existing in the same individual. Mariquita behaves like a distant relative of the Frau when she decides that nothing will stop her from reaching Andreas. She climbs a wall and tears the skin of her fingers so that blood drips on Andreas when she looks at him from above.[18] Hofmannsthal projects Maria/Mariquita's dual modes of being into what appears to Andreas first as two individuals. He limits himself, however, to the empirically researched phenomenon of schizophrenia as presented by Morton Prince in *The Dissociation of Personality*.

Ingeborg Bachmann goes one decisive step further. She provides her readers with all the necessary signals so that Malina and the Frau will be recognized as projections from the inner world of one person. When it comes to visualizing them, any reader will imagine them as being in two distinct bodies. To complicate matters, each of the two distinct entities develops separate dynamics which can no longer be explained psychologically. In the novel, Malina and the Frau are embodied as two separate beings who, to be sure, verbalize either directly that they are one or else hint at the source of their existence in one individual.

If we wish to respect the intentions of the author, we should not forget that we see before us, in the concrete images of Malina and the Frau, the battles that threaten to tear one person's mind apart. In view of this constellation, some of the questions that have been hotly debated become almost irrelevant. Several reviewers, be they male or female, find the Frau to be too hysterical for their taste. If we accept the thesis that this demanding text works, to some extent, like a scientific experiment, we will notice that the notion of hysteria cannot be applied. We are dealing with a literary figure whose essence lacks some of the elements that are integral to an individual.

Considering the genesis of Malina, I would tend to compare Bachmann to a scientist who discovers a puzzling substance (the female person who is also herself). She tries to determine the significant compounds (properties, attitudes, skills that can be grouped under the conventional names female and male) and after she has isolated them (female Frau versus male Malina), she tests their behavior, hoping that the observations may yield some insights into some aspects of the original substance.

If we try to think these things through (consciously ignoring recent theoretical debates which have been both enlightening and thoroughly confusing) we may find that, at different moments, we may either be able to derive reliable conclusions from the text or be forced to admit that we cannot go beyond vague feelings which a certain scene may have provoked. Such feelings, however, must be abandoned if a film director transfers a book into his medium. In view of the nature of the two central figures, one might suppose that a *Malina* film is simply not possible. A whirlpool of thoughts and feelings within one individual is projected into two literary beings whose effective polarization clarifies the disparity within. We are led through a text embedded in an environment of constant transitions.

How could Malina and the Frau endure the limitations of two actors' personifications? The director's task is fundamentally different from creating a film derived from, for instance, the Bachmann story *Eyes to Wonder (Ihr glücklichen Augen.)*[19] In this case, the director Margareta Heinrich had to transfer the story into the medium of television, a procedure through which everything remains within the framework of our everyday world. The director of *Malina*, however, was required to chart new territory. Schroeter's previous works seemed to have predestined him for tackling this awesome assignment. Through his films, he was renowned for disdaining traditional plots. Allowing fantastic images and unexplained gestures to meld with classical and contemporary music, Schroeter featured mysterious events, in which beauty and love, sex and violence are paramount.

I myself do not purport to be a Beckmesser, censuring any deviation from Bachmann's book or Jelinek's filmbook. Comparisons are certainly not useless; to their surprise, undergraduate readers often discover for the first time how much more a book can offer them. But faithfulness to the text can prevent a film director from creating a true work of art because it ties him down to the ground rules of the literary medium. It is more important that the director transfers those few presentable aspects of the book into about 120 minutes of film. This medium's great potential lies in the fact that it makes visual and acoustic phenomena directly accessible to our senses. In Germany it has become a matter of course that a stage or film director dealing with literature will be called to task if he merely produces a close-reading presentation. Of course, it becomes problematical if the production intentionally annihilates the spirit of the original text.

Since we cannot review the whole film with its dense visual and acoustic material within a few pages, the beginning and the end will be discussed in more detail in order to show Schroeter's approach. From the beginning, Schroeter makes it clear that the psychological categories of daily life will not suffice for this film. Even before the acknowledgments, a violent scene of less than two minutes (1:55) introduces the theme of war and mystifies the viewer.

On a roof garden at night, in whose background looms the dark shade of a huge flak tower (the bombing war is picked up acoustically when explosions intermingle with the atonal sounds of the violins), the father figure hits the Frau hard in the face yelling at her: "You feel you are something better, hey? Who do you think you are?"[20] He throws flower pots at her and then tries to push her over the railing. When he does not succeed, he grabs a little girl, whom we will meet repeatedly in the film as the Frau's childhood personification. A moment later, we see her from below falling towards the pavement. Then we realize that our perspective has been identical with that of the Frau who is standing and looking down at the spot where the child should have hit the ground. Instead, we hear another flowerpot break and, a split-second later, we see, next to it, a man lying apparently dead on the pavement. His face, drenched with blood, almost touches the legs of another man, whose face appears next. It is Malina addressing the Frau: "Your father almost hit me. This comes from him up there! You'll come with me now or we won't see one another ever again." She answers that she can't go along ("not now") because she wants to try a last time to calm the father down. Malina's response: "We'll see one another only after this has ended. He wanted to kill me!" All of a sudden, a police car halts and Malina explains that this is merely a boisterous family gathering, whereupon the police depart.

The Frau, suddenly alone, is lying on the pavement, her cheek resting in the blood on the dead man's face, and she speaks: "How have I come here? In whose power? It must not be a strange man. It must not be in vain, must not have been a fraud. It must not be true." This introductory scene of barely 115 seconds is fraught with implications. The corresponding scene in Jelinek's *Filmbuch* is Nr. 83 (of a total of 123) and is only one of the series of dream scenes. Schroeter uses it to get some of his most important messages across in the very beginning. The father figure is seen as the true threat not only to the Frau but also to Malina, who insists on an either-or between the father figure and himself. Thus Schroeter rejects from the very beginning any primitive division of Bachmann's world into the good female versus the evil male figures. The true antagonism exists between the violent ones (a woman will shoot and kill the girl in a later dream scene) and those who are seeking non-violence.

The dead man on the pavement is actually not a strange man. His face is Ivan's but this face, being bloated, resembles the father's, indicating that Ivan has certain properties in common with the father. At the same time, Malina's "He wanted to kill me!" points in two directions. Syntactically, it refers to the father but the tableau shows the dead Ivan figure and thus includes him in the pronoun *he*. Schroeter insists that we have to think in transitions, that he wants us to intertwine thought patterns usually kept distinct.

The attempt of our pragmatic reality to interfere is brushed aside. Against all expectations involving a police patrol's encounter with a dead man on the pavement, the officers leave without having asked a single question. Throughout the remainder of the film, one could interpret the injections of reality as mere props needed to narrate the story of two major forces in an individual which have gained independent life.

That Malina is not a real-life person is emphasized again and again. We have already referred to Sequence 2 and Malina's disappearance. In the apartment we do not see him walk away into his room but into a black background that could not be part of realistically presented living-quarters. In this respect Schroeter deviates from Jelinek who assigns personal emotions to *Malina*, thereby following Bachmann. Jelinek suggests, for instance, that Malina gloats *("schadenfroh")* when he refuses to help move the furniture (Scene 39). In the film he states calmly, as a matter of fact: "I am not a man!" (Sq 27, 0:41:09) In realistic terms this does not make sense; in reference to the genesis of the Malina figure, it is another of Schroeter's messages that may disorient the uninitiated while simultaneously informing those viewers who are familiar with the book. Malina is, in truth, not a man with a male body but the embodiment of the Frau's male/rational part of her mind.

Significantly, Malina's existence reaches beyond the book and the film and is part of Bachmann's autobiography as an artist. In the interview of April 9, 1971, she mentions that the book and this central figure had been on her mind as early as in her lyrical phase. She had known that this central figure would be male and that she was able to narrate only "from a male position." Not to renounce her "female I," yet to emphasize the "male I" had been for her like finding her own person.[21]

Schroeter's ingenious introduction to the film and his carefully controlled presentation of Malina as a male figure but not a regular man, indicate the manner in which he deals with the book and the filmbook, a truly legitimate approach of a director who respects Bachmann more than some radical feminists do. Fortunately, there is a sufficient number of women and men in the profession who will dismiss as irrelevant an outbreak of anger against Schroeter as Alice Schwarzer has published in *Die Zeit* and in *Emma* in 1991.[22] It was an embarrassment that one of her major assaults on Schroeter was caused by an unfortunate and serious error of translation of Jelinek's text into French for Isabelle Huppert. The original sentence, "Es war meine erste Erfahrung mit dem Schmerz und mit der Freude eines anderen . . . zu schlagen . . ."[23] was incorrectly translated into French; nobody caught the mistake when the French was dubbed into German: "Es war meine erste Erfahrung mit dem Schmerz und mit der Freude daran."[24] "It was my first experience with pain and with the pleasure of another. . . to beat . . ." versus ". . . experience with pain and the pleasure of it."

Schwarzer is carried away by her anger until she finally insinuates that Ingeborg Bachmann was sexually abused by her father. Ulrike Frenkel commented later in the *Stuttgarter Zeitung* that Schwarzer's innuendo is comparable to "the assertion that Franz Kafka was magically transformed into a beetle just because he wrote *The Metamorphosis*."[25]

Assaulting Schroeter is usually correlated with assaulting all men including Malina. Debating the correctness or incorrectness of certain assertions becomes sadly difficult when we can no longer trust quotes. Kathleen Komar breaks off a quotation in the middle of a sentence the moment it no longer fits into her line of thought. The Frau complains that she has been falsified: "Am Ende war ich eine einzige Fälschung . . ." (In the end I was one single falsification . . .)[26] Here the quote ends, without the original comma, because the continuation does not fit: "kenntlich darunter vielleicht nur noch für dich" ("underneath which I remained recognizable probably only to you").[27] In other words, the male figure represents the sole hope for the Frau to have her true nature recognized and validated. No wonder that Komar calls the film "a cruel travesty of Bachmann's novel," a verdict that becomes possible only because, interpreting the novel, she suppresses important evidence. She is the one who ignores Bachmann's statements, whereas Schroeter transfers them into his medium. Komar complains that Schroeter does not make "Malina's repressive and negative function" clear enough,[28] but Bachmann herself emphasizes the enormous significance of the Malina figure, even beyond the novel and for herself. Schroeter heeds Bachmann, especially her interview on April 9, 1971.[29]

It is simply absurd to conclude from one of Schroeter's sentences, in which he expresses his intention to keep "whimpering" (*"das Gejammer"*) out of the film version, that he "views the female subject's plight as simply 'Gejammer.'"[30] On the contrary, he wants to take her plight seriously. The one thing he does not wish to produce is maudlin kitsch. Isabelle Huppert concurs and drives Schroeter's argument[31] further: "I want to be responsible for my destruction myself. To be my own victim is more powerful and feminist than to assume that I am the victim of society or the victim of men."[32]

Kathleen Komar is supported by Kurt Bartsch when she sees the woman presented as "fragile, dependent, hysterical" and refers to the "film woman's hysteria."[33] Bartsch sees her presented, "from the first moment on, as a hysterical, neurotic, hectic and chaotic person, with masochistic tendencies shown later . . . in one word, she is (psychically) ill."[34] The "hysteria" thesis can be traced through a number of *Malina* film and book reviews. The reference to hysteria as a mental illness presupposes, of course, that we think of the Frau more in terms of an individual than of her appearance in a work of art. Since we think of the figures in the book/film anyway in terms of transitions between various conditions of being, this is doubtlessly acceptable. But even if I do accept this approach, I still disagree with the diagnosis. I could never see hysteria in the Frau, even after consecutive viewings of the film, because Isabelle Huppert's face prevented me from doing so. There is an enormous intensity and alertness in this face, and no fragility whatsoever in spite of the tears. The Frau seems to know exactly what she is doing and what she is feeling; she observes keenly what is happening to herself and is consciously running her experiment: She has decided to test whether a purely emotional state of being can prevail. I feel reminded of Sigrun Leonhard's perception of the Frau in the novel. According to her, the Frau is "anything but a woman loving sentimentally and caught in her private sphere, she is, at all times, exposed to her extreme perception of reality which she knows how to confront only by constructing her own anti-world." The interview with Mühlbauer demonstrates, "in addition to her verbal and intellectual brilliance as a writer, a considerable aggressiveness."[35]

We now approach a point at which verbal explanations ought to be complemented by a discussion within the context of the cinematic medium and its various visual and aural gestures. We can quote from the novel but we cannot (yet) quote from film. By focusing on a face and its various expressions, for instance, we might find more common ground than appears possible today. I venture to assert that major adjustments of verdicts quickly formulated after one viewing of the film would be revised if we could be locked away for a week, having nothing at our disposal but Bachmann's novel, Jelinek's filmbook, Schroeter's film (as well as Seiderer's postscript) and a representative selection of contradictory reviews and scholarly articles.

A more serious impediment overshadows our attempt to be scholarly and objective. We have experienced a similar problem in Holocaust discussions. Can we ask an Auschwitz survivor to be objective when she or he talks about the Germans? Objectivity is possible, as Ruth Klüger has demonstrated,[36] but nobody can *expect* a survivor to be objective. Can we then expect a rape survivor or someone close to her to be objective about men? Probably not, although objectivity may be achievable. In any case, hidden under the traditional form of our scholarly writing, there are very personal elements that influence perceptions and conclusions but that are protected by our conventional (and partially necessary) professional taboos.

To move the question out of the context of felonies: Women and men who have never enjoyed sex will respond differently to *Malina* than people for whom sex has been an enjoyable part of

their lives. We also react differently – and this has driven reviewers in different directions – to the individual actors, according
to certain undefined feelings. I was, for instance, so fascinated with
Isabelle Huppert at the first viewing and even more so with each
additional viewing that I cannot possibly understand why Kathleen
Komar writes: "In the film we only pity the female character, we
have no sympathy with her – whether 'we' are male or female."[37]

At this point, the scholarly debate ends. It could, however, be
continued by viewing and discussing the film, sequence by
sequence, at an extended workshop. We could then determine
which disagreements are due to lack of information or oversights
and which disagreements, in the end, would prevail. This again
could be considered scholarship in pursuit of the modest notion of
pragmatic truth (of which even a Wittgenstein would approve).
This note of hope will not make us forget the deeper level
addressed in Ingeborg Bachmann's dictum: "The real problems one
experiences in a different manner, they cannot be discussed at
conferences and congresses."[38]

One point of contention would be Schroeter's fire magic at the
end of the film. I remember that I distinctly resented it when I saw
it for the first time. I felt that Wagner-like reminiscences were
inappropriate to *Malina*. The more I became accustomed to it, the
more I was influenced by different associations from Goethe's
praise of the living that yearn for its death in flames in the poem
Selige Sehnsucht to Trakl's "hot flame of the spirit" which is
nourished by the agony of the warriors in his battle requiem, the
poem *Grodek*; not to mention biblical images of the Spirit appear-
ing in flames or Bachmann's own fire imagery throughout her writings. In her poem *My Bird* the lines: "when I am ablaze at night,/a
dark grove begins to crackle/and I strike the sparks from my body,"
lead to the signal of hope: "When I remain as I am, ablaze,/loved
by the fire ... that watch tower moves into the light ..." It is the
tower to which her "bird of belief," her "bird of trust" flies
"calmly, in splendid quiet."[39]

Fascinated by the fire imagery, Schroeter has the final events
take place in an ocean of cold flames until the Frau is swallowed

up, disappearing into mirrors that fill the screen. I cannot see the last scenes as having anything to do with hysteria. Since I truly believe that any artist deserves not only the benefit of the doubt, but also our honest, unbiased effort to understand him or her, I experience the tour de force of the final scenes as a kind of *Totentanz*, a *danse macabre*. Through these final scenes, Schroeter and Huppert express desperation over the conclusion of an ambitious experiment which leads to the annihilation of the beautiful being who tried to exist unfettered by control through our rational faculties.

The Frau joins the long list of others who have made similar attempts. I commemorate the young miller in the *Schöne Müllerin*, who retreats not into the crack in the wall but into the water. Was he "murdered" by the miller's daughter? I commemorate Werther who does not listen to his Malina, whose Ivan is named Charlotte and who shoots himself with the pistol delivered by Charlotte. And let us not forget those actual human beings of similar tragic fate, Hölderlin, who retreats from the world, or Günderode and Kleist, who kill themselves.

Does it matter that the majority of those I named, all of them cherished by Bachmann, were men? Hopefully not. For all of them, whether female or male, the words Kleist wrote before his death remain true: "The truth is that, on earth, I could not be helped."[40]

Their story has been told. And thus Schroeter takes his cue for the final sequence from Bachmann herself, even while deviating from Bachmann's book and Jelinek's filmbook. He shows the Frau becoming almost one with Malina, then being multiplied between mirrors, merging with the flames (of the Spirit?) and entering not a crack in the wall but the wall of books, as if Bachmann's *Werke* had been waiting for her ever since Ivan had looked at them disapprovingly in the beginning (Sq 8, 0:14:23). Malina stays behind, calm, a meditative, somewhat sad expression on his face. He picks up a few papers, then a book or notebook from the bookshelf, and leaves the apartment. Ingeborg Bachman on April 9, 1971: "Malina will be able to narrate what the other part of his person, the I, has left to him."[41]

Notes

Roman numerals for the volume plus arabic numbers for the page will refer to: Ingeborg Bachmann, *Werke*, eds. Christine Koschel, Inge von Weidenbaum, Clemens Münster (München, Zürich: Piper, 1978).

1. Ute Seiderer, *Film als Psychogramm: Bewußtseinsräume und Vorstellungsbilder in Werner Schroeters Malina* (München: dis-kursfilm Verlag Schaudig & Ledig, 1994) 19, footnotes 17 and 114. Seiderer counts 73 sequences and assigns them to 40 days. Her work makes more exact quotations possible than referring to the numbers of the video player. (Thanks to Peter Beicken, who gave me his copy of this most valuable book.)

2. *Malina* (München: Kuchenreuther Filmproduktion GmbH; Wien: Neue Studio Film GmbH, 1990. Artwork and Design: RCA/Columbia Pictures International Video, 1991). Transl. EA (This abbreviation indicates that the translation is by Elizabeth Austin).

3. Dieter Krusche, *Reclams Filmführer* (Stuttgart: Philipp Reclam jun., 1993) 740. Transl. EA.

4. Christine Koschel und Inge von Weidenbaum, eds. *Kein objektives Urteil - nur ein lebendiges* (München: Piper, 1989) 314. Transl. EA. Also in: Michael Matthias Schardt in cooperation with Heike Kretschmer: *Über Ingeborg Bachmann: Rezensionen – Porträts-Würdigungen* (1952-1992) (Paderborn: Igel, 1994) 411.

5. Ingeborg Bachmann, *Three Paths to the Lake, Stories,* transl. Mary Fran Gilbert, introd. Mark Anderson (New York/London: Holmes & Meier, 1989) 117-212.

6. Koschel/Weidenbaum, *Urteil* 318.

7. Koschel/Weidenbaum, *Urteil* 231. Transl. EA. The title includes a quote from the main character Charlotte's thoughts in *Ein Schritt nach Gomorrah*: "Das Reich erhoffen. Nicht das Reich der Männer und nicht das der Weiber." (II, 212) The translation poses two problems. "Reich" = "empire" is introduced a little earlier (II, 208) with an allusion to the Lord's Prayer: "Ihr Reich würde kommen" which would require in English: "Her kingdom

would come. "Unfortunately, kingdom implies that a man would rule, a notion which Charlotte definitely rejects. Cf. also Ingeborg Bachmann, *The Thirtieth Year,* transl. by Michael Bullock (New York: Holmes & Meier, 1987) 126 and 130. Secondly, *Weiber,* which often carries derogatory connotations, loses these in translation. It is difficult to explain why Bachmann uses the word *Weiber,* instead of the word *Frauen.* At any rate she is consistent. Although she turns from men as preferred major characters to women in her later prose works, she continues to apply the same critical stance towards men and women alike.

8. Koschel/Weidenbaum, *Urteil* 244. Transl. EA.

9. Deeply indebted to Ute Seiderer's *Film als Psychogramm/ Malina,* I will quote scenes and dialogue excerpts in reference to her *Sequenzprotokoll* (147-162) and her *Dialogliste* (163-226) by indicating: Sq = Sequence plus time of the beginning of the sequence.

10. Seiderer, *Film als Psychogramm/Malina* 166f.

11. Elfriede Jelinek, *Malina: Ein Filmbuch von Elfriede Jelinek nach dem Roman von Ingeborg Bachmann* (Frankfurt am Main: Suhrkamp, 1991) 11f. The numerous film photos in the book do not correspond to the sequence in the film.

12. Ingeborg Bachmann, *Wir müssen wahre Sätze finden: Gespräche und Interviews,* ed. by Christine Koschel und Inge von Weidenbaum (München, Zürich: Piper, 1983/91) 100.

13. Bachmann, *Wahre Sätze* 101f.

14. Ingeborg Bachmann, *Malina,* transl. Philip Boehm with an afterword by Mark Anderson (New York/London, 1990) 1.

15. The most influential reviews have been made easily accessible by Koschel/Weidenbaum and Schardt/Kretschmer.

16. Koschel/Weidenbaum, *Urteil* 164f.

17. Sigrid Löffler, "Undine kehrt zurück," *Der Spiegel* 46 (1995) 244. It is regrettable that Löffler, appropriating the *Spiegel* style of sarcastic aloofness, reinforces the polarization of male versus female. We can sympathize with her because we see her often humiliated by Reich-Ranicki in the immensely popular television program *Das Literarische Quartett.* But this does not

redeem statements such as: "*Undine leaves* – and condemned men. Her male community of adorers has never forgiven her for that" (244). Undine resents women as much as men in the famous farewell speech *Undine leaves*. And today one may reject, but cannot ignore, Bachmann's dictum: "Undine is not a woman, not even a living creature, but, as Büchner says, 'art, alas, art.' And the author, in this case I, is to be sought on the other side, that is, among those who are named Hans." Transl. EA. / "Die Undine ist keine Frau, auch kein Lebewesen, sondern, um es mit Büchner zu sagen, 'die Kunst, ach die Kunst.' Und der Autor, in dem Fall ich, ist auf der anderen Seite zu suchen, also unter denen, die Hans genannt werden." Koschel/Weidenbaum, *Wahre Sätze* 46 (Interview on November 5, 1964).

18. Hugo von Hofmannsthal, *Andreas oder die Vereinigten* (Frankfurt: Fischer Bücherei, 1961) 70f.

19. Bachmann, *Three Paths to the Lake*, 75-94. Original text: II, 354-372.

20. Quotes from the introductory scene: Seiderer, *Malina*, 164 (Vorspann, 0:00:05) Transl. EA.

21. Bachmann, *Wahre Sätze* 99f.

22. Schardt/Kretschmer, *Über Ingeborg Bachmann* 415-420.

23. Jelinek, *Malina* 75.

24. Seiderer, *Malina* 194.

25. Schardt/Kretschmer, *Über Ingeborg Bachmann* 421.

26. Kathleen Komar, "The Murder of Ingeborg Bachmann," *Modern Austrian Literature* 27, 2 (1994) 95.

27. Bachmann, *Malina*, transl. Boehm, 197. Original text: III 297.

28. Komar, *Modern Austrian Literature* 104.

29. Bachmann, *Wahre Sätze* 95-100.

30. Komar, *Modern Austrian Literature* 105.

31. In an interview with Stefan Grissemann, Schroeter is quoted: "I respect the fantasies and the trauma of Ingeborg Bachmann and also the trauma of Elfriede Jelinek. However, my own I must also respect. Inside myself, I revolt against this image of the man, I see men completely differently." That he is a homosexual

adds another dimension. He also talks about some friction between himself and Isabelle Huppert, "because she is not haunted by these torments of the soul. That's why I wanted her. On the one hand she is my exact opposite, on the other a mirror: She has at her disposal a high degree of sensibility and steeliness. This steeliness I share with her. Therefore working on the film is a great pleasure." *Die Presse*, 8/9 September, 1990. Schardt/Kretschmer, *Über Ingeborg Bachmann*, 399.

32. Schardt/Kretschmer, *Über Ingeborg Bachmann* 408.

33. Komar, *Modern Austrian Literature* 103f.

34. Kurt Bartsch, "'Mord' oder Selbstvernichtung? Zu Werner Schroeters filmischer *Malina*-Interpretation," John Patillo-Hess & Wilhelm Petrasch, *Ingeborg Bachmann: Die Schwarzkunst der Worte* (Wien: Verein Volksbildungshaus Wiener Urania, [1993]) 88. Transl. EA.

35. Sigrun D. Leonhard, "Doppelte Spaltung: Zur Problematik des Ich in Ingeborg Bachmanns *Malina*," Gudrun Brokoph-Mauch & Annette Daigger, eds. *Ingeborg Bachmann. Neue Richtungen in der Forschung? Internationales Kolloquium, Saranac Lake, 6-9 Juni 1991* (St. Ingbert: Röhrich, 1995) 149. Transl. EA.

36. Ruth Klüger, *Weiter leben: Eine Jugend* (Göttingen: Wallstein, 1992) und *Katastrophen: Über deutsche Literatur* (Göttingen: Wallstein, 1994).

37. Komar, *Modern Austrian Literature* 105.

38. Bachmann, *Wahre Sätze*, 66. Interview of May 29, 1969.

39. Peter Filkins, transl. *Songs in Flight: The Collected Poems of Ingeborg Bachmann* (New York: Marsilio, 1994) 139-41.

40. Heinrich von Kleist, *Briefe 1805-1811, Lebenstafel, Personenregister* (München: DTV, 1964) 133.

41. Bachmann, *Wahre Sätze* 96.

The Role of Austria Will Be Played by... Ingeborg Bachmann's *Requiem for Fanny Goldmann* as Sociopolitical A llegory

Robert von Dassanowsky

Much analysis of Ingeborg Bachmann's work has been centered on a psychological and feminist understanding of her characters and topics. However, for an author who has so often written about Austrian consciousness and identity, it is surprising that scholarship has only recently turned to the historical and sociopolitical critique that may be found in her fiction. Short stories such as *Youth in an Austrian Town (Jugend in einer österreichischen Stadt)* and *Among Murderers & Lunatics (Unter Mördern und Irren)* have always attracted inspection of Bachmann's particular view of Austrian political development in this century, but even this has been subordinated to questions of psychology. Specific attention has been paid to issues pertaining to ego, alienation, childhood trauma, gender roles and patriarchal oppression. A more historically aware critique arrived with Sara Lennox's essay on *Franza's Case (Der Fall Franza)*,[1] but it is Lisa de Serbine-Bahrawy's recent book-length examination of Bachmann's work, *The Voice of History*,[2] that now allows Bachmann to be seen less as a German-language pre-feminist and more as an Austrian writer who continues the tradition of critical sympathy for Old Austria and its post-1918 incarnation.

In *Literature as Utopia (Literatur als Utopie)*, Bachmann, who approached the Hofmannsthalian crisis of language in her own "despairing progress/advance toward language"[3] still found great hope in the written word as a mechanism for social and political renewal. De Serbine-Bahrawy understands this as "neither a denial of the historical past, nor a break with the literary traditions of her land."[4]

Clearly, Bachmann's knowledge of Austrian history is extensive. Although she is highly critical of the conservative tendency she finds in the Second Republic's political, religious and social aspects, she addresses these relationships from a standpoint which takes into consideration the complex and problematic influences of imperialism, Catholicism, class consciousness, and multiculturalism on contemporary Austria.

Like Ilse Aichinger, the only other woman member of *Gruppe 47*, Bachmann focuses on the negative aspects of gender roles as they influence Austrian social development. Bachmann, however, differs from the abstract, often cryptic Aichinger and practically all other Austrian writers of her time in that she is not afraid to deal directly with Austrian Nazism, the love/hate relationship with Germany, the seemingly taboo subject of the Dollfuß /Schuschnigg corporate state,[5] and even the positive elements of imperial or Old Austrian sociopolitical and cultural identity. This latter focus is something quite unique for a writer of her generation. There is an unusual sense of mourning in Bachmann's excavation of Austrian history, one which connects her with an older generation of Austrian writers (Hofmannsthal, Schnitzler, Broch, Roth, Lernet-Holenia) who found themselves scarred by the fall of the Habsburg Empire and, for those who survived, by the Anschluss. The victims of identity crisis in Bachmann's works often echo Joseph Roth's alienated Old Austrian characters who appear lost in the post-1918 world. Her critical view of a provincial and static post-1945 Austria also recalls Lernet-Holenia's meditations on the death of a "true" Austrian identity in the historically escapist early Second Republic.

For examination of Bachmann's sociopolitical and historical

evaluations and to see how she continues this tradition of concern over Austrian identity, no text is quite as revealing as her novel fragment, *Requiem for Fanny Goldmann*.[6] The scholarly neglect of this text is apparent in the many studies of the author, and even de Serbine-Bahrawy does not utilize the fragment to support her sociopolitical angle. Written during the late 1960s, it was planned as a companion piece for *Franza's Case* and *Malina*, all elements of "a large study of all possible types of death."[7] It is the story of the tragic personal relationships of the fictional Viennese actress Fanny Wischnewski whose life becomes preoccupied and ultimately destroyed by unfaithful male companions. Fanny's fate, however, differs from that of her literary sister, Malina. Although psychological torment eventually brings on Fanny's alcoholism, career collapse, and death by pneumonia, it does not reduce her persona to the vanishing point, as in the case of Malina, who is introduced here as Fanny's young nemesis. While Fanny identifies herself as an important theatrical figure and member of a fading upper class, she is nevertheless a self-destructive woman who cannot allow herself autonomy or even much pride in her artistic accomplishments. Although she demands independence and recognition in her work, she fully embraces the traditional image of a woman fulfilled only through the love of a man. This subservience is part of the Old Austrian class-conscious codes Fanny identifies with. Bachmann thus presents a provocative critique of imperial and corporate state Austria by embodying them in a female protagonist at odds with the archaic roles of a patriarchy.

Fanny does not stand alone in this text as the singular representative of the Austrian past. As in *Malina*, the men in Fanny Goldmann's life appear as alter egos of the title character, not in the specific psychological manner of that novel,[8] but rather as sociocultural and political allegories, who together with Fanny, enact the changes in the Austrian national image just prior to 1938 and after 1945. These roles will be examined in a sociopolitical and historical reading of the text, as I attempt to extract the very political message Bachmann presents. The novel fragment will be shown to mirror Austria's confused national direction following

World War II and the subsequent roles or reinventions that Austria undertakes in its escape from historical image and identity.

It is most fitting that as the representative of post-imperial Austria, Fanny is an actress, an attractive and versatile one whose roles range from the epitome of classical beauty and harmony, *Iphigenie*, to the romantic kitsch of *Thank You for the Roses (Danke für die Rosen)* (161). Bachmann's figure of role playing and reinvention is, however, not praised for any great acting talent, but instead for her masterful manipulation of her image. The conceit of Fanny-as-Old Austria is carefully created to reflect the republican Austrian evolution in microcosm. Fanny is introduced as a Wischnewski, more exactly, as the daughter of the Austrian Colonel Wischnewski, who shot himself in March 1938. She is also described as having removed her German flak uniform in 1945 to don mourning dress for her martyred father. De Serbine-Bahrawy points out that Bachmann appreciates and is most sensitive to the multicultural heritage of Austria. This is most obvious in Bachmann's use of the Polish name, Wischnewski, which she uses to denote the non-German element in Austria and which she places in opposition to the German Anschluss. Along with the nod to the Central Europe (Mitteleuropa) of Hofmann-sthal's *Austrian Idea*,[9] this indication of a strong non-German Austrian heritage conjures up the ideology of the Dollfuß /Schuschnigg corporate state, which attempted to promote Austria as the sociocultural nexus of a reborn Danubian identity. The corporate state also considered restoration of the Habsburg monarchy and found its mission in being the "better" German state, one that through clerico-authoritarianism, celebrated Alpine provincialism but desired the Central European high culture of a cosmopolitan Vienna.[10]

That Fanny's mourning dress is more pose than sincere ritual, a costume intended to pass her through denazification (161) and allow for employment or further education without difficulty, implies a double-edged attack on post-1945 Austrian historical escapism. It not only suggests the postwar slight of Austrian martyrs against Nazism, owing to their participation in the

Austrofascism of the corporate state, but also the soft denazification process in Austria and the national advocacy of the
Moscow Declaration. The pro-Anschluss crowds of 1938 notwithstanding, the accuracy of the Moscow Declaration's finding that
Austria was a victim of Nazi aggression despite its active participation in Hitler's war has only been questioned in popular discourse since the Waldheim era. The ambivalent victim/collaborator status, as uncomfortable as it was for occupied Austria, nevertheless allowed for a window of opportunity in the interpretation
of history. The German aggression against Austria and ultimate
annexation would come to represent the totality of Austrian
involvement with Nazism, and thus little dealing with the past
(*Vergangenheitsbewältigung*)[11] would be required. Furthermore,
Soviet interest in an independent and neutral Austria helped
encourage this self-view.[12]

Bachmann's rejection of this cursory interpretation of history is
to be found in the character of Harry Goldmann, an exiled Austrian
Jew who returns as the American Forces cultural officer.
Representing the fading Old Austrian cosmopolitanism, Goldmann, a witness to Austrian Holocaust guilt, subverts the quasi-
official Austrian victim image. As an Americanized capitalist, he
moreover suggests a Western oriented route for an Austria intent
on escaping from the control of the Soviet forces. Additionally,
Goldmann stands as Fanny's alter ego, the other half of the
Austrian experience between 1918 and 1945. The coupling of
Harry and Fanny Goldmann thus embodies the naive hope of the
entire embryonic Austrian political spectrum (excepting the
Communists) as distilled by the writers of the immediate postwar
era. The conservative author Alexander Lernet-Holenia said of the
newly liberated Austria: "We need only to continue from where the
dreams of a lunatic interrupted us. Indeed, we do not need to look
beyond–but rather into the past."[13] Progressives also looked back.
In her *Aufruf zum Mißtrauen* (1946), Ilse Aichinger demanded a
critical inspection of Austrian tradition, culture and history, not
only to trace the road to disaster, but also, hopefully, to recapture
the best of Old Austria.

The Wischnewski's *Vergangenheitsbewältigung*, their coming to terms with the suicide of Fanny's father, is a dark comedy of assumption, injured pride, and inconclusive information – Bachmann's microcosm of the Austrian emotionality and difficulty in dealing with Austrofascism in the Second Republic. As the last generation of identification with, and loyalty to, the military/class superstructure of the Austro-Hungarian concept, Fanny's mother and her two maiden aunts guard the image of Colonel Wischnewski's martyrdom. Fanny, a child of the First Republic, adaptable to change and conditioned by the loss of Austrian identity to the Third Reich and the horrors of a belligerent war, takes no tradition beyond surface value: notably it is she who discovers her father's close link with corporate state Minister Emil Fey, who was suspected of involvement with the failed Nazi putsch signaled by the assassination of Chancellor Engelbert Dollfuß.[14] Fey also committed suicide after the Anschluss in 1938 and Fanny understands: "that her father was not the hero he would be resurrected as, rather, he was an unfortunate man, driven by fears, miscalculations, shame, and hopelessness"(163). This evaluation of her father can well describe the final years of the Schuschnigg regime: the Chancellor, having lost the support of Mussolini with the Berlin-Rome Axis of 1937[15] and intimidated by Hitler, increasingly accepted German agents and Austrian Nazis into his government.[16] The heroic attempt of Schuschnigg to maintain a free Austria is often countered by the claims of his indecision, miscalculations and hopelessness, often by former Schuschnigg supporters themselves.

Fanny's attempt to suppress her mother's desire to rehabilitate her father speaks of the discomfort Second Republic Austria has had with confronting the immediate past. The general silence which has surrounded the corporate state and the Anschluss in Austria until recent decades is symbolized in Fanny's diversion: "one now has other concerns, (namely) that the Allies certainly did not comprehend what transpired in Vienna in 1934 or even in 1938...they are a complete bunch of idiots..."(163). The Second Republic, in seeking to escape from its own history, hopes to develop a new identity untainted by the Austrofascist or Nazi past. Bachmann suggests that this new image was privately detested by most Austrians who were either snobbish over Austria's historical importance or self-deceptive over its more recent historical foibles.

Bachmann further smashes the Austrian self-image of a resurgent national "high culture" by underscoring Fanny's new experience with books and her position with the writers' organization, where she gives identification cards intended for writers to non-writers for the sake of a housing allowance. That this hypocrisy should be Fanny's "first contact with literature in Vienna" (163) certainly exposes the anti-intellectual nature of Fanny's Nazi education. It also reflects a lack of substance in the cultural elitism of the Viennese bourgeoisie and postwar cultural institutions, including the stages upon which the unread Fanny becomes a star. Bachmann's reference to "Hiroshima" (164) as the caesura for traditional understanding of what a writer is and how he/she exists, is a cynical reference to Theodor Adorno's dictum, "Nach Auschwitz kann man nicht dichten" (one cannot create literature after Auschwitz),[17] since all of the "writers" Fanny has met in her organizational work were either not writers or had only vague connections with the art.

Equally revealing of postwar Austrian, specifically Viennese, cultural elitism is Fanny's dislike of Goldmann's Christian name, Harry: "It sounded like the tango or the Jimmy from the 1920s or 1930s..." (164). This rejection of the American-jazz inspired, but primarily Berlin-based cabaret culture of the Weimar Republic is the first of many attacks against German socioculture which Fanny makes in support of an Austrian quality represented by her odd notions. It is strongly implied that Fanny considers only Mozart, Beethoven, and the Romantic music of Beethoven to the waltzes of Johann Strauss as authentic Old Austrian music. Her "German music" is an incongruous collection of baroque, rationalist, atonal, and modernist concepts offered by Vivaldi, Bach, Webern, Boulez, and various jazz composers (185). Fanny's image of the gentle and cultured Austrian, and the harsh, even martial German is supported by criteria as arbitrary and spurious (the "Austrian" Beethoven is in fact German, the "German" Webern is Austrian) as that of the racist Nazi culture Fanny apparently despises.

Fanny's animosity toward Germany surfaces most spectacularly when her lover Anton Marek is suspected of having an affair with a German woman, Karin Krause. Ever vigilant of Austrian acceptance of German leadership in Central Europe, even in the postwar era, Fanny finds such a match to be in bad taste and recalls with venom the Austrian difference from Germany, even during the Anschluss: "The Taunus, the Taunus, doesn't concern us at all, that is what they sang in the high schools during the Nazi period..."(179). Karin is the product of that which Fanny believes to have destroyed the traditions and elitism of Old Austria, and she reduces Karin's persona to a fulfillment of Nazi propaganda slogans: "a thousand-year-Reich child, survival child. People-without-space child. Tall and attractive, conceived under the portrait of Hitler, something that was not the child's fault" (180).

Karin's relocation to Austria is attacked as the result of her father's "half and half-successful denazification"(181) which makes his theatrical profession apparently more feasible in Vienna. The suggestion that unrepentant Nazis and those who unjustifiably claim innocence from Nazi involvement are more at home in Austria because of its unwillingness to confront the Nazi period totally eludes Fanny, but Bachmann intends to underscore the sort of official laxity demonstrated here and at the Viennese writers' organization.

Through examination of her nemesis Karin, Fanny ultimately and without any actual historical understanding, recognizes the postwar similarity between Austria and Germany. Although this situation is based on a general internationalism in Western Europe and an increasing proletarian focus, Fanny, as a member of a pre-Anschluss bourgeois Viennese family, interprets this similarity as pure German hegemony: "from the automobile brands to the fashionable drinks, in many ways everything we have is the same, naturally with exception of the language; and there is a vulgarity which had seldom existed before. Yes, you are very irritated" (187).

Fanny's insistence on the language difference is a result of what de Serbine-Bahrawy analyzes as Bachmann's awareness of the connection of language and religion/culture in Austria, from the Catholic *Kanzleisprache* that differentiated itself from *Lutherdeutsch* to the power of language in supporting class structure and patriarchal values, notions which Bachmann highlights so successfully in *Unter Mördern und Irren* and *Simultan*.[18] It is also a nod to the post-1945 concept of the Austrian Nation, which in addition to making a convincing claim to historical sociocultural development outside the German Nation, also took into account the Austrian version of the *Hochsprache* with its Slavic and French loan-words as indicators of the different nationhood.[19] To prove her point, Bachmann allows this consideration of Austrian/German similarities "mit Ausnahme der Sprache" (with the exception of the language) to conclude with the word "agaciert," which is an example of a French-based Austrianism not found in any German dictionary.[20]

The various sociocultural elements of pre-Anschluss Austria represented by Fanny Wischnewski and Harry Goldmann which come together as the postwar Austria of "Herr und Frau Goldmann" survive only briefly, more as ideal than actuality. Although Harry obviously loves Fanny and their coupling is an allegorical reestablishment of an idealistic postwar Austria based in the traditions of the past, it fails, because according to Bachmann, these elements are no longer representative of Austria's sociopolitical reality in the post-1945 era. Fanny's heavily promoted self-image as a member of the Old Austrian elitist bourgeoisie which, despite her Nazi experience, celebrates the myth of a lasting Viennese imperial culture, is subverted by Malina, the young girl from Klagenfurt. Malina is representative of the provincial Austria which gains increasing national influence in the postwar era, while the cosmopolitan, Central/Eastern European quality of Vienna fades in the wake of the communist Eastern bloc. Having a raw passion and instinctive ability that would make her a truly great actress, Malina eclipses Fanny, who is a celebrity less for her acting than for her aging image of Viennese charm. Malina also undermines Fanny's dominance in her relationship with Harry and is partially responsible for destroying their marriage.

Fanny, who has based her professional life and her very existence on carefully controlled image, resents Malina's lack of image consciousness and her pragmatism: "Have you ever noticed that if she desires someone, she is always helpful and friendly. She is nothing more than an instrument, she is apparently not alive" (165).

The new Malina-Austria is hardly urbane and is devoid of any emotional investment in Austria's past, but can pragmatically adjust and adapt to what is expected of her. The result, however, seems artificial: Austria's postwar neutral alpine republic image is inspired by Switzerland, a country with which Austria shares little sociohistorical commonality. This emulation placed a welcome emphasis on Alpine/provincial culture as the national image, and it afforded an escape from the Central European cosmopolitanism of Austria's historical identity.[21]

Fanny and Harry's divorce is satirized as an operetta-like story by a cabaret artist who summarizes what their allegorical break indicates: the reduction of Old Austria to a romantic Hollywood-type cliché in the consciousness of the postwar Austrian (167). Bachmann indicates that following the divorce, Harry returned to America and then traveled to Israel. Upon his reappearance in Vienna, Fanny is alienated by his difference, in particular, his interest in Judaica and his strong desire to attend the Adolf Eichmann trial. In Harry Goldmann's disillusionment with the romantic image of Fanny and Vienna (170) Bachmann conveys the Jewish and Israeli disappointment with the Second Republic's lack of dealing with the past regarding the Holocaust and a lingering anti-Semitism which would eventually surface more blatantly in the neo-Nazi organizations of the post-Waldheim era.[22] Harry's new Jewishness renders him incapable of identifying with Austria and enjoying the romanticized images (Fanny) of what he now regards as an unrepentant people once involved in the destruction of Jewry: "He no longer required an embrace from her; as with the emigration, so the return to Vienna, [there was] no longer a most beautiful Viennese woman and no night in Nußdorf" (170).

To complete the allegory of Austria in the 1960s, Bachmann pairs post-Goldmann Fanny with Anton Marek, who, like Malina, represents a provincial Austria (172). Fanny, however, also needs to continue her image as a relic of a romantic, cultural Vienna for the sake of her theatrical career. It is an insightful parallel to the Austrian showcasing of its Habsburg heritage for the sake of tourist income at the same time that it denied the widow of the last Emperor and their son, Otto von Habsburg, the right to visit their homeland for unsubstantiated fear of a monarchist resurgence.[23] Certainly, given the allegory which Bachmann constructs, her view of the Second Republic in the 1960s and 70s as portrayed by Anton is as vitriolic as her rejection of Fanny-as-Old-Austria facade: "A sly, small-time criminal so unscrupulous that he could adapt to the scruples of a desired society and accept all their dogmas, their very best, which so suit a provincial" (173).

Like Malina, Anton is an opportunist and a pragmatist, free of the traditions and memories of an Austria before his time. Unlike Harry Goldmann, who doted on Fanny in an attempt to recapture his lost pre-1938 world, Anton's creativity and self-importance upstages Fanny's somewhat tired image and he emerges as the dominant figure in their relationship. Fanny becomes subservient to Anton, as she hopes to gain love by catering to his ego and expectations, something she did not attempt with Goldmann. Her quaint and manipulative frivolity is not appreciated by the modern and cynical Anton (174).

What follows are Anton's affairs with Helga Hobaluek and Karin Krause which ultimately shut out the aging, self-deluding Fanny from his life and stunt her personal growth and artistic accomplishment. Like the Second Republic which in its early decades tended to commercialize its historical culture while its historical escapism stunted true sociocultural development, Fanny discovers she has lost the ability to learn or comprehend, that her eyes disclose her tendency "not to understand, towards petrifi-cation, towards incomprehension" (184). The Austrian provincialization and according to Fanny's intimation, proletarization, has even affected her own family. Her sister, Maria Pilar, has married below her class and has raised two children, Burschi and Mädi. Devoid of the expected social decorum of a Wischnewski, they speak in a Styrian dialect and are thus scornfully noted as the "product of a new style of rearing" (186). Fanny detests these children for their boorishness, but although she is obsessed with perpetuating the myth of her family and her own image of social elitism, the actual disaster here eludes her recognition: as the only offspring of the Wischnewski daughters, Burschi and Mädi are the sociocultural heirs of the Old Austrian upper class in the Second Republic. The family's, and by representation, the social caste's traditions, historical connections, and status end with the extinction of the Wischnewski name.

The concluding chapter, "The Stolen Years," retells the troubled relationship between Fanny and Anton, mentions Maria Pilar (here known as Klara) and Karin, but the style is not the allegorical one of the earlier text; it resembles far more the rambling, existential musings of the *Malina* novel. Nevertheless, the love/hate relationship between Austrians and Germans as embodied in Anton's relationship with Karin Krause, now his wife, and in his literary dealings continues. Anton is seen by a German friend as "a fossil . . . something pitiable, astonishing, indescribable even with the adjective arch-conservative" (199), while his German wife is regarded as "progressive"(199). In fact, the German view of Anton is that he is "thirty years old and dead" (199). Bachmann finds the non-role of Austria in the 1960s and 1970s destructive to its sociopolitical development and damaging to its reputation in the international cultural arena, especially when compared to the West Germans, who contend not only with a strong self-criticism in the arts, but with sociopolitical upheaval, radicalism, and terrorism. Austria's reinvention of itself as the *Alpenrepublik* in order to escape the historical baggage and worthless mythologizing of a lost cultural heritage (Fanny) has made its art far less political and socially conscious than that of Germany. The Austrians offer instead an intense look inward with the existential and linguistic examinations of the *Wiener Gruppe* (1946-1964) and the Graz-based *Forum Stadtpark* (1959-   ), as well as with literary and pictorial Fantastic Realism during this socially tumultuous period in Western European history.

Although *Requiem for Fanny Goldmann* is a provocative dirge for Old Austria which does not shy away from confronting the identity problems of the Second Republic – Austria's alternately damaging rejection or banal mythologizing of its imperial heritage and the West German domination of German-language culture – it is only a partially successful allegory. Naturally, it is difficult to imagine what Bachmann's finished novel would ultimately consist of, but given the large fragment that survives, the author's love/hate attitude toward a patriarchal Old Austria as presented in her sympathy toward Fanny, does not allow her any clear critical conclusion in feminism. This is even more revealing of Bachmann because she initiated what Hélène Cixous now encourages: that a woman writer can best expose the missing history of women by placing herself into the text so that her personal history blends with women's history and thus embodies the history of female oppression.[24] Lisa de Serbine-Bahrawy rightly claims that Bachmann not only addresses problems specific to female experience but that, "like her great Austrian predecessors, her empathy extends beyond her own sex."[25] This is most apparent here in Anton's death in the "battle" of cultural politics. Bachmann's proto-feminism generates a Fanny Goldmann who is destroyed by the very sociocultural concepts she defends and a Malina who is eventually negated by her lack of strong identity and complicity in a male-dominant world.[26]

Nevertheless, the author's concern for the devolution of a specific Austrian identity based in patriarchal tradition is equally strong, often outweighing the feminist messages of the text. The collision of the two impulses in this novel fragment results in a fulfillment of the work's title and its role in the "Todesarten" concept: it is a mourning piece for Old Austria as well as for the women and men destroyed by an oppressive patriarchy. There is, however, no closure or healing here; Bachmann's allegorical dirge sings of national self-destruction. Austria's social and political burial of its difficult past has not rid it of the archaic codes and values which brought about the disasters it desires to forget. It has only served to smother the seminal and often problematic cosmopolitan and polyglot nature of Old Austria, a legacy which would have nourished the early Second Republic into becoming a truer representative of the desired "Austrian Nation."

Notes

1. Sara Lennox, "Geschlecht, Rasse und Geschichte in *Der Fall Franza*," *Text + Kritik Sonderband: Ingeborg Bachmann*. Ed. Heinz Ludwig Arnold (München: Edition Text + Kritik, 1984) 156-179.

2. Lisa de Serbine-Bahrawy, *The Voice of History: An Exegesis of Selected Short Stories from Ingeborg Bachmann's* Das dreiigste Jahr *and* Simultan *from the Perspective of Austrian History* (New York: Peter Lang, 1989).

3. Ingeborg Bachmann, *Werke, Bd. 5*. Eds. Christine Koschel, Inge von Weidenbaum, Clemens Münster (München: Piper, 1978) 268. All English translations are by Robert von Dassanowsky unless otherwise noted.

4. de Serbine-Bahrawy 143.

5. The *Ständestaat*: 1934-1938.

6. Ingeborg Bachmann, *Requiem für Fanny Goldmann* (Frankfurt am Main: Suhrkamp, 1979). All quotes from this text are translated and cited parenthetically.

7. Ingeborg Bachmann, *Wir müssen wahre Sätze finden. Gespräche und Interviews*. Eds. Christine Koschel and Inge von Weidenbaum (München: Piper, 1983) 66.

8. For an insightful exploration on the male/female relationship, see Kurt Bartsch, "Es war Mord: Anmerkungen zur Mann-Frau-Beziehung in Bachmanns Roman *Malina*." *Acta Neophilologica*, 17 (1984).

9. Hugo von Hofmannsthal, "Die österreichische Idee," *Gesammelte Werke in Einzelausgaben, Prosa III* (Frankfurt am Main: Fischer, 1952).

10. This is symbolized in Dollfuß's choice of a Christian-feudal *Kruckenkreuz* to represent his Austrian state, which would subvert the pagan swastika of Hitler's Germany. See: Irmgard Bärnthaler, *Die Vaterländische Front: Geschichte und Organisation* (Wien: Europa Verlag, 1971) 28.

11. A popular term referring to the examination of the Nazi past.

12. See: Gerald Stourzh, "Der Weg zum Staatsvertrag und zur immerwährenden Neutralität," Österreich: Die Zweite Republik Vol. I. Eds. Erika Weinzierl and Kurt Skalnik (Graz: Styria, 1972).

13. In: Joseph McVeigh, *Kontinuität und Vergangenheitsbewältigung in der österreichischen Literatur nach 1945* (Wien: Braumüller, 1988) 56-57. Lernet-Holenia, however, did not demon- strate the possibility of continuity in his pessimistic 1948 novel, *Der Graf von Saint-Germain*. See my analysis, "A Destiny of Guilt: The Crisis of Postimperial Austrian Identity and the Anschluss in Alexander Lernet-Holenia's *Der Graf von Saint-Germain*," *The Germanic Review*, Fall (1994) 156-166.

14. Major Emil Fey, who became State Secretary for Security under Dollfuß in 1932, is not well remembered in Eva Dollfuß's biography of her father. Although the leader of the Rightist *Heimwehr* militia, Prince Ernst Rüdiger Starhemberg, first suggested Fey to Dollfuß as the "verlä licher Österreicher" (reliable Austrian) who could stand up to the Nazis, he was wary of Fey's dangerous "Ehrgeiz" (ambition) (104). By 1934, Dollfuß would recognize the "unverhüllte Machtstreben" (obvious striving for power) of Fey, and Carl von Karwinsky recalls that there was an unclear relationship between Fey and the National Socialists (312). Five days before his assassination, Dollfuß drew up plans for the reorganization of his government in an effort to better combat National Socialism. Among these plans were a rapprochement with the Social Democrats and the "Ausschluß Feys aus der Regierung" (exclusion of Fey from the government) (316). See: Eva Dollfuß, *Mein Vater: Hitlers erstes Opfer* (Wien: Amalthea, 1994).

15. The July 1936 German-Austrian agreement for friendly relations was soon overshadowed by the German-Japanese Anti-Comintern Pact in November of that year, which was joined by Austria's ally Italy in 1937. With the Berlin-Rome Axis, it became clear that Austria had lost its only protector and that sovereignty would now be imperiled.

16. Chancellor Schuschnigg allowed such Nazi sympathizers as future *Reichsstaathalter* of the *Ostmark*, Arthur Seyss-Inquart, Guido Schmidt, and General Edmund von Glaise-Horstenau "who

enjoyed both the confidence of Hitler and the Reich Foreign Ministry" into his cabinet. See: Radomir Luña, *Austro-German Relations in the Anschluss Era* (Princeton: Princeton University Press, 1975) 31-32.

17. Walter Jens, "Laudatio auf Nelly Sachs," *Das Buch der Nelly Sachs*, Ed. Bengt Holmqvist (Frankfurt am Main: Suhrkamp, 1968) 381.

18. de Serbine-Bahrawy 25ff.

19. The question of language as source of nationhood is questioned in the context of Austria vis-à-vis Germany by many authors writing on the concept of the Austrian Nation. An excellent summary is given in Gerald Stourzh, *Vom Reich zur Republik: Studien zum Österreichbewußtsein im 20. Jahrhundert* (Wien: Edition Atelier, 1990). Austria has continued to promote international recognition of Austrian German as is evident by the article "AATG Annual Conference and Austria: 'Paradeiser' instead of 'Tomaten'" in the official publication *Kooperationen: Culture, Science and Education: Austria's Cooperation with the United States*, ed. Österreichischer Akademischer Austauschdienst (Wien: ÖAA, 1994) 24.

20. The word is an Austro-Germanization of the French *agacer*, meaning "to irritate."

21. See: Stourzh 71-98.

22. For a superb presentation of such pan-German and racist impulses in contemporary Austria see: Dokumentationsarchiv des österreichischen Widerstands, ed. *Handbuch des österreichischen Rechtsextremismus*, 2. Auflage (Wien: Deuticke, 1993).

23. The political and financial actions against the former Imperial House by the First Republic continued into the Second Republic despite the outspoken anti-fascism of the Habsburg family, the victimization of the dynasty by Nazi propaganda, and the involvement of Otto von Habsburg in President Roosevelt's plans for the re-establishment of a sovereign Austria. In the 1960s, the political dealings behind the anti-Habsburg stance of the SPÖ (Social-Democratic Party) became a scandal of major proportions, but Otto von Habsburg was finally allowed to return in 1966. Ex-

Empress Zita was not allowed to enter Austria until 1982. See: Hermann A. Griesser, *Konfisziert: Österreichs Unrecht am Hause Habsburg* (Wien: Amalthea, 1986).

24. Hélène Cixous, *The Laugh of the Medusa.* Transl. Keith Cohen and Paula Cohen, *The Signs Reader: Women, Gender & Scholarship.* Eds. Elizabeth Abel and Emily K. Abel (Chicago: University of Chicago Press, 1983).

25. de Serbine-Bahrawy 148.

26. Gabriele Bail, *Weibliche Identität: Ingeborg Bachmanns "Malina"* (Göttingen: Edition Herodot, 1984) and Saskia Schottelius, *Das imaginäre Ich: Subjekt und Identität in Ingeborg Bachmanns Roman "Malina" und Jacques Lacans Sprachtheorie* (Frankfurt am Main: Peter Lang, 1990) offer comprehensive discussion of female identity in *Malina.* Also enlightening as to the various literary and cinematic interpretations of this character and Bachmann's feminism is Kathleen L. Komar, "'Es war Mord': The Murder of Ingeborg Bachmann at the Hands of an Alter Ego" *Modern Austrian Literature* 27/2 (1994) 91-112.

The Ruins of an Illusion.
Intertextuality and the Limits of Friendship in Bachmann's *The Cicadas*

Sabine I. Gölz

With her 1954 radio play *Die Zikaden*, Ingeborg Bachmann draws the limits of the economy of friendship, i.e., of the fundamentally homosocial mode of operation of our representational order.[1] With the help of intertextual excursions into two Shakespeare plays, she both articulates this critique and with surprising clarity marks her difference from the existing literary economy. Under the gaze of her critique, the struggle for poetic transcendence which drives even such "deconstructive" writers as Kafka or Celan, and which crucially relies on the notion of the "friend," loses all force – leaving but "the ruins of an illusion."

Since Bachmann does not "explain herself" in explicitly theoretical terms, any study of her theory of language, power, and subjecthood must proceed by interpreting her literary texts. If we do so, we find that Bachmann inhabits language only temporarily and reluctantly – just enough to convert "what has already formed itself out of language" into "the white, blank page where that which is yet to be gained seems to be also inscribed."[2] In representation she is a prisoner. Unrepresented, she can assume a strong readerly position, reclaiming the possibility of change in and through reading. From there, Bachmann can take issue with the founding law of the Western symbolic order: the male homosocial link between "friends" or "brothers."

The text I will discuss – Bachmann's radio play *Die Zikaden* – offers a strange landscape, a world whose laws seem weird and unfamiliar. That strangeness of Bachmann's literary world is due to a profound revaluation, a (self-)critical reassessment of both the historical Gestalt of the literary order which confronts her (and us), and the readerly practice with which we as readers surround, inhabit, and perpetuate that order. The play's perspective differs radically from the one informing the world of interpretive business as usual – so radically that it becomes invisible to that world. Yet the play does not construct that invisibility as victimization, but rather as a blindness of that world which is ultimately (also) a blindness of that world to itself. It is also our own blindness insofar as our mode of reading remains unreflexive, and as long as we continue to trust the ability of language to name anything at all.

Several strategies – indispensable in reading Bachmann's texts – inform my procedure: a very literal relation to metaphor, careful attention to the composition of the text and to the (strategic) use of intertextuality, and an intense awareness of the potential for repetition to insert difference.

The Composition of *Die Zikaden*

Bachmann's radio play *Die Zikaden* is set on an island populated by some rather eccentric characters, dominated by the noonday sun, and pervaded by the swelling and fading of a "music" which is painful to the ear: the screaming of the cicadas. That music is part of the phenomenon of noon which governs the island: "She [it, the music] came out of the earth in summer, when the sun stood desperately high, when noon stepped out of its conceptuality and entered into time" (1, 221). The play opens with the voice of the narrator who comments that the music begins to sound. It closes with a similar remark on the fading of the music. In the postscript to the play proper, the clamor of the cicadas is only a memory shared by "you" and "me."

The first character we "meet" on the island has just received a letter from a woman, asking him to return to the continent. Of him the narrator says that he goes a bit too far – farther than most of the islanders – in withdrawing from society. He does not even read the island's newspaper anymore. Nor does he read the woman's letter. We encounter him at the moment of noon, which seems to paralyze him: he lowers his hand with the letter, for "now he cannot think" ("er kann jetzt nicht denken"; Bachmann 1, 225). At the very end of the play, the man is (jokingly) named "Robinson" by Benedikt, the editor of the island's newspaper.

The play's only sustained plot is the story of an encounter between "Robinson" and an escaped "prisoner" from a yet farther outlying island. The prisoner is the most mysterious personage of the play, and the key to understanding it. Suffice it at this point to note that he is the only figure in the play who has no proper name. At issue in this figure is a fundamental resistance to language as representation. Three sections of the play are devoted to exchanges between the prisoner and "Robinson." These three sections are interrupted by two blocks of three "scenes with Antonio" each.

Antonio is the newspaper boy who calls out the headlines of the island's paper. His voice fills the news items "with the barbaric magic of old hunting-calls" (see Bachmann 1, 230). He is also involved in many other business deals. Beyond that, the narrator knows nothing about him: "Of Antonio, by the way, I know nothing, except that in addition to distributing the newspaper he is involved in many a business transaction" (1, 231).

The scenes with Antonio create the most heavily repeated pattern in the play. The first of the two blocks contains the exchanges between Antonio and, successively, Mrs. Brown, Mr. Brown, and the painter Salvatore. The second block contains his interactions with Prinz Ali, Jeanette, and with a little boy called Stefano. At the end of the play, before the concluding words of the narrator, Antonio returns one more time in a scene with the newspaper editor Benedikt. Most of the people who live on the island (and no longer talk to each other) each turn to Antonio for help in pursuing their desire for transcendence. The stage directions call for the "scenes with Antonio" to have a special quality that sets them off from their casual and "realistic" beginning without letting them become unreal (*irreal*). They should sound intimate, as if someone were speaking in your ear (see 1, 219). Each of the solipsistic islanders is possessed by some impossible desire: to speak with a lost voice, to bring back a dead son, to plant a new star in the sky, to remain eternally young and beautiful, or to paint the unpaintable – the gaze (*den Blick*). Each hopes for help from Antonio, and he obliges them up to the moment when they ask for the fiction he enacts for them to become real and permanent. At those moments Antonio's accommodating "Yes" turns into an impervious "No!" The pattern of his responses – "yes, yes, yes, ... no!" – is varied only in two cases: in the scene with Stefano, there is no "yes," and the "no" sounds hesitant and qualified. Stefano has discovered something which no longer requires confirmation by Antonio, and something which Antonio therefore can also no longer deny. Benedikt's scene with Antonio is also different: his demands on Antonio are pragmatic, perhaps even cynical. They involve no transgression of the possible, hence the scene does not end in a "no." Robinson is the only islander who has no "scene with Antonio." But he likes to listen to Antonio's voice from a distance.

The cicadas' clamor, the glare of the noonday sun, and the scenes with Antonio set the stage for the encounter between Robinson and the prisoner.

Two Islands

What island is this? How is it that the people brought by the noonday ship do not even know about the place where they thus arrive? "They all know nothing about the island, which they consider a piece of earth of a higher order; they look back at the continent, this gray strip of cellotape on the horizon, from which they have escaped, and they thank God that he has placed the sea between them and the land" (1, 222).

The islanders and the narrator have radically different views of what constitutes a ground. To the former, the island is a piece of ground of a higher order. If they believe in a "higher" ground, by implication they believe that what they have left is also a ground – albeit a lower one. The narrator, by contrast, identifies what they take to be higher ground as an "island" in the open sea, and goes on to remove the promise of a more extensive terra firma by identifying the "continent" as a mere strip of cellotape on the horizon. And the narrator goes on to pull not only the firm ground out from under the islanders' feet, but also the shaky boards which – as long as they held together – formed a ship. The people who have left the continent and arrived on the island, are (according to the narrator) not only unaware of the island – they also do not realize that they have been shipwrecked. "For it is still the shipwrecked who seek refuge on islands" (1, 222).

That they arrive aboard the white noonday ship does not contradict this. "One" – the generalized subject of established and thoroughly automatic interpretive practice – does not see what the narrator sees: "that they are already without strength and will sink down on the beach, when nobody sees them, with closed eyes, and that they will thank God for their miraculous rescue (1, 222).[3] The subjects constituting the position of that "one" (man) are not seen because they keep their eyes closed: they are not seen by each other and themselves. The problem is a profoundly entrenched lack of self-reflexivity, a lack of consciousness.[4]

The word "continent," etymologically considered, means – something that "holds together." Nobody who leaves that strip of cellotape behind can still hold a ship together. To leave the "continent" by definition means shipwreck. The horizon springs open, language becomes fluid, a changeable ocean, and there is no longer any ground to stand on. From this situation, the island appears to provide a miraculous rescue. The island is a site of encounter. It is situated between two horizons, belonging to neither: the glued-together horizon of the continent, and the opposite horizon from which the prisoner has temporarily escaped. The island lies at what we might call the "crack of noon": here noon "enters into time," the continent comes unglued, and two horizons meet and become legible in their difference.

The first island is not "out there" at all – it is "here" and "now," where language offers indexical contact to the world. If I am here, reading this now, the noon of representation enters into time. But the time it thus enters is always the same: it is Today. Tomorrow is subject to a perpetual deferral. "Tomorrow everybody will receive his letter. But what does 'tomorrow' mean on the islands? One day comes up like the next, comes up like one great and singular Today after another" (1, 224-225). The temporality of the island is the temporality of noon: an open succession of Todays. The second island, from which the prisoner has escaped, is smaller, rocky and arid. Wine and figs do not grow there, only a few brown blades of grass – so few that one could count them. But that is not worth the trouble. "It is better to stick to the tall and strong cacti with their finger-long thorns that stand in for the earth against the sky"(1, 223).

In an ambivalent relation of advocacy or representation, the cacti and their thorns represent (vertreten) the earth for or against the sky. The gesture that founds the second island is a deictic pointing at something else – at the sky, at the earth, at tomorrow, at you. The first island indexically invites an effect of presence. The second island is founded by a pointing which enforces a thorny distance. I am here and you are there. The letter will arrive tomorrow. On a banner (Transparent) over the harbor, the prison island displays a promise: "This is a place of deliverance. Thus it stands written on the banner which is attached to two rusty posts to the left and right of the small bay" (1, 223).

Reversal and Leap

During his first conversation with "Robinson," the prisoner tells a short tale which contains the name Robinson – but the name is not attached to any particular person outside of the story.

> *The Prisoner* Once upon a time there was an island on which Robinson got stranded, and he built himself a

> hut out of the stones ... He gazed into the distance, and
> an old Writing appeared on the sky, across the stage set
> of infinity: You are Orplid, my land!
> *Robinson* What did you say?
> *The Prisoner* You are Orplid, my land.
> *Robinson* I have never heard of it.
> *The Prisoner* I have been there. It is this, a place of
> deliverance. (1, 227-228)

These lines contain at least two allusions – one to Daniel Defoe's
Robinson Crusoe, the other to the poetic fantasy island Orplid.
Orplid – the island, its peoples, culture, wars, religions, and gods
– is the product of a poetic friendship between Eduard Mörike and
Ludwig Bauer.[5] "You are Orplid, my land!" is the first line of
Mörike's poem *Weyla's Song (Gesang Weylas* see Härtling, 7), and
the words are thus attributed to the goddess Weyla, who protects
the island Orplid, and who eventually decides to depopulate it. The
name Orplid has become a topos for the poetic fantasy of an "other
world."

In Bachmann's play, the line from Mörike's poem first appears
as a conscious citation on the horizon of (the prisoner's rendering
of) "Robinson's" world. When the prisoner cites the line a second
time, he does so in response to his interlocutor's incomprehension.
By then the line has lost the narrative bubble of "Robinson's" story
and (reported) perspective. In a second, "naked" repetition, the line
suddenly appears directly addressed to the prisoner's interlocutor:
"You are Orplid, my land." The deferral reverses its direction. The
postulate of a poetic Other is mirrored back whence it came,
inverting the I-You relation between the literary order and its
readers. Someone from the island "you" claims the island "I" as a
utopia. Writers have traditionally addressed their hopes for
transcendence to readers. Bachmann turns literature into a utopia
for a reading subject.

But the reversal alone is not enough. There is more to the
prisoner's feat – and that "more" also marks Bachmann's difference
from deconstruction. The prisoner comes to the island neither on
the conventional noonday ship, nor driven by a Robinsonian desire
to withdraw from the world. He manages the passage by means of

a leap which "cannot repeat itself" (see 1, 229). The leap takes him out of the order of naturalized metaphor,[6] out of the faith that any glue could hold together the horizons of reading. Thanks to that leap, the prisoner is "free" in Hannah Arendt's sense of the term: here is someone who breaks with the automatism of repetition and reclaims initiative in, of and for reading.[7]

Yet Mörike's is not the only citation repeated by the prisoner. The earlier line from the banner on the other island also returns: "This is a place of deliverance." It returns with a small variation registering a displacement: "This is ..." becomes "It is this ..." Since the speaker has moved, the referent of the word "this" has shifted as well. It no longer coincides with the other island: "I have been there. It is this, a place of deliverance."

Only in combination with the "leap" can the reversal defeat the ability of the "I" to keep its "other" at bay. The departure/arrival of a free subject abruptly arrests the deferral and transports the noon "into time." Tomorrow is today. The actual reader departs from language to arrive in the place of the written "I."[8] Substitution of subjects instead of an indefinite deferral of "tomorrow": a reader usurps the writers' "I." That usurpation can only occur as an event. It is readable only to those who perform it. The order of representation – and those faithful to it – will never know it happened.

There is a site in Bachmann's play which marks the "zenith" of what is possible in representation. That site is located in the central one of the three sections on the encounter between the prisoner and "Robinson." The prisoner creates a second narrative "bubble" – a hypothetical dialogue between an "I" and a "you" which doubles their dialogue and opens the possibility for them to switch positions. In that "dialogue," the substitution of subjects is announced: "I speak of myself as one who is another" (1, 240-241).

Bachmann contests the viability of a poetic procedure that leaves the continent behind in the hope for a "time which will come" (see 1, 222-223), but which nevertheless deludes itself into thinking that such an opening of language onto the future implies anything less than the opening for a radical and unrecuperable difference.[9] The addressee of her critique is any stance that endeavors to colonize future reading, and which – upon finding that such colonization remains impossible – installs a deferral or *différance* (Derrida) to keep at bay the difference which appears in and as reading. Bachmann's point is that *différance* is a strategy which turns the site of reading into a prison island, and which turns into cicadas those who leave the continent to live on islands in the pursuit of poetic transcendence: "For the cicadas used to be people. They ceased to eat, drink, and love, to be able to sing forever. In their flight into song they became dryer and smaller, and now they sing, lost to their desire – enchanted, but also damned, because their voices have become inhuman" (1, 268). The clamor of the cicadas which fills the islands at noon is the clamor for transcendence which fills literary history. At the end of Bachmann's radio play, that clamor fades away.[10]

The Friend

Despite everything that has been said in recent decades about the deconstruction of Western Metaphysics, the door which Bachmann closes on the desire for "transcendence" has generally remained open. This has been the case because of a certain procedure of exchange by which readers bind themselves back into language as "one of the boys." The endeavor to colonize reading takes the form of an attempt to co-opt readers into dressing up as one of the "brothers" whose language this used to be. Bachmann takes issue with the "deal" which is thus constantly struck between the past and the future/ present.

At the end of the play, Robinson offers his suit to the prisoner in order to facilitate the latter's escape to the continent. The prisoner makes his most telling choice when he refuses that offer. His decision has two consequences: it returns the prisoner to the island whence he came, and it leads to Robinson's return to the continent. When the deal falls through, each must return to where he came from. The prisoner's "arrest" towards the end of the play, and his return to the other island, are thus his own decision. He is no victim, but someone who makes choices in the framework of the possible.

The prisoner turns down the offer of Robinson's suit on the basis of a principle: he disapproves of a particular kind of cross-dressing which passes off one "brother" for another and obscures the fact that a substitution of subjects has taken place. The prisoner identifies as appropriate both his place on the "outpost" to which "she" (the world) has assigned him, and the nakedness which he preserves by refusing to put on the suit which is exchanged "between brothers."

> *Robinson* Take it [him]!
> *The Prisoner* A respectable piece. It is too bad that it [he] doesn't fit me.
> *Robinson* Try it.
> *The Prisoner* No. It [he] can't fit me. It is your suit.
> ...
> A suit is exchanged between brothers. The deal is no good. For I am not lost to this world; it [she] has only relocated me, transferred me to the outpost ... My suit is appropriate and as little negotiable as yours. (1, 262)

In order to understand what "deal" the prisoner refuses at that moment, and what the consequences of that refusal are, we have to pursue another intertextual lead. The names of two Shakespearean characters make their appearance in the play: Antonio and Horatio. In Shakespeare's texts, the characters with these names both play important roles as friends.

Antonio is the name of the friend in Shakespeare's *The Merchant of Venice*, who with his very life and body will stand in for those he loves. He is willing to give a pound of his flesh for Bassanio, and he is only saved from having to deliver on his pledge by the intervention of Portia who, disguised as a lawyer, decides the case and saves Antonio.[11]

Portia can play the role of the judge only by cross-dressing as a man. Indeed, all of the female characters in *The Merchant of Venice* at some point dress up as men: Jessica to escape with Lorenzo, Portia and her maid Nerissa to appear as the lawyer Balthasar and his clerk.

Horatio's name makes only a single and surprising appearance in Bachmann's play, and it functions as a strong intertextual signal. The one appearance of the name is prominently placed in the mentioned "zenith" of the hypothetical conversation between Robinson and the prisoner:

> *The Prisoner* I would be telling you: "My friend, let us eat and drink ... " And you would answer me: "I feel weak, Horatio, my insides are burning, but I require different fare ..."(1, 241)

"Horatio" is thus the name by which the prisoner has his hypothetical interlocutor – "you" – address him.

In the tale which the prisoner told on his arrival, the only proper name was "Robinson:" it marked the position of one who lives on an island and envisages another utopian island on the "stage set of infinity." In this second hypothetical dialogue, the only proper name is "Horatio:" it marks the position complementary to "Robinson's" – the position of the friend and supplement, and thus the very other from whom "Robinson" desires completion. The role of Horatio is the suit which the prisoner is offered.

In Shakespeare's *Hamlet*, Horatio's is a strangely sketchy presence.[12] He establishes the connection between Hamlet and the ghost of his father. During most of the play, he serves as a backdrop or support in exchanges with Hamlet. Sometimes he is reduced to the role of an "aye-sayer" to such a degree that Bachmann's Antonio begins to look like a parody of him. Horatio is there to observe the reactions of the King to the performance of *The Murder of Gonzago*, helping Hamlet establish "truth" by confirming his perceptions. He is also linked to Hamlet by a relation of prefiguration and similarity. The two see eye to eye, and descriptions can echo from one to the other. Thus, Hamlet first introduces the simile of the man who is "not a pipe for Fortune's finger/To sound what stop she pleases" to characterize Horatio,[13] before he later uses the same simile with reference to himself in his famous rebuff of Rosencrantz and Guildenstern (III. ii. 371-380). Only at the end of the play, however, does Horatio's most important role emerge. His loyalty and ability to serve as proxy for

Hamlet are never more important than after Hamlet's death. When Hamlet is dying, he calls upon Horatio to go on living in his service:

> *Hamlet* Horatio, I am dead;
> Thou livest; report me and my cause aright
> To the unsatisfied.
> ...
> And in this harsh world draw thy breath in pain,
> To tell my story.
>
> (V.ii. 339-41; 348-50)

Horatio's most important function as a friend and alter ego is to ensure the afterlife of Hamlet's name, to preserve memory and honor, to establish its "truth." Retrospectively, we can recognize that as his function from the moment he brings Hamlet in contact with the ghost of his father.

Horatio's "almost silent" (Halverson, 66) presence is the supportive presence of the "friend" authorized to speak in the name of the dead, and to represent them to and in the future. Without him, there would be no lineage from father to son and beyond, and no "truth." In his article *Heidegger's Ear. Philopolemology*, Derrida discusses the function of the "friend" in the constitution of Dasein and of world:

> If hearing the friend's voice constitutes Dasein's opening to its ownmost potentiality-for-being, that means there is no Dasein without it, no properness, indeed no self-proximity of Dasein without this "bei sich Tragen" of the different other, of the other-different as friend but of the other ... No ear without friend. No friend without ear.[14]

Without the friend, Dasein is not possible. In seeking Horatio's ear ("Dost thou hear?" III, ii, 64), Hamlet seeks the ear of the world in the desire to be.

To Be or Not to Be a Piece of Him

What form does the presence of the friend take? At the beginning of Hamlet, one of the guards asks whether Horatio is "there."

Horatio responds: "A piece of him" (I.i.19) – confirming that there is something systematic in the partial character of his presence. Yet given Bachmann's allusion to both Antonio and Horatio, the word "piece" also recalls Antonio's predicament – the risk of having literally to give "a piece of himself" for Bassanio. The prisoner in "The Cicadas" (*Die Zikaden)* rejects Robinson's suit with the words: "A respectable piece. It is too bad that it [he] doesn't fit me" (1, 262).

The logic of that "piece" (of the friend) is essentially the logic of the supplement which has been influentially analyzed by Jacques Derrida. The "supplement" is added to a whole which it constitutes as a whole (since it is merely "added on"), yet of which it also implies that it is incomplete (otherwise there would be no need for "supplementation"). Horatio's supplementary presence as a friend stabilizes Hamlet as a figure (see Halverson). It constitutes him as a "whole," ensures his place in history, convicts the "usurper," and maintains the proper lineage in the name) from father Hamlet to son Hamlet. Derrida's point concerning the "dangerous supplement" is that it both enables and disables the "whole" to which it is added. He reads the effect of the supplement as an "undecidability" between openness and closure. For Bachmann, what is at stake in the question of the "piece" is not the openness and closure (hemorrhage or Band-Aid) of the "one world" of fathers and sons. For her, the undecidability is between wholes, between worlds.

Let us return one more time to Horatio's response – "A piece of him." An important equivocation is at work in the word "him." To whom does it refer? Given that H⁻ ⲟⲟ (as Hamlet's supplement) is indeed constitutive of Hamlet's viability and trustworthiness as a hero – of his "being there" (Dasein) in the future – it would seem entirely appropriate for Horatio to introduce himself as "a piece of him" – i.e., of Hamlet. Yet in order to fulfill the function of the supplement which constitutes and "completes" Hamlet, Horatio also has to exist as a "whole" himself. He could not have the authority he does as a witness of "unimpeachable" integrity (Halverson, 66) if he were a mere appendix and prop to Hamlet. A mere "piece" of Horatio thus appears in the play. Most of his being and significance are located off stage. The same is true for the bond between the friends. Halverson points out that Hamlet's remark "I have told thee of my father's death" has no passage in the text to refer to, thus implying that a "powerful bond between [Hamlet and Horatio] has been cemented entirely off-stage" (Halverson, 62). Also, Horatio's most important role is to ensure the future life of Hamlet's name. That task, too, begins where the play ends (both in terms of the temporality of the plot, and in the sense that it is Horatio's support which makes Hamlet credible with the audience). Only insofar as Horatio exceeds the limits of the play can he function as Hamlet's "anchor to reality" (Halverson, 66). It is thus just as possible to read the "him" as referring to Horatio himself.

The supplementary relation between Horatio and Hamlet comes to fruition in the undecidability of the word "him." In "him," they become inseparable, the Inside and Outside of their world indistinguishable.

The prisoner, by contrast, refuses to become a "friend" in this sense. He will not mend the incompleteness of the "one world" by dressing up as a "piece of him." He declines the invitation to assume the male-gendered subject position around which the one world coheres. And since that is the only subject position for which a "suit" is available which will facilitate a return to the continent, the prisoner chooses instead the nakedness and unrepresentability of the "outpost."

Only on the outpost is a repetition possible which substitutes a different subject for the one which would only be yet another piece of him. Therefore, the moment of the leap with which the prisoner ("I") escapes from the prison island coincides with the recognition that "He cannot repeat himself" ("Er kann sich nicht wiederholen." Bachmann 1, 229).

If the prisoner is not one of the "brothers," he is also not a "woman reader." He is a temporary vehicle for a self-conscious reader who refuses to wear any one gender-suit. Gender-suits belong to the continent only. They do not apply to the "outpost."

As a result of the prisoner's decision, therefore, the woman's wish articulated in the letter which Robinson received at the beginning of the play is fulfilled: "*The Prisoner* What does she want? *Robinson* To put an end to this" (1, 242). At the end of the play, Robinson returns to the continent, the music fades, and the narrator tells us that the island and the people in the play "do not exist" (1, 267). Looking back from here, we see: "It is the hour of noon, the hour without an essence (*wesenloseste Stunde*) on the islands. Then, they look like the ruins of an illusion. Colorless, playing into brown" (1, 262).

While it lasted, that illusion tended towards a certain poetic totalitarianism, granting "being" only to those willing to be a piece of him. As we survey its ruins, therefore, we see that its colorlessness was playing into brown.[15]

Notes

1. For a discussion of the "friend" in a philosophical context see, for example, Derrida's recent book *Politiques de l'amitié* (Paris: Galilée, 1994).

2. See Bachmann, Ingeborg *Werke*, 4 vols., eds. Christine Koschel, Inge von Weidenbaum and Clemens Münster (Mün-chen: Piper, 1982 [1978]) 4, 258. Translations are my own.

3. For my use of the term "consciousness" see my *The Split Scene of Reading* (Atlantic Highlands: Humanities Press, 1997).

4. I have drawn on the convenient selection of materials about Orplid which was recently edited by Peter Härtling: *Du bist Orplid, mein Land. Texte von Eduard Mörike und Ludwig Bauer*, gesammelt und mit einem Nachwort versehen von Peter Härtling (Darmstadt: Luchterhand, 1982).

5. On literature as utopia see Bachmann's fifth Frankfurt Lecture on Poetics: Ingeborg Bachmann: "Frankfurter Vorlesungen: Probleme zeitgenössischer Dichtung. 5 Literatur als Utopie," in: *Werke*, eds. Christine Koschel, Inge von Weidenbaum, and Clemens Münster (München: Piper, 1982), 4, 255-271.

6. For example, he has to "overtake the night" (see Bachmann 1, 229).

7. Hannah Arendt, "What is Freedom?" *Between Past and Future. Eight Exercises in Political Thought* (New York: Penguin, 1993) 143-171, 169.
This reading is confirmed by the stage directions, according to which the prisoner is "very 'free'" in everything he says, he says it "straight out," for he has nothing to lose. ("Er ist sehr 'frei' in allem, was er sagt, sagt es 'heraus,' denn er hat ja nichts zu ver-lieren," Bachmann 1, 219f.) This moment of disconnection occurs elsewhere in Bachmann's work, as well, for example as the "tear-ing loose" of the bear in "Invocation of the Great Bear."

8. Compare also Bachmann's third Frankfurt Lecture on *Das schreibende Ich*.

9. That model is articulated particularly clearly and influentially in Osip Mandelstam's essay *About an Interlocutor,* which was first

published in the journal *Apollon* in St. Petersburg in 1913 (*Osip Mandelstam: Selected Essays*. Transl. Sidney Monas [Austin: University of Texas Press, 1977] 58-64). Paul Celan was instrumental in bringing about its translation into French. Mandelstam argues that poetry must exceed the realm of the known and write itself towards a future *destinataire*. The poet addresses himself to this *destinataire* to the exclusion of his "mere contemporaries." To turn towards a known addressee, Mandelstam argues, is to clip the poem's wings. To a specific person, you can only say specific things, and thus your poem fails to transcend the realm of the known.

The "island" in Bachmann's play is the site established in the effort to transcend the continent of the known which is theorized (for example) by Mandelstam and which was developed by Celan (see Martine Broda: *Dans la main de personne. Essai sur Paul Celan* [Paris: Les éditions du Cerf, 1986]. That site is irreducibly open to reversals of the kind Bachmann performs.

The most important "Robinson" for Bachmann's writing – a specific addressee of *Die Zikaden*, were I to postulate one – is Paul Celan himself. He is one who goes "perhaps a bit too far," and to his (highly gendered) poetic strategies Bachmann's work is responding.

10. Elsewhere, I have discussed Friedrich Nietzsche, Franz Kafka, and Jacques Derrida insofar as they, too, are representatives of that stance which is subject to Bachmann's implicit critique. (See my "One Must Go Quickly from One Light into Another: Between Ingeborg Bachmann and Jacques Derrida," Margaret R. Higonnet, ed. *Borderwork: Feminist Engagements with Comparative Literature* [Ithaca: Cornell University Press, 1994] 207-223, as well as my book *The Split Scene of Reading* (see note 3 above).

11. Shakespeare, William. *The Merchant of Venice* (New York: Penguin, 1965) IV.i, 304-311, 323-331.

12. John Halverson gives a concise summary of the role of Horatio in Hamlet in his "The Importance of Horatio," *Hamlet Studies*, vol. 16, 1 and 2 (1994) 57-70.

13. Shakespeare, William. *The Tragedy of Hamlet, Prince of*

Denmark (New York: Penguin, 1963) III, ii, 64-73.

14. Jacques Derrida, *Heidegger's Ear. Philopolemology*," John Sallis, ed. *Reading Heidegger. Commemorations* (Bloomington: Indiana University Press, 1993), 163-218, 173-74.

15. The allusions here are also to Paul Celan's use of color adjectives in his earlier poetry, especially *Mohn und Gedächtnis*, which culminates in the self-effacing "water-color" of the "wasser-farbene Vließ" (the "water-colored fleece/flowing") of language. (For this analysis see my dissertation: "Legenda Feminina. Ingeborg Bachmanns verschwindende Poetik." Diss. Cornell [1987], especially 84-129.)

"Flying Blind": A Neglected Early Essay by Bachmann

Geoffrey C. Howes

Bachmann's status as an essayist has now been well established, along with the literary qualities of her essays and their importance within her oeuvre, at the latest by Malgorzata Swiderska in her 1989 book *Die Vereinbarkeit des Unvereinbaren. Ingeborg Bachmann als Essayistin.*[1] The essay is experimental, it treads the brink between literature and philosophy and between literature and science, and it combines lyricism and discursiveness, all of which points to the genre's centrality to Bachmann's approach to language and writing. Swiderska regards Bachmann as a creative essayist in the sense that Musil described in *The Man without Qualities* (93), and notes that like all great essayists, she is an individualist, an outsider, a marginal figure, and someone who mediates between various seemingly irreconcilable fields of knowledge and culture (93-94); hence Swiderska's title "the compatibility of the incompatible."

Swiderska discusses Bachmann's philosophical essays, her essays on Musil, the Frankfurt lectures on poetics, her addresses, and her essays on music, indeed, nearly all of Bachmann's published and unpublished essayistic texts, yet she passes over two outwardly unassuming early essays, merely noting their existence:

What I Saw and Heard in Rome (*Was ich in Rom sah und hörte*) and *The Stowaways (Die blinden Passagiere)*, both 1955. The elision is understandable, since these essays do not directly address aesthetic or philosophical problems, and hence are not so interesting for Swiderska's dual purpose of reviewing Bachmann's essayistic production and thereby establishing something like a poetics of the essay in Bachmann. Yet in spite of their mundane "travelogue" themes, these are just as interesting, just as literary as Bachmann's other essays, and just as reflective of her general concerns.

In discussing one of these essays, *The Stowaways*, I will emphasize that it is ultimately *how* Bachmann uses literary means to approach reality, rather than *what* she writes about, that distinguishes her from lesser writers. Her main theme is also her main method, that is, critically revising the relationship between language and the world. She presents the world, using language in a way that cuts through the coercion of everyday linguistic habits to get to a truth that these habits, in the arrogance of their currency, obscure. This is a trait that the criticism has acknowledged, but it bears repeating, especially in view of the difficulty critics have met with in trying to align Bachmann with one form or another of feminism.[2] Like it or not, political and critical languages are also forms of everyday language, and Bachmann offers alternatives to these too. Her job is to invent a world; the discourses of politics and criticism must already assume the existence of a world that encompasses their terminology and conceptual systems.

However important Bachmann may be as an influence on others' political thought, it is not politics qua politics that absorbs her attention. Her role is simply (and hence complexly) that of the writer. "Some people do not exist to make realpolitik. They exist in order to invent. The world must be invented, it is the material" (333).[3] Any political questions, since they are dependent on the composition of that world, are secondary to its creation in the artistic act. The essay *The Stowaways* represents the creation of a world at the same time that it is a lesson in cultivating the open, naive, original attitude that one must assume to place oneself at the point of creation, at the beginning of a world.

The essay recounts the first airline flight of the author (or more precisely, of the "essayistic self," which corresponds to the narrator in fiction or the lyric "I"; but for simplicity's sake, let us call her the "author"). The author's fellow passengers are "blind" because they ignore the wonder of what they are doing. The urge to feel normal is much stronger than the sense that one is engaging in a miracle, or at least in what a few decades earlier would have been regarded as such. The essay appeared in 1955, less than ten years after mass air travel started to become prevalent, and the writer can be fairly certain that she is relating a brand-new experience to much of her audience. Modern technology, however, and the corresponding ease with which social engineering has made flight accessible to the public, masks the romantic aspects of the achievement. As Musil, one of Bachmann's mentors, writes in *The Man without Qualities*:

> If it is the fulfillment of man's primordial dreams to be able to fly, travel with the fish, drill our way beneath the bodies of towering mountains, send messages with godlike speed, see the invisible and hear the distant speak, hear the voices of the dead, be miraculously cured while asleep, see with our own eyes how we will look twenty years after our death, learn in flickering nights thousands of things above and below this earth no one ever knew before; if light, warmth, power, pleasure, comforts, are man's primordial dreams, then present-day research is not only science but sorcery, spells woven from the highest powers of heart and brain, forcing God to open one fold after another of his cloak; a religion whose dogma is permeated and sustained by the hard, courageous, flexible, razor-cold, razor-keen logic of mathematics.[4]

Because our "normal" versions of primordial dreams and sorcery are imbued with hackneyed fairy-tale imagery and are generally no longer believed possible, we do not recognize them when they are realized in the guise of modernity. And because we can adapt so quickly to new conditions, we do not even notice that they have taken us across an epochal border. The author of *The Stowaways* has two purposes: to examine the nature of "normality" as it persists (and as it is constituted in language) even in the highly abnormal circumstance of flying in an airplane; and to offer a fittingly anomalous point of view (and fittingly anomalous language) for regarding the experience as the source of an invention of a world.

The title *The Stowaways (Die blinden Passagiere)* can be translated literally as "the blind passengers." Since *The Stowaways* does not directly suggest the willful ignorance of clinging to normality that the metaphor of blindness connotes, I would prefer to translate the title as *Flying Blind*, which takes a dead metaphor like Bachmann's original title and revivifies it. The notion of "stowaway" – the conventional meaning of the dead metaphor *blinder Passagier* – is also an important part of the title's meaning, however, for it plays with the notion that there is a more legitimate use of the airways than just getting somewhere (the normal use): to see the world with new eyes (the aesthetic use). The former use is purposeful yet ordinary; the latter is pointless yet extraordinary. Most passengers are mere stowaways precisely because they are *not* "just along for the ride." The author, whose ride even makes her forget her destination, is one of the few who are focused on the ride itself, and hence fully *here*, not merely between here and there.

Perhaps out of character for this genre, which is traditionally bent on particularity, the essay *Flying Blind* begins with generalizations about "all" airports. Bachmann's generalizations are not prejudices, templates against which to compare and correct the view of experience. Rather they are generalizations born of experience, careful observations biased only against careless normality, careless in the sense of uncaring, carefree, incurious. For Bachmann, normality is at times amusing or charming, sometimes stupid, but often brutal. She is fascinated by normality as an all-too-human frailty, but impatient with its limits. She constantly sees new frameworks and perspectives that are usually unavailable to the person who takes a normal point of view, and she can therefore be accused of a sort of aesthetic elitism. Either you are in touch with these alternative perspectives or you are not, and the line between these two is the line between those who see and those who are, ethically and aesthetically speaking, blind. Social isolation is the price of discerning, without compromise, a dimension of experience that our social constructions of reality exclude from consideration. In its milder forms, this isolation is the sort of amused distance that Bachmann suggests in *Flying Blind*. In its most extreme forms, the isolated person, the one with the alternative perspective, falls victim to the sort of everyday brutality described in the late novels of the cycle *Ways of Death* (*Todesarten*).

As tenuous as this connection might seem, there is a continuum between the wish to spend time on an airplane reading a newspaper and acts of misogyny. Both attitudes refuse to acknowledge evidence for the existence of a second reality alongside the one-dimensional everyday condition that we conspire to take for granted. Artists are likely to be in touch with this second reality, and so are women, since the dominant culture has so often given them reason to question its premises, which square so poorly with women's experience. In Bachmann, the artist's sensibility and the woman's sensibility are one and the same, both isolating her, both leading her to extraordinary, indeed radical, conclusions about the way things are. If there is nothing particularly feminist about this early essay, still it can be seen on this continuum with later, more overtly gender-related works.

Bachmann's essay alternately presents the normal attitude and attempts to break away from it. It modulates between a dispassionate portrayal of banality and a buoyant portrayal of unheard-of possibilities for experience. It shifts between precise generalizations and precise representations of singular experience. The essay opens in the key of commonplace: every airport has the same kind of bazaar with supposedly exotic, but actually trashy, trinkets. And the same music, the thin music of music boxes, pursues the traveler from airport to airport, making her believe that she has kept the melody of the last airport in her head, when in fact she is simply hearing it over again. Consciousness, awareness, is replaced by filler, and the work of memory is performed for you.

The modern miracle of flight and its accompaniments is thus a great paradox: at the same time that it makes new and distant places more accessible than anyone ever imagined, it levels out the sense of place and the uniqueness of places. This accounts for the abruptness and seeming unconnectedness of the opening paragraph, which evokes a bizarre, tasteless sameness and debunks the prosaic idea of travel as "getting away." Against the background of this sameness a certain postmodern drama is played out: the disjuncture between the quality of our experiences and the mental tools available to us for understanding them. We can travel farther, faster, and cheaper than ever. Automobile travel was an advancement over carts and horses, but air travel seems like a quantum leap. Yet even within the first decade of mass air travel, flying had produced not a new consciousness that matched this massive change, but a sameness that guides old attitudes safely into the future. This sameness or emptiness of experience is the space within which the author is isolated, but it is also a space of negative potential. The space of enforced ordinariness is where extraordinary experience can take shape.

It is not easy to admit, but banality is not chiefly a function of the triteness of available experience; banality is a function of our mentality, which often does not rise to the possibilities it is presented with. We blame the landscape, and not our imaginations, when a cornfield is not as stimulating as an alpine scene. Only a glowing, uncompromising imagination like Bachmann's transcends the moment as it is proffered by the culture at large. The exclusivity and privacy of such a vision is one reason it is difficult to make political and feminist claims on her: her feminism is not the desire for social equality with men, but the desire for a utopian transformation of society that includes what has been excluded. This transformation seems to take place in single acts of creativity, in art.

This does not mean that art itself is the only route to getting beyond the deadly everyday sameness. Flying in a plane, at least for the first time, is a chance to see the difference between the normal attitude and another attitude, to develop what Musil called the sense of possibility. Hence we can learn as much about Bachmann's poetics from this "travelogue" as we can from her more clearly aesthetic essays on music and literature. Parallels between *Flying Blind* and the essay *Wondrous Music* (*Die wunderliche Musik*), also of 1955, can help make this evident. For instance, the blind passengers who do not see that they are doing something wondrous correspond to the concert-goers in the essay *Wondrous Music* who "check their hearing" with their coats (W 4, 46), and whose ears are "deaf ones, sound cemeteries" (47).

Like *Flying Blind*, *Wondrous Music* explores gradations between absolute triteness and transcendent awareness. The section on "Conductors," for example, presents a series of maestros: one who is surprised by his own productions; one who wields the baton like a butcher knife; one who loses his composure; and one who conspires to make the musicians look bad so he will look better. Another conductor is a magician, but only an illusionist. Finally, there is conductor who "is so famous that he can dare to perform what is written in the score" (49). He no longer needs to worry about "getting there," and so he sacrifices style for substance, in order to approach a style yet unimagined, a style beyond the wishes of his musicians and beyond his own. In this he coincides with Bachmann's own attitude. The demands he makes on his orchestra are similar to the demands Bachmann makes on her readers. "Your god isn't worth a damn!" he yells, and "My God is alright." The "alright" is in English in the original, and this message from another language has authority that surpasses the personal authority of the conductor.[5] Both he and the musicians break down and weep in frustration, but in the last rehearsal "he passes the test together with all his musicians before his God, whom he has also made into theirs" (50).[6]

Bachmann demands that the reader submit to her god, because it is the god of the music as it is "written in the score," the god of experience that has nothing to do with how we expect or hope it to be. In the second paragraph of *Flying Blind* we are met with a remarkable image that propels us out of our normal relationship to language and hence to what we experience. (One should also note Bachmann's ironic whimsy in such passages.) On the morning when she is to take her first flight, the author has left all her friends at home, "although I would have liked to wave to them." She is thus free to experience flight without social obligations interfering; this permits her to have "eyes for everything" (35). The signal that this is not a cliché is an audacious extended metaphor that tugs our normal modes of language and experience off their tracks, even by literary or poetical standards: "The air was champagne-colored, and the pop with which the cork of the night had shot up still hung in the stillness. I waved my hand through the sparkling element and in my joy I would have sprinkled the plane – if it hadn't been so far off – and given it a name" (35). The air is transformed by metaphor into an intoxicating fluid whose stimulation is felt even on the skin, and the social function of champagne as a prelude to the new is then derived from its metaphorical presence. This elaborate image should feel as heavy and busy as a second-rate baroque altar, but it does not, for it floats on the joy it expresses. This joy feels so unprecedented that the plane, which the author has "picked out" for herself, needs christening with the champagne. It needs a new appellation if it is to match the originality of the instant.

After this personal observation the next paragraph modulates back to a more objective remark on the location of airports "outside the cities, where there is a lot of air" (35). This sentence teases the reader. We know that there is more *space* outside the city, but the idea that there is more *air* turns this statement about city planning into a subjective comment on how it feels to get out of the city. Indeed, the essay's modulation between observation and ecstasy, between the extraordinary and the ordinary, always retains a trace of one phase in the next phase, so that the categories "subjective" and "objective" are mixed up and finally suspended. This also means that logic and emotion are commingled. Otherwise, what are we to make of non sequiturs like the ones in this paragraph?

> In my own way I was also still, and my patience was not a matter of chance. I no longer had any baggage with me, when I learned from the loudspeaker that the two ladies who were standing next to me at the bar and had ordered a martini were Miss Carter and Miss Herman. They were called to customs, and they went without a moment's hesitation. Nobody drank their martinis. The bartender furtively put them under the bar; later he poured them back into the bottle. I rediscovered the two ladies when I was sitting in the plane with my seat belt on. They had taken seats behind me and were burying their heads in photo magazines and seemed incapable of the slightest infraction. (36)

Somehow the author's patience is connected with two logically unrelated facts: she no longer has any baggage with her, and she has discovered the names of two of her fellow passengers. She is peaceful because she is unencumbered; she no longer is weighed down by luggage, and hence she is in a mode of transition, not really anywhere. In this state, other people are interesting in and of themselves. Their names somehow provide access to their worlds. Helga Meise writes that names are places for the writer, primary units that create nodes of significance in Bachmann's texts (102), and only after reading this statement, which actually refers to Bachmann's late fiction and not to her early essays, did I start to sort out this curious paragraph.[7] Equipped with the names of the two women, the author can follow their tiny drama)they leave pleasure for duty, strand two martinis that secretly make their way back into circulation, and then turn up unharmed and harmless in the plane.

The almost magical power of names arises elsewhere as well, in the near-christening of the plane (35), and later when the copilot whispers something to the stewardess. It is not the whispering that excites the author's curiosity, but the names she is able to give to the two crew members: "Our curiosity was piqued for a moment, for we knew that his name was Maos and she was Mlle. Baumann" (42).

As with Misses Carter and Herman, a name, a designation that lifts these persons out of their anonymity and into particularity, makes them available as objects of – disinterested – interest.

This disinterested interest is much different from the indifference of the "blind passengers." The author conveys the meaninglessness of their routine actions through two types of rhetorical devices: collective descriptions and negations of apparent fact. Here are some collective descriptions:

> Before the passengers walk onto the airfield, they drop their cigarettes as one man and stamp them out (36). The passengers read or try to sleep. Rarely, one of them looks out the window, and if he does, then he does it with a look that says: "Oh, we're only at Garden Street." (37-38)

The collective passengers act mechanically and do their cool best to ignore the fact that they're doing anything more than riding a streetcar. This leads the author to make the puzzling statement: "The passengers aren't flying" (38). She immediately explains this patent contradiction of fact: "they are moving forward and taking it easy, even though they are in a big hurry" (38). They are moving forward, but as long as they are in a big hurry (worrying about getting where they are going) and taking it easy (ignoring their circumstances), they are not flying.

For the author in her reinvented world, flying means something else. It means paying exquisite attention to the details of an experience that is available for the first time only this once. Nothing in previous experience suggests how to behave here; the author cannot decide where to sit (37) – should she follow the other passengers and sit in the back? Should she sit near the pilot? Should she sit near the wing, since that is what holds the plane up? Even superstitions must be made up out of whole cloth for this new situation.

The plane seems animated, and this is how the author interprets its behavior. Anthropomorphism suits its struggle to leave the ground, perhaps because the airplane is, after all, an extension of the human. The plane has to exert lots of energy (37); it strains to become light so it can float (37). The craft shudders and seems about to burst, "as if it was trying to destroy itself and plunge into the earth or into hell" (37). This is a moment that fascinates Bachmann again and again, the *Zerreissprobe*, the experience that one either survives or does not survive, but which one cannot avoid, for avoiding it means to avoid the truth. It is the difference between regarding the plane's leaving the ground as a successful takeoff or as a crash avoided. "An airplane that has ventured this far can no longer be stopped" (37). The finality of this situation lurks in nearly every experience, as Bachmann writes in the essay *People Can Face the Truth (Die Wahrheit ist dem Menschen zumutbar)*:

> In any circumstance, even in the most everyday circumstance of love, there is an extremity, which we, upon closer examination, can see, and perhaps we should make an effort to see it. For in everything that we do, think, and feel, we would sometimes like to take it to its extreme.(W 4,276)

Flying in the airplane seems also a chance to take experience to its extreme.

Yet once this mortal moment is past, the plane settles into its purpose. It is, after all, "a plane for the air" ("ein Zeug zum Fliegen," 37), and this etymology comforts the author, who now sits down to the show of watching the world from the air. She has a strong desire to see the ocean from above (37). Her attention then modulates again to her fellow passengers, who try to humanize the sky by sleeping, reading, and even eating, which reminds them they are aliens in this element. One stops eating and looks distracted, upset by the air "that he has so often hungered for" (38).

The ambivalence of flying is as strong a theme as its thrills. A chart is passed around, but clouds obscure the objects whose names one can identify with it, and the connection with the ground, which could have been established with names (as the names of Miss Carter and the copilot Maos created connections) is lost. The author also makes a curious discovery about speed: "Time is compressed over the distances"(38). With air travel, "two hours" is no longer a measure of distance, for these two hours can separate two houses, two countries, or even two seas. The distances, however, remain the same. "Otherwise a rapid step toward another person would have to bring me closer to him"(38). The author recalls two moments when this distance remained despite the efforts of language to bridge it. The modern lack of affiliation with places and with people cannot be remedied by adding more efficiency; indeed, efficiency can increase the alienation. This theme binds the essay with Bachmann's later prose, or a work such as *The Good God of Manhattan*, in which the distance between persons under modern circumstances is a chief theme.

Flying can perhaps offer another perspective on our earth-bound lives, but it does not remove illusion. In fact, it supplies some illusions of its own. You do not feel as if you are moving along quickly, but in fact you are. The markers along the way (the clouds, dark and light) register their own mysteries, but not a feeling of speed (39). Later she writes that there is nothing to compare one's progress to, and the plane seems to be standing still. And so some subjective impressions bring us closer to the truth, and some increase our illusions. Yet the next illusion "comes close to the truth": one can see the curvature of the earth (42-43). "One will see for this one time and this one time only that the world is round"(43). But this direct perception of a truth that is out of all human scale is repressed, written off as an optical illusion, or simply forgotten by the passengers (43).

Although most of her fellow passengers remain "blind," Bachmann records or invents a conversation between a father and his son that shows that the dialectic between "ordinary" and "extra-ordinary" is just that, a dialectic, and not an absolute polarity. Bachmann shows the syntheses, the transitional zones, in the struggle between comfort and truth. We start to hear the dialogue *in medias res*, but it becomes quickly apparent that they are talking about Icarus. The boy asks whether he looked like a bird, and his father explains the waxen wings. The child: "'Oh! like an angel!' The father: 'Angels don't have wax wings.'" This gently ironic conversation hovers at the edge of the fantastic: it is fine to talk about a myth as if it happened, but let's not bring theology into it. But at the same time, even if he did not look like an angel, Icarus's wish was certainly to be like an angel. So the trajectory of the child's thought is right, even as the father tries to bring it back down to earth. When the man explains the fate of the wax wings in the sun, it is the boy's turn for mundane realism: "'How could he do it? Your heart isn't a motor. Have you ever heard a heart roar?'" The father says no, but corrects himself: he has heard a heart roar. The child is suspicious: was it when he was flying? And the father answers: yes (39).

Thus the modern experience of flight intersects with the ancient myth, and the roar of the heart is the appropriate response to this brazen undertaking: it roars and throbs in fear and excitement, and even if this is not what gets you off the ground, it is what allows you to fly in the conscious sense that Bachmann intends here. But the air is an element in which "nobody is at home," and the earth calls Icarus, and even birds, back to itself (40). The classical myth of failed flight is balanced later by the Christian myth of the Madonna of Loretto, the patron of those who fly, who knows how they must feel because she was borne across the sea by angels. This explains her traditionally black face: it has "touched the heavens where they are darkest" (42).[8]

The ambivalence and ambiguity of flight are further apparent on a long stopover, when one "forgets where one is coming from and where one is going"(40). This purposelessness, as we have seen, is the negative space where possibilities are born, but it is also uncanny, for the airports are cut off from the cities and the passengers are cut off from the world, in "quarantine" (40). Scenes of flying, airports, of being between places, are essential to much of Bachmann's oeuvre. Helga Meise speaks of her protagonists as "artists of orientation in strange spaces" (94), and the "I" of *Flying Blind* is such a protagonist. Again, this is an ambivalent role: creative, but condemned to the sense that nearly everywhere is a strange space. This strangeness or emptiness releases the artist from prejudice and allows her fleetingly to perceive truth, but it can be frightening and depressing too.

To draw the parallel again between flying and music, both are a "gesture against an element in which no one is at home" (40). In flying this is the lofty air; in music it is the space between sounds, silence. Hearing music, one hears what one could not otherwise hear, when the music is over: "Quiet!" (*Wondrous Music*, 58). Like air, stillness is an element in which no one is at home, yet which accompanies our life. The "tragic world" (W 4, 58), death, that which is repressed from consciousness, reverberates in the stillness that the sounds of music create. And so flying puts us to the test: will you fly blind or will you acknowledge the extraordinary, which is extraordinary not because it is unusual (it is there in every circumstance) but because we refuse to allow it to enter our awareness. Can you face the truth?

By the end of the essay the euphoria of the first champagne-drenched scene has receded. The original chance for new perception, the first flight, has passed. Her second flight, a few months later, already finds the author reading a newspaper while waiting for the plane, "even though it was cumbersome to read while standing. But it was better than just standing" (43). Before, just standing was enough, because it allowed her to observe. But now when the gate is opened she drops her cigarette and crushes it with her foot, precisely the mechanical gesture she noted in the passengers on her first flight. Next to her, however, is a young man with a distressed look on his face and wide eyes (43-44). Now he is the one with the potential for extraordinary experience, and if he were not twenty years old and surrounded by others, he would press his hands to his heart and cry into the wind: "I have no idea why I shouldn't fly today" (44). To fly in Bachmann's sense of engaging his full awareness.

How difficult it is to engage in and maintain this awareness is shown both in the author's slide into normality and the ambiguous situation of this young man: he is duly scared by the potential to really fly, yet his socialized sense of sophistication and his awareness of others inhibit him.

In *Flying Blind* Bachmann sees air travel for the masses as a potential for unparalleled experience, as a sort of music or poetry. There are two attitudes: one can become blasé and act as if one were on a street car, or one can imagine what is truly happe ing – we are traveling with seven-league boots. Yet one also has this choice at a concert, in a gallery, or when reading a novel. The potential for new perception is squandered by clinging to normality, to the old language, to social self-consciousness. For Bachmann, these are chances to arrive at a new language, not because style stirs up our mundane existence and makes it new, but because this existence is always already new for those who perceive its hidden significance:

> A new language always confronts reality where a sudden moral, epistemological shift takes place, and not where someone tries to make language itself new, as if language itself could drive home knowledge and express an experience that one has never had. (192)

For a moment in 1955, flight was a moral, epistemological shift.

This shift in perception and language is valuable not just as a deepening of individual experience, but as an ethical model. We open ourselves gladly to a complex, unique, subjective experience when hearing a concert or reading a poem. But this means that we paradoxically treat objects (works of art) subjectively and subjects (persons) objectively. In *Flying Blind* Bachmann suggests a model for a type of experience that abandons this distinction, that applies the aesthetic attitude to all experience, and hence to our dealings with people as well. Even when one is merely flying, an experience that is for many now more common than riding the streetcar, one should take life as seriously as art.

Notes

1. Malgorzata Swiderska, *Die Unvereinbarkeit des Unverein-baren. Ingeborg Bachmann als Essayistin. Untersuchungen zur deutschen Literaturgeschichte* 49 (Tübingen: Niemeyer, 1989).

2. See Sara Lennox, "The Feminist Reception of Ingeborg Bachmann," *Women in German Yearbook 8* (1993) 73-111.

3. There is no published translation of Bachmann's essays, so I will quote from volume four of the German edition of her works and translate the quoted passages into English. Ingeborg Bachmann, *Werke*, eds. Christine Koschel, Inge von Weidenbaum, and Clemens Münster, 4 vols. (München: Piper, 1982). Quoted passages will be identified in the text by page number in parentheses.

4. Robert Musil, *The Man without Qualities*, Transl. Sophie Wilkins; editorial consultant Burton Pike (New York: Knopf, 1995) 35-36.

5. On the role of foreign languages in Bachmann see Helga Meise, "Topographien: Lektürevorschläge," *Ingeborg Bachmann*, ed. Heinz Ludwig Arnold (München: Edition Text + Kritik, 1984) 104-105.

6. In German Bachmann makes a pun on "Probe," which means both "rehearsal" and "test"; this word choice transforms a practice session into a test, a struggle with "God," with the ultimate questions posed by performing music.

7. Meise, 102-104.

8. Karen Achberger notes that such mythological inlays in Bachmann's fiction are a "corrective or utopian counterpoint to the narrative" that offers "glimpses of a timeless, mystical realm where real limits are suspended while fantastic possibilities are entertained." See "Beyond Patriarchy: Ingeborg Bachmann and Fairy Tales," *Modern Austrian Literature Vol.* 18, Nos . 3/4 (1985) 211.

"A Favorite Selection at the Beauty Parlor?"
Rereading Ingeborg Bachmann's
Oh Happy Eyes

Linda C. Hsu

Oh Happy Eyes appeared in *Three Paths to the Lake*, Ingeborg Bachmann's final collection of short stories published in 1972.[1] That same year, Marcel Reich-Ranicki wrote the following in a review of *Three Paths to the Lake*:

> Do these stories, in which the chic and the bizarre dominate, the mundane and the melodramatic triumph, in which everything is caught up in a sentimentality combined with a snob appeal that is hard to surpass, can these stories claim to be anything more than reading material for those ladies who leaf through illustrated magazines at the beauty parlor or in the waiting room of their dentists?[2]

Reich-Ranicki's dismissive comments served as a provocation for me to take a closer look at Bachmann's late prose, and in particular her short story, *Oh Happy Eyes*. Elsewhere in the same review, Reich-Ranicki writes: "With the exception of a few passages, these five short stories are simplistic and completely transparent, offering clear, plain writing rather than mysterious ciphers."[3] But are Bachmann's stories really as simplistic and transparent as Reich-Ranicki claims? Deceptively simple is perhaps a more apt description.

The title of Bachmann's story, taken from Goethe's *Faust*, was originally a line sung by Lynkeus, the tower watchman, whose name is "connected etymologically with the lynx, an animal known for its sharp eyesight:"[4]

> Oh happy eyes
> What all you have seen,
> Be it, as it may,
> Yet it was all so beautiful![5]

Why did Ingeborg Bachmann choose one of Lynkeus' lines as the title for a story about Miranda, an extremely nearsighted woman who also suffers from astigmatism? And why did she dedicate the story to Georg Groddeck (1866-1934), whose work on vision and the eye has remained obscure? Groddeck's paper, *On Vision, the World of the Eye and Seeing without Eyes*, published in 1966 in *Psychoanalytic Writings on Psychosomatic Medicine*, provides the answer to these questions; but more significantly, it appears also to have been the impetus and source for Bachmann's *Oh Happy Eyes*.[6]

Bachmann had written the stories in *Three Paths to the Lake* during the late sixties, and it was during this time that she had first become acquainted with Groddeck's works.[7] In 1967 she wrote the draft of a review of his works, one year after his *Psychoanalytic Writings on Psychosomatic Medicine* was published. Bachmann regarded Groddeck as one of the forerunners, if not in fact the father of psychosomatic medicine.[8]

In her review Bachmann was particularly struck by Groddeck's ideas on the cause of illness: "Groddeck's first and most keen assumption has proven itself correct: there is no illness which is not produced by the patient, not even a broken leg or a kidney stone. It [illness] is a production, like an artistic one, and illness has meaning."[9] According to Groddeck, illness is a nonverbal expression of the *Es:*

> the *Es* is for [Groddeck] a heuristic term, not a thing in itself, but rather denoting something which is present

> and . . . much stronger than the ego . . . the ego is
> a mask . . . which each of us wears, and we are
> governed by the *Es*, the *Es* . . . speaks illness
> through symbols.[10]

Groddeck did not believe in external causes of illness, but rather in internal causes which stemmed from the *Es*. For him, the distinction commonly made between mind and body was not a fruitful one. Instead, he proposed that the *Es*, as he termed it, controlled both mind and body and affected mental as well as physical health.

In 1920 Groddeck gave a talk on vision and visual disorders at the Sixth International Psychoanalytic Conference in The Hague to an incredulous audience. Groddeck espoused the view that visual disorders, especially nearsightedness, developed from an individual's repressed complexes. Visual disorders "were efforts to defend against forbidden wishes and to express them."[11] This talk, which gained him notoriety in psychoanalytic circles, also established him as an independent thinker, or "wild analyst," as he himself acknowledged to his audience.[12] Freud, who had invited Groddeck to the conference, wrote to him asking him for confirmation of his novel ideas on vision. In his response to Freud, Groddeck compared the development of visual disorders to that of antitoxins: just as antitoxins overcome toxins, visual disorders help an individual to overcome repressed complexes.[13]

Kurt Bartsch has acknowledged Groddeck's influence on *Oh Happy Eyes*. He, however, surmises that Groddeck's *Book of the Es* served as Bachmann's source.[14] Although Groddeck does discuss his theory that visual disorders are caused by the Es in *Book of the Es*, vision is not the central focus of the book. A more plausible catalyst is Groddeck's essay *On Vision, the World of the Eye, and Seeing without Eyes*, in which such ideas are specifically articulated.

Groddeck read this paper at a conference of the Swiss Psychoanalytical Society shortly before his death in 1934. In it Groddeck claimed: "For us, visual disorders are an aid to the *Es*, so that we are able to repress even when normal aids to repression prove insufficient (overlooking, not remembering, turning one's gaze away etc.)."[15] His beliefs about visual disorders as well as his etymological discussions of visual metaphors seemed to have served as inspiration for Ingeborg Bachmann's *Oh Happy Eyes*.

Groddeck argues that the repressed symbolism individuals harbor finds expression in the visual metaphors found in language. In his view, the abundance of visual metaphors shows the significance of the visual organ as an outlet for repressed emotions. He begins his etymological discussion of such metaphors with the opening lines of *Deep Night*, Goethe's poem from which Bachmann also took the title of *Oh Happy Eyes*: Born to see, Summoned to look and envision.[16]

Human vision, according to Groddeck, is a mixture of both "seeing" and "looking" or "envisioning"; an examination of the envisioning aspect of vision yields the internal or unconscious cause of visual disorders. He explained the distinction between seeing and envisioning thus: whereas seeing is a biologically determined, physical act, envisioning is constituted through a creative act on the part of the [viewer]: "Seeing [is] the passive affect of the sense of vision, envisioning a conscious act of will, which directs one's gaze to something or someone . . ." In other words, one either envisions or looks at something which does not exist external to us, or one alters a given situation or condition through means of poetic envisioning.[17] For Groddeck, seeing and envisioning are the two components that comprise vision. He called seeing the "outside-inwards" component and envisioning the "inside-outwards" component.[18] He maintained that an understanding of the "inside-outwards" component of vision is crucial in determining the cause of visual disorders, which is consistent with his claim that all illness originates from internal causes. The difference between seeing and envisioning also parallels the distinction Groddeck made between clinical and psychoanalytic approaches toward the diagnosis and treatment of visual disorders. He believed that ophthalmologists should receive training in psychoanalytic methods, in order to make diagnoses based not on the physical condition of the eye, but rather on the psychological state of the patient.

The title *Oh Happy Eyes* thus refers both to Goethe's poem and to Groddeck's discussion of the two components of vision. It seems an ironic title for a story in which the main character's eyes can hardly be construed as happy. Miranda, however, considers herself fortunate to be spared from seeing. From her point of view, her eyes could therefore be described as happy in their blindness to reality. The textual irony emphasizes Miranda's inability to make sense of her world. She views the world solely via the envisioning component of sight, since her myopia and resulting behavior rob her of the faculty of seeing. In this regard, *Oh Happy Eyes* can be read as a literary representation of Groddeck's envisioning component of sight and its manifestations in psychosomatic illness.

Bachmann's text begins with a clinical, somatic description of Miranda's lack of visual acuity. In addition to being myopic, she also suffers from astigmatism. This second condition worries her, because she cannot understand why her vision is "distorted." As she tells her lover, Josef: "Having distorted vision, you know, that's worse than being blind."[19] As the story unfolds, we learn why astigmatism, or the inability to see without distortion, is worse than being blind while at the same time serving as a mark of an albeit dubious distinction.

The narrator then abandons the clinical explanation of Miranda's visual disorders for an intuitive one, corresponding to Groddeck's psychosomatic view of illness. Miranda perceives her nearsightedness as a "gift from heaven." She is grateful that she is prevented from having to confront reality visually. Within the story several motives for her myopia can be discerned. Most critics have assumed the primary cause to be Miranda's inability to cope with the provincial Viennese society in which she lives. Although this is the initial reason for her psychosomatic condition, her relationship to Josef and his betrayal of her assume greater importance in light of Groddeck's ideas.

According to Groddeck, nearsightedness is proof that a serious conflict has arisen between an individual's personal moral views and those of her social milieu. When such an individual tries to submit to given social mores, she is forced to repress her own. This repression in turn affects her vision, since she unconsciously desires to be blind to those aspects of her society which she finds intolerable.[20] Given this theory of nearsightedness, the proper treatment would require a resolution of the moral conflict. The ophthalmologist would prescribe glasses, a solution Groddeck must find unacceptable. In his opinion, glasses should be worn only when absolutely necessary, since "corrected" vision only defeats the purpose of myopia: wearing glasses only further aggravates the individual's subconscious predisposition, which opposes convention and cannot meet societal demands, by reversing the effect of the impaired vision which the *Es* deems desirable and necessary.[21]

Miranda is especially sensitive to social outcasts whom she tries to avoid seeing along the streets of Vienna:

> If she isn't careful things might enter her field of vision which she can never forget: a glimpse of a crippled child or a midget or a woman with an amputated arm, but those are the most glaring, conspicuous apparitions in the midst of a mass of unhappy, malicious and damned faces marked by humiliations and injustices, nightmarish faces.[22]

Miranda attempts to help herself by wearing glasses only when absolutely necessary, in keeping with Groddeck's ideas on visual disorders. She even admits to punishing herself by wearing them: "Once, as a form of self-punishment, she walked all around Vienna with her glasses on, through district after district, and she feels it wouldn't be right to repeat that walk. It would go beyond her strength, and she needs all her strength to cope with the world she knows."[23] Her distorted vision provides her with an avenue of escape from the "nightmarish faces" of the Viennese streets to the safety of an "acceptable and private world" in which she only has eyes for Josef.[24] Miranda's perception of Josef is, at best, hazy: "Unlike others, she doesn't need to see him in a sharp outline . . . . She fell in love with him at first sight, although any eye doctor would have shaken his head at that, because Miranda's first glances only result in catastrophic errors."[25] The relationship between Josef and Miranda becomes yet another source and catalyst for Miranda's psychosomatic illness.

Miranda needs Josef to look after her and help her make sense of the world. She prefers him to the glasses that her body rejects – prolonged wear causes her headaches, . . . her eyes water, she is forced to lie down in a dark room.[26] In an effort to please and surprise Josef, she tries wearing contact lenses. The advertising slogan of the manufacturer, "Never lose sight of the good things in life," becomes Miranda's ironic motto.[27]

This episode reveals another aspect of Miranda, namely, that she is vain and envies "beautiful" people. Miranda surrounds herself with "beautiful" people and is herself an attractive woman. Wearing contact lenses would allow her to please and surprise Josef because she would not be wearing glasses, which she feels makes her less attractive. She has a host of admirers; even the driver of the streetcar cannot help but notice her shapely legs and smart figure. Yet Miranda is blind to her own attractive qualities and admits reluctantly to herself that she prizes beauty over all other characteristics: "But doesn't she profess to liking only beautiful people? No one knows more beautiful people than Miranda, she attracts them because she places more emphasis on beauty than on any other quality."[28]

Her name serves an another indication of her vanity; "Miranda" is Latin for "the admired one."[29] She finds fault with herself because she cannot see the blemishes and wrinkles of those around her. Miranda's friend Anastasia – Greek for "overthrower" or "destroyer" – is the antithesis of Miranda.[30] She sees "properly" or "decently," has "beautiful and properly functioning blue eyes" and is "discerning." Miranda reasons that Josef's interest in Anastasia is caused by the latter's attractiveness: "If she is abandoned – and Josef is now in the process of leaving her – then it will be because Anastasia is more beautiful or especially beautiful . . . She was simply more beautiful than I am."[31]

Miranda's obsession with beauty points to a further connection between Bachmann's story and Groddeck's paper on visual disorders. In his etymological discussion, Groddeck links "envision-ing" to "beautiful:" "There are other words which are associated with [envisioning]. For instance the word *beautiful* which shows up best what [envisioning] means since nothing else is quite as subjective-objective as beauty."[32] Miranda's preoccupation with beauty and her vanity thus provide additional motives for her myopia. Yet being blind to her environment does not allow her to see the faults of others as clearly as her own, and this ultimately works against her.

Bachmann created Miranda's identity via the idiomatic expres-sions found in German which make use of visual metaphors. Miranda enacts visual idioms, but always in a distorted fashion. As Sigrid Schmid-Bortenschlager has noted, Miranda is both passive in her refusal to "see" and aggressive in actively redesigning her reality in order to fit her world of limited perception.[33] Miranda thus sees only what she wants to; however, her other senses still subject her to unwelcome external forces. As Josef's betrayal be-comes increasingly apparent, her other senses begin to display psychosomatic symptoms as well.

Miranda's first awareness of Josef's relationship with Anastasia occurs through her sense of hearing, as his conversation centers more and more on Anastasia. Sensitive to subtle changes in Josef's behavior, she suffers silently as his visits with Anastasia become more frequent. Her pain and disbelief find expression in physical and behavioral abnormalities.

Her sense of hearing, for example, which had given her pleasure in the past, has become a bane. With Josef she had enjoyed attend-ing concerts where she could relax and "rest her eyes," whereas other "rest their souls."[34] At concerts she was impervious to the social intrigues going on around her, blissfully happy to be listening to the music rather than wondering what the people were thinking about her. With the realization of Josef's betrayal, she has become overly sensitive to noise: "Lately this city seems to be made of noise: radios, TVs, young yapping dogs, and those small delivery trucks, wait, Miranda stops short at that: she can't wish to lose her hearing on top of everything else!"[35] Her eyes have also continued to suffer under the strain: "It hurts her eyes, this act he's putting on for her, she doesn't have the aches other people do: it's not her heart, her stomach or her head. Her eyes alone have to stand all the pain, because seeing Josef had been the most important thing in the world for her."[36] Miranda can no longer bear to look at Josef, nor can she stand to hear his voice, however much she longs to do both.

To save face and avenge her injured pride, she decides to bow out gracefully and make it appear as if she, too, has no need of their relationship. She conspires to have Anastasia see her kissing Ernst, a former boyfriend, and Anastasia gives Josef an eyewitness account of what she has seen. At first Josef is disbelieving, then relieved that he has been absolved of any guilt.

Josef accompanies Miranda to her apartment after their last concert visit together, "acting as though it isn't the last time."[37] He is unable to tell her that their relationship is over, and he studiously avoids her gaze, suddenly aware that he will hurt her by terminating the relationship. Consumed by his guilt and by the look of forgiveness in Miranda's eyes, he is forced to shut his eyes to his own cruel behavior. Miranda is despairing, and her vision and hearing have become severely impaired: "She no longer wants to live imprisoned in this noise, this cell of light and darkness, her sole remaining access to the world by way of a droning headache that forces her eyes closed: they have been open too long. Now what was the last thing she saw? She saw Josef."[38] The end of her relationship with Josef quells any hope of a speedy "recovery" from her psychosomatic illnesses.

The final scene of *Oh Happy Eyes* is a *mise-en-abyme* of Miranda's story. She has run into Anastasia and Josef in a café in Salzburg, and in her embarrassment at seeing them together and in her rush to exit the café, Miranda runs headlong into a revolving door. Amid shattered glass and with an injured face, she thinks of the lens manufacturer's slogan: "Never lose sight of the good things in life."

Critics remain divided as to the meaning of the advertising slogan for Miranda. Obviously, Miranda cannot hope to subscribe to the saying literally, as one critic has suggested, because she is physically incapable of doing so.[39] Nor can she correct her skewed perception of reality so that she only sees the "good," as another critic speculates.[40] The slogan has also been interpreted as simply another one of the many lies Miranda fabricates in order to make sense of her irrational world.[41]

In my opinion, the irony of the "motto" is aimed against Miranda herself – she knows that she cannot literally keep sight of the good things in life, especially now that Josef is lost to her. She must learn to take care of herself, and the story suggests she will be unable to do so successfully. Miranda's collision with the revolving door illustrates the self-injurious nature of her relationship with Josef.[42] Miranda's attempts to help herself are thwarted by an insensitive, uncaring world. Unfortunately, her self-protective myopia does not serve her well.

Although Bachmann finds no "cure" for Miranda in her text, she does offer the reader a "diagnosis" and elaboration of Miranda's psychosomatic condition. In keeping with Groddeck's tenet that ophthalmologists would do well to heed their psychoanalyst colleagues, Bachmann's text illuminates psychosomatic illness in ways that are beyond the grasp of modern medicine. Instead of trying to alleviate Miranda's symptoms, Bachmann attempts to show the root causes of her character's illness in narrative fiction. In so doing, Bachmann fulfills her vision of the task of the writer in the modern era, which she wrote about in a speech entitled *Humanity Can Be Expected to Bear the Truth*:

> It cannot be the task of the writer to deny pain, to erase any trace of its existence, to mask it. On the contrary, the writer must perceive pain and render it once again for us, so that we are able to see it, because we all want to become aware. And such secret pains sensitize us to experience, especially to the experience of truth. We say very simply and quite correctly, when we enter this state, the lucid, aching state in which pain becomes fruitful: my eyes have been opened. We do not say this because we have perceived an event or object external to us, but because we have grasped that which we are

> unable to see. And this is what art should bring
> about: that in this sense, our "eyes have been
> opened."[43]

In *Oh Happy Eyes*, Bachmann shows us that which cannot be seen except with the mind's eye.

Groddeck's holistic approach toward illness earned him Bachmann's admiration. In her review of his works, she criticized modern medicine's impersonal methods and increasing bureaucratization and lauded Groddeck's wholehearted, almost fanatical concern for the mental and physical well-being of his patients. She also expressed the belief that his ideas and methods would gain appeal, and in *Oh Happy Eyes* she rendered a literary application of his ideas on vision. By presenting a character whose physical ailments are a direct result of her interactions with specific individuals and the mental distress such interactions cause, Bachmann offers an alternative to a strictly physiological or medical view of illness.

Irene Holeschofsky has accused Reich-Ranicki of a superficial reading of the stories in *Three Paths to the Lake*; the same can be said of many readings of *Oh Happy Eyes* which thus far have neglected to explore the connection between Bachmann's story and Georg Groddeck's work in psychosomatic medicine.[44] And what about the reading material of "those ladies who leaf through illustrated magazines at the beauty parlor or in the waiting room of their dentists?"

For my part, Bachmann's story is well worth the wait. Amidst the cosmetic distortions in the name of beauty and aesthetic appeal, Bachmann's Miranda serves as an ironic reminder to take a hard look at ourselves and our language: "Never lose sight of the good things in life."

Notes

1. Ingeborg Bachmann, "Eyes to Wonder," *Three Paths to the Lake: Stories by Ingeborg Bachmann*, Transl. Mary Fran Gilbert (New York: Holmes & Meier, 1989) 75-94. I have translated the title of the story much more literally than Gilbert, who translated the title *Ihr glücklichen Augen* as *Eyes to Wonder*. Unless otherwise noted, all translations of Bachmann's text are taken from this edition.

2. Marcel Reich-Ranicki, *Die Dichterin wechselt das Repertoire, Christine Koschel and Inge von Weidenbaum, Kein objektives Urteil – Nur ein lebendiges: Texte zum Werk von Ingeborg Bachmann* (München: Piper, 1989) 189-90 (translation my own).

3. Ibid., 189.

4. Ann White, *Names and Nomenclature in Goethe's Faust*, diss., Institute of Germanic Studies, University of London, 1980, Bithell *Series of Dissertations 3* (London: 1980) 123.

5. Johann Wolfgang von Goethe, *Faust*, pt. 2, act 5, *Tiefe Nacht*, lines 11300-11303 (translation my own).

6. Georg Groddeck, *Vom Sehen, von der Welt des Auges und vom Sehen ohne Augen, Psychoanalytische Schriften zur Psychosomatik*, Ed. Günther Clauser (Wiesbaden: Limes Verlag, 1966) 263-331 (All translations of Groddeck's text, unless otherwise noted, are my own).

7. Andreas Hapkemeyer, *Ingeborg Bachmann: Entwicklungslinien im Werk und Leben*, Österreichische Akademie der Wissenschaften Philosophisch Historische Klasse Sitzungsberichte, vol. 560 (Wien: Verlag der Österreichischen Akademie der Wissenschaften, 1990) 145.

8. I have chosen to use the term psychosomatic to describe the kind of "medicine" Groddeck was practicing, in keeping with his own self-description and Bachmann's understanding of his work.

9. Ingeborg Bachmann, *Werke*, eds. C. Koschel, I. von Weidenbaum, C. Münster, vol. 4 (München: Piper, 1978) 351 (translations my own).

10. Ibid., 352. See also Georg Groddeck, *Das Es und die Psycho-analyse, Verdrängen und Heilen: Aufsätze zur Psychoanalyse und zur psychosomatischen Medizin* (Frankfurt am Main: Fischer Taschenbuch Verlag, 1988) 60-70. In it Groddeck gives a definition of the *Es* and contrasts it with Freud's term *Unbewußt* or the unconscious: "The term *Unbewußt* does not mean the same thing as the term *Es*. That which is unconscious was at one time part of consciousness . . . *Es* and *Unbewußt* are, I repeat, two completely different concepts: the unconscious is a part of the psyche, the psyche a part of the *Es*" (67).

11. Carl M. Grossman, M.D. and Sylvia Grossman, *The Wild Analyst: The Life and Work of Georg Groddeck* (New York: George Braziller, Inc., 1965) 97.

12. Ibid., 95. The term "wild analyst" has a negative connotation; it was used to designate "analysis by untrained persons."

13. Georg Groddeck and Sigmund Freud, *Briefwechsel* (Wiesbaden: Limes Verlag, 1970) 44.

14. Kurt Bartsch, *Ingeborg Bachmann,* Sammlung Metzler, vol. 242 (Stuttgart: J.B. Metzlersche Verlagsbuchhandlung, 1988) 165. See also Sara Lennox's discussion of Groddeck's term *It* in connection with Bachmann's *Malina* in: "In the Cemetery of the Murdered Daughters: Ingeborg Bachmann's Malina," *Studies in Twentieth Century Literature*, 5 (1980) 75-105.

15. Groddeck *Psychosomatik* 285.

16. Ibid.

17. Ibid., 289.

18. Ibid., 275. I have borrowed Gertrud Mander's translation of the two components of vision from her partial translation of Groddeck's text in: Lore Schacht, ed., *Vision, the World of the Eye, and Seeing without the Eye, The Meaning of Illness: Selected Psychoanalytic Writings by Georg Groddeck*, Transl. Gertrud Mander (New York: International Universities Press, Inc., 1977) 174.

19. Bachmann, *Eyes to Wonder* 75-76.

20. Groddeck, *Psychosomatik* 307-08.

21. Ibid., 308.

22. Bachmann, *Eyes to Wonder* 77.

23. Ibid.

24. Holger Pausch, *Ingeborg Bachmann, Köpfe des XX. Jahrhunderts*, vol. 81 (Berlin: Colloquium Verlag, 1975) 74.

25. Bachmann, *Eyes to Wonder* 76-77.

26. Ibid., 80.

27. Ibid., 94. The advertising slogan might also be rendered as "Always look on the bright side" to parallel the idiomatic quality of the German expression.

28. Ibid., 91.

29. Robert Pichl, "*Rhetorisches bei Ingeborg Bachmann: Zu den 'redenden Namen' im 'Simultan'-Zyklus*," *Jahrbuch für Internationale Germanistik 8.2* (1980) 298-303. Bachmann herself gave a lecture on naming and names in literature as part of her Frankfurt lectures (cf. *Der Umgang mit Namen, Werke*, vol. 4, 238-54).

30. *Anastasis*, Liddell and Scott's Greek-English Lexicon, 1870.

31. Bachmann, *Eyes to Wonder* 91.

32. Schacht 182.

33. Sigrid Schmidt-Bortenschlager, "*Frauen als Opfer-Gesellschaftliche Realität und Literarisches Modell: Zu Ingeborg Bachmanns Erzählband 'Simultan',*" *Der Dunkle Schatten, dem ich schon seit Anfang folge: Ingeborg Bachmann-Vorschläge zu einer neuen Leüthre des Werkes*, ed. Hans Höller (Wien: Löcker Verlag, 1982) 85-95.

34. My translations of Bachmann's phrases "Augenruhe" and "Seelenruhe," respectively.

35. Bachmann, *Eyes to Wonder* 91.

36. Ibid., 90.

37. Ibid., 92.

38. Ibid., 93.

39. Irene Holeschofsky, "Bewu8tseinsdarstellung und Ironie in Ingeborg Bachmanns Erzählung *Simultan*," *Sprachkunst: Beiträge zur Literaturwissenschaft 11.1* (1980) 63-70.

40. Christa Gürtler, *Schreiben Frauen Anders? Untersuchungen zu Ingeborg Bachmann und Barbara Frischmuth*, eds. U. Müller, F. Hundsnurscher and C. Sommer (Stuttgart: Hans-Dieter Heinz Akademischer Verlag, 1985) 262.

41. Gudrun Mauch, "Ingeborg Bachmanns Erzählband *Simultan*", *Modern Austrian Literature,* vol. 12, nos. 3/4 (1979) 273-304.

42. Bartsch 165.

43. Ingeborg Bachmann, *Die Wahrheit ist dem Menschen zumutbar: Essays, Reden, Kleinere Schriften* (München, Zürich: Piper, 1981) 75; my emphasis.

44. Holeschofsky, 64.

The Intellect of Love: Female Thought and Presence in the Poetry of Ingeborg Bachmann

Manfred Jurgensen

A key poem in the writings of Ingeborg Bachmann, *Tell Me, Love* from the second collection of *Invocation of the Great Bear,* offers the most immediate and powerful access to the author's understanding of herself as a woman of intellect and artistic creativity. The original German carries a more precise meaning of the poem's programmatic title lines: "Explain to me, Love," perhaps even "Explain, Love, to me." They summarize the female poet's lamentation over the conflict between nature and consciousness, sexuality and intellect, biology and identity:

> Tell me, love, what I cannot explain:
> should I spend this brief, dreadful time
> only with thoughts circulating and alone,
> knowing no love and giving no love?
> Must one think? Will one not be missed?

Again, the English translation is imprecise and misleading. "... und allein/nichts Liebes kennen" carries a deliberate emphasis: "and be the only one not knowing love" would have done the text greater justice. The theme is the woman artist's forced detachment from the natural passions of her gender. She is suffering an isolation which is the very basis of her artistic calling. It is paradoxically only by means of such alienation that the poet's own creativity transforms consciousness into literary art. Hers is the passion of knowledge that redefines and reinvokes its losses.

There is a sense of longing informing all of Ingeborg Bachmann's poetry which can only be understood in these terms. "I watch the salamander/slip through every fire" is a statement epitomizing the artist's knowing position: she is "watching," observing and witnessing a nature her poems can celebrate only in passions of mythology and imaginative transformation. Unlike the salamander, Bachmann is burned by the fire, she feels its pain and dreads its destruction. There is no need to perpetuate the myth of the poet's death by fire in a Roman hospital; this is not a case of life imitating art. The fire motive runs throughout Bachmann's oeuvre with the same specific allusion: the surrender of identity and independence in the fiery passions of sex and love. It is a paradoxical, cruel and illogical love which threatens her very being as a female artist.

Borrowed Time, Bachmann's first collection of poems, also carries in the original German the existentially and poetologically specific meaning of "measured time," the "hourly" grace of existence as well as the lyrical concept of recording and verifying an extended history. "Smoke" is one of the first images invoked in the opening poems of that collection. The tone of *Journey Out* is overwhelmingly descriptive ("Smoke rises from the land..."), with an early reminder that "the sun will sink." And already the poet offers advice, not least to herself: "Even when the ship pitches hard/and makes each step uncertain,/stand calm on deck." A (life) boat carries the woman above "dark water." She does not escape nature, but lets herself be raised above it by a consciousness of detachment and imaginative, transformative observation. In the fourth stanza the daily life of "men" is described, starting with an account of ritualistic meals and ending with an invocation of the bread of dreams. There is a daring identification with the natural landscape – for it is female: "The dark water...opens its white-foamed lashes," its waves reach the poet who soon can no longer see land and who now seeks to re-enact a oneness with her natural gender she appears to have lost: "With your hand you should have dug into the sandbank or tied yourself to the cliff with a strand of hair."

Interestingly, her own poetic womanhood aims to reunite with a female nature she finds both threatening ("sea monsters float") and, in a deadly defeatist way, curiously reassuring ("a red trail/ remains in the water, where sleep takes hold of you"). The poet's "senses" are "spinning" because she struggles to remain awake, to continue to be conscious of the creative and the destructive forces of womanhood. The poem ends with a call to repair the craft "that sail far away." But they are the boats of men fishing the sea, now calling upon the woman to be of assistance. Like her sisters, Bachmann is anxious to oblige. Read properly, the following three lines are among the most powerful feminist statements made in modern German literature: "But then something happens with the ropes, you are called and you are happy that you are needed." The full pathos of this admission becomes apparent when it is compared with the equally moving outburst in *Tell Me, Love*: "Must one think? Will one not be missed?"

The fear of being left "alone" informs the natural, pathetic joy of being "called." The "guarding" of the "freight" remains ambivalent because it is not clear whose freight it is, the man's or the woman's. On one level, the final seven lines of *Journey Out* may indeed be read as a poetic description of a woman's daily challenges as wife and mother. But it is the complexity of Bachmann's images which introduces further, less "accepting" readings of the text. The *Journey Out* is partly an encouraging act of defiance, partly a lament of the seemingly inescapable pattern of female existence.[1] In the broader context of Bachmann's poetry and feminism her language embodies both the nature and consciousness of womanhood. In terms of the poem's own imagery there are different possibilities for women "to lift the ship over the waves" – in support of male craft, or "to awaken clear to the first light." Enlightenment and despair, knowledge and imprisonment, being and death are always causally interrelated in the poetic and social consciousness of Ingeborg Bachmann.

As in all good poetry, description transforms itself into vision, the image becomes a metaphor, the metaphor a symbol. It is a central feature of Bachmann's poetry to incorporate womanhood into nature in such a way that both redefine each other. Neither in poetry nor in social politics can there be simple equation. The nature of woman (and the "femaleness" of nature) defines itself in complex imaginative and self-assertive terms. *Fog Land (Nebelland)* is one of many love poems in which Bachmann invokes a presence of intelligence which is created and composed. The female lover emerges as her own invention; the poet "makes her" a complex design, a pattern of uniqueness of imaginative strength and independent passion. It is easy to see how the descriptive landscape gives way to a nature anima embodied in female adaptation. In constantly changing appearance the beloved woman will not be trapped by social or cultural pre-definition, her nature remains defiantly untamed. She resides in *Fog Land*, in "winter" and in a wilderness of carnal knowledge. It is in the brutal natural passions, "the bird's hunting call," that love between man and woman leads to a shared defeat.[2] In a seeming reversal of traditional role imagery "she plucks/the hens" to let him "walk off through the bitter down." With characteristic ambiguity Bachmann both celebrates and laments a love which makes her "think" (cf. *Must One Think?*, *Tell Me, Love*). In *Fog Land* love does speak directly: wooing the beloved leads to a recognition of the brutality of desire, the ambivalent powers of nature and the elusiveness of a womanhood under siege.

Perhaps one of Bachmann's most powerful love poems carries a defining title highlighting the difficulty of coming to terms with the nature of human love: *Love: Dark Continent*. The image invokes a realm of barely civilized rule; its "black king holds aloft the panther's claws" and "he chooses and rejects you without grounds." The poet yet again points to the tyranny of love, the lack of defense against its willful rule. The natural landscape of this poem is entirely composed of poetic vision, it is a curiously attractive place of execution ("You stare transfixed, seeing where you will die."), seductive in its violent knowledge and the "secret" of its powerful beauty. In an extraordinary exercise of self-restraint Bachmann, perhaps incongruously, employs rigid classical meter and pure rhyme. The wildness of vision remains firmly controlled by the poem's formal structure. *Love: Dark Continent* carries the ambivalence and fascination of Conrad's *Heart of Darkness* linked to Blake's *Songs of Innocence and Experience*; fairy tale and horror story intermingle. Sexual passion is invoked as worship and sacrifice. "From every jungle recess: sighs and screams. He lifts the fetish. You have no reply."

Bachmann's preoccupation with *Todesarten* derives almost exclusively from the realm of human sexuality. The poem's imaginative strength is inseparable from its vision of horror. Its final stanza amounts to an apotheosis of "the panther" who "crosses over from the valley of death,/trailing the heavens' fabric in his claws." Love is his territory, his rule and his prey. Bachmann knows that violence is an inherent part of love. It is a discovery carrying its own terror – and the inspiration of the poem's female thought and presence. Must the woman be in collusion with such intimidation, must she inherit the "insignia from the black king's hands"? Defiantly the poet asserts "You can deprive the kingdom of its king." But the poem itself contradicts this apparent confidence. It reads a powerful document of the fascination of woman with the animalistic, male-dominated "nature" of love, carrying with it the erotic horror of Joseph Conrad's vision.

Bachmann recognizes the nature of this territory, she describes it and she judges it in visionary imagination. Can she (re)claim it as her own? In *The Native Land* she awakens to a "light" of knowledge, but even then it is the sight of recognition which liberates her. She does not rule even her native realm, she comes alive in bearing witness and inspiring regeneration. "And when I drank of myself/and my native land/rocked with earthquakes,/I opened my eyes to see./Then life fell to me." Certainly there is promise and hope: drinking her own communion causes earthquakes within herself. Here, and elsewhere, Bachmann's poetry is one of Annunciation.

Her dilemma is that of a woman whose knowledge is, in the first instance, a "seeing." She finds that conveying her thought she begins to live "in another tongue." *How Shall I Name Myself?* records the difficulties of that situation – and Bachmann's determination to overcome the suppressive pattern of patriarchal language. In an attempt to find her own expression the poet's nature imagery undergoes a further process of transformation, one in which the very course of change assumes the character of woman's true identity. The historical and ideological implications of the opening stanza are unmistakable: "Once I was a tree that had been bound,/and then I slipped out as a free bird; /chained up in a ditch I was later found,/laying an egg that was covered with dirt."

The promise of a new beginning grows out of a consciousness of bondage and servitude in the past. The "egg" is dirty, but symbolizes a hope carrying its own shell. And that shell is not broken. Thus the poem reaffirms not merely the need, but also the possibility of creative liberation for suppressed womanhood. Yet, tragically, inevitably, this need to grow a new voice interacts with Bachmann's poetic genius which still relates to concepts of imaginative language designed by the aesthetics of patriarchy. Put simply, Bachmann faces the problem so characteristic of most so-called "women writers": to what extent, and in what manner, does the social and cultural liberation of women determine the literary, artistic expression, its form and structure, its very language, the quality of the poet's imagination? Is it possible to create a poetry recognized by men, but of a quality which allows her to say "I can once more see myself?" The answer, in Bachmann's case, is triumphantly clear. Precisely because of its inherent conflict her poetry possesses an imaginative complexity in which language, images and ideas constantly question each other, lending her work the overall quality of an invocation, a revision, or appeal. When Bachmann writes "But a beginning sings inside me still – or an end – and it prevents my escape," she points to a dilemma which in fact does not merely imprison her but is also the source, the realm of her special creativity. For it is here, between the "beginning" and an "end," that Ingeborg Bachmann's woman resides, where she finds herself in conflict, but in the knowledge of an authentic self. "For what we are can only be imagined," writes the Australian poet James McAuley.[3] Bachmann's greatness lies in her ability to articulate imaginatively her gender's collective need to redefine itself within a continuing patriarchal cultural discourse while expressing the searching, gradual liberation of her own authentic self. Her poem states the challenge categorically, though not without deliberate ambiguity: "How shall I name myself/without living in another tongue?"

In fact she is "naming" herself in the "other tongue" of man,[4] with the aim of using its complexity ("Dichte") to find a "tongue" of her own. That is the freedom poetry does allow her. There is in all of Bachmann's poems a "female presence," instantly recognizable and powerfully effective, turning the language of men against itself, authoring the woman in that very process.

It was clearly easier for Bachmann to adopt the traditions of patriarchal poetry to transform the act of "naming" than it proved in her later attempts to do the same in prose. The violent response of male critics to her *Todesarten* trilogy of novels confirms the difficulty of writing "in another tongue." Bachmann's very attempt to introduce into narrative prose forms poetic qualities of imaginative liberation and creative transformation must be recognized as female aesthetics challenging the rigidity and lack of authenticity in male concepts of literary art. Bachmann's biography demonstrates the difficult but essential union of life and literature. The poet suffered her writing, as her art remained her life. It is worth quoting those lines again, this time with special emphasis on their verbs: "How shall I *name* myself/without *living* in another tongue?" Ingeborg Bachmann lived the conflict of "authoring" herself and her gender in a male-dominated culture "binding its trees." The haunting, urgent question "What am I now?" is posed on behalf of all women; its courage lies in the poet's own determination to find herself in the realms of creative freedom left by patriarchal culture. The language she employs is both hers and the "others," the complexity of her poetry, its very own *Dichte*, derives from a transformation of alienation into appealing intimacy, an act of identification which proves to be detachment, negation and metamorphosis.

Thus it is not surprising that Bachmann uses a number of symbolic images which recur throughout her work. They are codes of consciousness and change. Light, high noon, the sun and fire convey vital stages of recognition, understanding and alteration. The most important images are derived from nature, acknowledging its basic importance in a female culture of liberation) but also the need to free itself from the confines of biology. Darkness appears as a correlative (cf. *Darkness Spoken*) in the process of conscious transformation. As fluidity is a central feature of natural change, water, harbors and rivers play an important part in Bachmann's lyrical vocabulary. These images are the language of her naming, the passwords of her creative liberation.

Bachmann's affirmation of light ("where we are not, is night," *Paris*) grows out of an intimate knowledge of its challenge and the terror of nothingness that is its opposite. "Lifted onto the wagon of light/... we are lost," the poem declares; conscious existence holds its own fear and intimidation. For the "light" can be "cold." But it is here that the woman artist has to prove herself. It is a "heavy cargo." In the poem of this name Bachmann writes "you'll drown, open-eyed, in the light you'll drink." The senses of meaning can also be the senses that mislead, that drown the nature of womanhood into oblivion. In different seasons women submit "to rain and also at last the light" (*March Stars*). The love poem *In Twilight* invokes in its very opening the creative ambiguity of the senses:

> Again we both swear to what we each hold as true, you reaching for the wine of the seasoned night, I for morning's wellspring that knows no winery.

These lines assume their full impact only when it is realized that the poet's voice is both the "you" and the "I," that, as with *Tell Me, Love*, the woman artist (and intellectual) is torn between the senses of nature and the sense of identity and meaning. For it is in love that this conflict emerges most radically, most brutally. Bachmann knows the experience she describes in *Theme and Variation* with these two lines: "Already the sun had struck/and spun around death." The "noon" of warmth and light, of love and regeneration can come "early," revealing the brutality of man (*Early Noon*). For the poet it becomes the height of recognition articulating a brutality of sight. It is a noon "in embers." Along with the ashes "hope" is "blinded in the light." Bachmann's poetry records such pain of seeing. It carries a vision of despair: "Of the great storms of light, none has come to life."

But it is also an invocation of faith, a force of enlightenment residing in the image of promise and terror. "Where fear leaps up inside me/and blinding light opens before me," Prince Myshkin confesses in his monologue, "I discover/the horror...." (*A Monologue of Prince Myshkin to the Ballet Pantomime The Idiot*). But the poet also knows that "In an overbearing age/one must flee from one light into another." (*Curriculum Vitae*) Her art consists of the shaping of light, transforming it into an imagery of self-definition, self-consciousness and self-transformation. The motive plays a central part in enacting Bachmann's imaginative creation of womanhood. The "new language" remains both assertive and ambivalent. It is its questioning quality which is at the same time its critically affirmative claim. Bachmann's searching and liberat- ing process of "naming" is precarious for women as much as for men: "Oh the ascent of clouds, of words,/entrusted to the shard pile's pyre!"

This "Mound of Shards" is the very medium a female intelligence and creativity needs to work in; out of the fragments of patriarchal language, ideas and assumptions, her new "pleading words" will grow and compose a re-unified identity, an art form which is recognizably, challengingly, affirmatively an expression of womanhood. Occasionally "the light foams" (*Spoken and Rumored*), but the poet's prayer like invocation will find fulfillment:

> Word, be that part of us
> enlightened, clear, and beautiful.

> Certainly an end must come,
> so take it as warning.

There can be little doubt about Bachmann's faith in woman's power to transform the culture of patriarchal language. It is a struggle she defines in many of her poems as well as in her prose. "The beast will not be caught by the one who mimics its call," she warns. Contrary to the popular myths about Bachmann's early accidental death, the imagery of fire in her poetry is a code of transformation, knowledge and passion, even purification by self-defiant renewal. If "this hand will fall into the fire," as one of her poems asserts, it will be delivered by "my word," a triumphant phoenix-like rebirth into authenticity. *Deliver Me, My Word!* is an appeal uniting light and fire, enlightenment and passion, reflection and creation. The poet no longer spends "this brief, dreadful time/only with thoughts" (*Tell Me, Love*); she becomes part of a nature recognizing her consciousness and being. Her "word" releases her into authenticity.

The central image of fire gains further impact from its intertextual significance in Ingeborg Bachmann's work. In her *Songs from an Island* she alludes to an all-embracing, apocalyptic transformation. "There's a fire under the earth," she reminds herself, "and the fire burns clean." In deceptively simple language, precisely codified and contextualized, she anticipates the end of the world in both scientific and traditional religious terms: "There will be a great fire./There will be a great flood." The remarkable thing about this affirmation of fiery change is that it is totally free of associations of terror and fear. Bachmann's tone is that of a statement, even in the poem's final line: "We shall witness each." There is a calmness which derives from certainty, the confident acceptance of knowledge and belief. It is impossible not to be reminded of her earlier lines: "I see the salamander/slip through every fire./No dread haunts him, and he feels no pain."(*Tell Me, Love*) Bachmann's artistic and moral integrity lies in her total identification with words, her faith in the poetic logic of imaginative thought. She projects herself, albeit longingly, into the fiery salamander of "no pain." The fire she invokes in her writing is the end of a male-dominated world and the re-formation of life on a fundamental scale. Her own creativity proves a vital part of its energy, along with the cleansing and at times terrifying strength of vision of other women in other fields of human endeavor. Out of the burning of one culture a new world, a new quality of being will emerge. Occasionally her poems carry lines of warning in which men are gently, almost lovingly, alerted to the changing of the world and their need to participate in this fundamental process of redirection. *North and South* ends with the haunting reminder: "Then you knocked it away. Its season left you/as soon as, with the birds, I fled your land."

The female writer and the self-conscious, self-reliant woman remain "in the midst of it" (*Letter in Two Drafts*); they articulate and assert their own consciousness in drafts of new versions, hoping for a "goodbye without insult." Bachmann uses self-quotations and variations in her poetry to express the path to a new, her own language. She reinvokes one of her most powerful poems in lines like "and autumn in a land of fog the gaudy tatters." Bachmann's *Fog Land* is a vital part of her "female landscape" which reinterprets and replaces predefined concepts of nature and identity. Its ambivalence is the very basis for a new process of identification.

In *Under the Grapevine* this new poetic interpretation of nature is linked again very forcefully to a feminist discourse of redefinition. It is a natural process which will bring about the fruition of woman's true identity.

> The night must turn over the leaf
> when the peel bursts open
> and out of the pulp there presses the sun.

Each stanza repeats the programmatic line "The night must turn over the leaf," emphasizing the importance of light and darkness symbolism in Bachmann's codified nature poetry. She remains confident that "the light pours out its seeds" (*In Apulia*) and that it is "a light that never recedes."

Fluidity, the other recurrent central image of Bachmann's poetic female consciousness, shares with the light symbolism the promise of purity in change. Again, she operates in terms of coherent objective correlatives: her art transforms the meaning of a natural landscape.

> The purified water held within its hands,
> at midday, under the eyebrows of its white caps,
> the river gazes deep into its depths...

> > *(At Agrigento)*

Light and water together build a composed residence of female spirituality and creativity. The poor translation of the line "wird der Fluß die tiefren Töne lieben" as "the river begins to love the sea's deep thrust," hides or distorts the specific allusion to the deeper meaning, the more embracing dimensions of the poem's process of transformation and redefinition. It is only with that inherent direction in mind that the poem's final stanza can be fully recognized as a celebration of woman's return to a sacred being, her own discovery grown out of the basic elements of life, water and fire:

> Consecrated by light from silent fiery brands, the sea
> still holds the ancient temple open,
> as the river, returning to its origin,
> with purified water held within its hands,
> takes consecration from the silent fiery brands.

As in earlier poems (*The Native Land* etc.), allusions to self-consecration, a communion of spiritual, sacramental identification, a transubstantiation into authentic being affirm Bachmann's belief that the liberation of women is in itself an act of sanctity, a holy duty and a natural blessing. This sacred task may be fulfilled by political action and revolutionary force, but to Bachmann it is essentially a religious calling. No other German-language poet has celebrated the spiritual dimension of women's liberation to the extent that Bachmann does. It remains one of many gaps in contemporary Bachmann criticism and scholarship.

This poet's glorification of light is expressed most powerfully in her lines *To the Sun*. In what amounts to an officiation of her faith Bachmann invokes a nature "colorful, shapely, come into the world on a beam of light." The German "mit einer Sendung von Licht" explicitly refers to the missionary casting of such light, its divine origin and purpose) worshiping the sun which makes her see, and lamenting "the inevitable loss of" that precious "sight." For her, light carries a spiritual presence, the divine power to be and to define, to be in identity. Even in love it is essential to "illuminate...the dark" (*Songs in Flight*, VI). The fluidity of her being turns the woman into Undine, elusive in change: "swim, look and dive," she appeals to her lover, "I am not the one./I am." (*Songs in Flight*, XIII). Fire and water are of course the key symbols of enlightenment, of baptism and sanctification, the elements of reason and the deification of sense. It is such rationalism which informs the spirituality of Ingeborg Bachmann's poetry and prose. Her vision of liberated womanhood combines imagination and intellect, being and consciousness, invocation and annunciation. It is the faith of this "sight" which gives her art of "naming" the power of creative integrity.

Notes

All quotations are from *Songs in Flight. The Collected Poems of Ingeborg Bachmann,* transl. Peter Filkins (New York: Marsilio, 1994).

1. The journey image is, of course, a strong indication of development and change.

2. It is significant that in the structure of patriarchal power both man and woman are losers in love.

3. James McAuley, *Against the Dark, Surprises of the Sun* (Sydney: 1969) 47.

4 Cf. Manfred Jurgensen, *Ingeborg Bachmann. Die neue Sprache* (Bern: Peter Lang, 1981).

5. Cf. Kurt Bartsch, *Ingeborg Bachmann* (Stuttgart: Metzler, 1988).

Ingeborg Bachmann's *Death Styles*: A Narrative Historiography of Fascism and the Holocaust

Kirsten A. Krick

> My story and the stories of everybody who
> indeed constitute the larger story, where do
> they join the larger one? – *Franza's Case*[1]

Anyone who has seen Leni Riefenstahl's 1935 film documentary of the 1934 Nuremberg Party Congress *Triumph of the Will* experiences an uneasy chill when the overwhelming German masses chant in adoration of their *Führer*. Similarly Thomas Bernhard's character Frau Professor Schuster in *Heldenplatz* slowly loses her mind as she constantly recalls the masses crying out "Sieg Heil" in unison below her apartment after German troops march into Vienna in 1938.[2] Gerhard Botz points out that Hitler's troops were not the ones screaming and displaying brutality in the streets of Klagenfurt, but in fact thousands of Carinthian Nazis who greeted the tide of German troops.[3] When Hitler spoke from the balcony of the Hotel Sandwirt in Klagenfurt on April fifth, Bachmann was in the hospital suffering from diphtheria. Is it any wonder then that Bachmann, who was twelve years old at the time, describes the "Einmarsch" of Hitler's troops into Carinthia as the first traumatic experience of her childhood and, more importantly, that this experience triggers the "origin of her memory?"[4] It is the brutality, the roar of the crowd, the marching into her peaceful Carinthia, as she calls this intrusion, that brings on her first feeling of deathly fear. In fact, it is precisely this moment in Bachmann's perception of history that becomes a focal point in her unfinished trilogy *Death Styles* (*Todesarten*), more specifically in the novel fragment *Franza's Case* (*Der Fall Franza*), begun in 1963.

The process of remembering and writing intersects with the memory of the historic events surrounding the Austro-fascist rule from 1934 to 1938 and the Nazi rule from 1938 to 1945 in Austria. "Vergangenheitsbewältigung" literature, narratives which come to terms with the past,[5] has been criticized for portraying the "trivial daily struggles and idylls of the family and almost ignoring concentration camps, slave labor and the role of the technology and industry in the Nazi events."[6] Bachmann, however, explores Nazism from within the personal relationships of her female non-Jewish narrators, as well as portrays historical details such as gas chambers and the deportation of Jews. While Bachmann's work should thus be read in the wider context of her participation in the politically active *Group 47*,[7] the author was careful to emphasize her independence from this particular literary scene, calling their political involvement less than adequate.[8]

When Bachmann's *Malina* first was published in 1971, most literary critics agreed that the novel was far from depicting historical, political, and social reality. Bachmann, however, was well aware of the impact of history in writing, being well-read in many fields, including, but certainly not exclusively, German literature, philosophy, psychology, and history. When asked in 1963 what she was reading at the time, Bachmann replied: "Many factual books, documentations which explore the recent war and concern contemporary history; in general everything tends to encompass history, the philosophy and writing of history."[9] Ten years later Bachmann would state that a writer could in fact not afford to write within a vacuum: "History is indispensable for a writer. One cannot write if one does not see all the socio-historical connections which have led us to our present time."[10]

The public, who had first embraced Bachmann as a poet, was

highly critical of the new style and content of the novel *Malina*, perhaps feeling somewhat uneasy about its subject matter. Much of Bachmann's narrative involving the Holocaust can be found in the fragment, as well as in the central dream chapter of *Malina*, where the father figure is portrayed as a Nazi in some sequences. Although there is much controversy concerning Bachmann's posthumously published novel fragment edition of *Franza's Case*, one cannot overlook the many questions and concerns Bachmann raises in her narrative about the Holocaust. *Franza's Case* seems built on the memory of the historical trauma in Bachmann's own life, as well as the history surrounding the Nazi past of Austria as perceived by the author in the 1940s and 1950s, a time during which the complex nature of individual responsibility came to be explored in German-speaking literature.

There seems to be a certain resistance involved in writing about this not so distant past both for Bachmann and for myself writing about an author who takes up the issue of the Holocaust in her narratives. The last few decades have brought about a mass of literature on the Holocaust and the Third Reich, so that one has a frame of reference, if only partial, of this history with which to discuss this past. Though James Young contends that the widely televised Eichmann trial in Jerusalem 1961 became a prospective trope of the Holocaust for the literary imagination,[11] it must be emphasized that Bachmann did not have a popular public discourse with which to discuss the Holocaust at the time she began writing her trilogy in the late 1950s and early 1960s. How does one then position Bachmann's trilogy in post-WWII literature? What motivated Bachmann to present her characters transformed by the events of the Holocaust? More specifically, how is the character Franza linked to this event in that she seeks out a doctor, a former Nazi in the euthanasia project in the Third Reich, to give her the lethal injection he once forced upon his victims? Finally, in which way does the Holocaust influence Franza's progressive "murder" by her husband and society?

Numerous difficulties arise when discussing the works of an author writing about the Holocaust, especially when she is not

Jewish, specifically because she is a member of a western European culture that murdered people for their alleged cultural, religious, and linguistic otherness within this society. In order to situate Bachmann's work one can begin by examining her interest in and knowledge of Judaism and Jewish identity, as well as her concern for the role that Nazism and the Holocaust played in her personal life. Key factors can be traced which might have influenced Bachmann's concern for crimes committed against the Poles,[12] specifically Jews and the mentally ill.

Very disturbing and distressing is the conclusion that Bachmann seems to draw concerning women and Jews in their desire and drive towards victimhood. In other words, the blame is placed on the victim and not on the aggressor. Bachmann equates women with Jews in their position as victims within society, parallels which psychoanalysts such as Otto Weininger, Otto Rank and Bruno Bettelheim draw in their psychoanalytic writings concerning Judaism and women (works Bachmann was surely familiar with when she wrote her trilogy). Otto Weininger's *Sex and Character*, translated from the 1903 *Geschlecht und Charakter*, was one of the first psychoanalytic works to compare the situation of women to that of Jews. His negative views of women have become almost legendary. With statements such as "I must again assert that the woman of the highest standard is immeasurably beneath the man of lowest standard,"[13] one can assume that his views of Jews were equally low. He found that Jewish women in particular captured the essence of the woman perfectly and that Jews and women were similar as a "genre." The "fear of the other" that Weininger discusses describes the hate Jordan demonstrates for his wife Franza, who realizes that it is her otherness that Jordan desires to extinguish: "Why was I so hated? No, not me, the otherness in me . . . . "[14]

A later work which compares women to Jews is Otto Rank's first work in English *Beyond Psychology*, published in 1941. Rank's observation of the importance of the father figure in the Judaic tradition reflects Bachmann's analogy of the role of the father figure in the lives of her women characters in the *Death Styles* trilogy:

> The overwhelming importance of the father, likewise a characteristic of Jewish tradition and mentality, represents the rational aspect of Freudian psychology, whereas the vital relationship to the mother is conceived of as merely an "infantile" fixation.[15]

Despite Rank's realization that both Freud and Weininger's views of women are derogatory and based on what Rank calls "the outgrowth of the patriarchal attitude in the Old Testament,"[16] he also holds the view that women have "suffered from the very beginning a fate similar to that of the Jew, namely, suppression, slavery, confinement and subsequent persecution . . . . "[17] Rank, however, traces this analogy to the entire tradition behind Freudian psychology, which projects upon the woman the specific Jewish psychology, "who therefore is depicted as enslaved, inferior, castrated, whereas the psychology of the male the masculine qualities appear exaggerated to the point of caricature in a libidinal superman."[18]

Rank states that it was the Jew who "invented" the first psychology as an explanation of evil in the human being. Furthermore, that it was the Jew who took over the "curse" of being persecuted for all human evils from women who had historically had the role of the scapegoat. Rank traces the "feminine" fate of the Jews to Freud's psychoanalytic tradition: "What Freud attempted unconsciously in his ideology therefore was the projection of those feminine characteristics of the Jew upon the woman, thereby achieving a kind of therapeutic self-healing for the Jewish race."[19] Although I cannot be sure what specific psychoanalytic works Bachmann was familiar with at the time she wrote her trilogy, it can be assumed that she was knowledgeable of the Viennese psychoanalytic tradition of Weininger and Freud and well read in Rank's studies, a selection of whose works were found in her personal library.

Highlights from Bachmann's political involvement throughout her literary career show her political activity and her desire for peace, marked – despite her critical distance – by her membership with the *Group 47*. In 1965 Bachmann wrote a letter to Simon Wiesenthal in Vienna, pleading for a lengthening of the appointed time set for those having committed crimes under the Nazi regime.[20] In the early 1970s Bachmann turned her back on the Piper Publishing house, where her first works had been published, protesting their attempt – successfully – to include the poetic works of one of her favorite poets, Anna Achmatova, in the translations of the former Nazi author, Hans Baumann.

Bachmann's visit to Poland in the early 1970s transformed the way she would perceive the past. It is known from interviews with Bachmann that she was very interested and informed about the tragic destruction in Poland during the Nazi regime. In a 1973 Warsaw radio interview Bachmann spoke to Alicja Walcka-Kowalska about her large collection of documentations about Poland from 1939 on. Although *Malina* had been published two years prior in 1971 and she had by this time written a large part of her trilogy *Death Styles* in which she had referred to the Holocaust, her visits to Auschwitz and Birkenau had rendered her speechless:

> I was in Auschwitz and Birkenau. Now nothing helps when one knows this, because in that instant, when one is standing there, everything is very different. I can't speak about it, because . . . there is nothing to say. It would have been possible to speak about it earlier, but since I have seen it, I think I can't any longer . . . . [21]

In another interview in Warsaw with Karol Sauerland in May, 1973 Bachmann expressed her horror and silencing by her experiences during her reading tour in Poland: "To be there is different than reading about it . . . . There is nothing to say about it. Truly it makes one speechless."[22]

The repetitive cycle in the power structure of domination and subjugation in *Death Styles* is played out on the terrain of political paradigms such as fascism and colonization to illustrate the relationships between the individual and society, more specifically between men and women. The grounding of this hegemonic power structure seems to always fall back upon the father figure, who is one of the three central figures in *Malina*, and a marginal character yet a powerful source of destruction in *Franza's Case* and *Requiem for Fanny Goldmann*. The destruction by the father precludes any possibility of a future harmonious relationship between a man and a woman, as well as between the individual, male or female, and society. Bachmann states in an interview that the father figure is just one type of "murderer" who commits that crime which society itself commits: "Everything comes together in this one large person who commits that which society commits."[23]

The society in which Bachmann's female characters are situated is one where criminality and war are a part of every day life, for as Bachmann emphasizes in her introduction to *Franza's Case*, the crimes of the postwar era are more subtle but therefore more destructive than the visible and "obvious" war crimes committed during WWII[24] Later in the novel the narrator concludes that society itself is the greatest murder scene,[25] in which peace is a dangerous illusion, as Bachmann warns in an interview: "It is such a big mistake to believe that one is only murdered in a war or in a concentration camp – one is murdered in the middle of freedom."[26] In *Franza's Case* the motif of fascism is carried over to the relationship between Franza and her dominating and destructive husband Jordan, as Franza tells her husband:

> You say fascism, that is strange, I have never heard it used as a word for personal behavior, no, pardon me, I have to laugh, no, I am definitely not crying. But that is good, since it has to begin somewhere, of course, why does one only speak of it when it is about opinions and publications.[27]

Bachmann once said in an interview regarding her novel *Malina* that fascism is the first element of relationship between a man and a woman.[28] Fascism is clearly alluded to in *Malina*, in whose central dream segments the father attempts to exterminate his daughter in a gas chamber.[29] Franza also has a dream in which Jordan exterminates her in a gas chamber: "Tonight I dreamt that I was in a gas chamber, all alone, all the doors are locked, no window, and Jordan is fastening the tubes and is letting the gas stream in and, how can I dream such a thing . . . . "[30]

The identification with fascism that Bachmann clearly makes in *Death Styles*) in which history becomes "her story" – raises some important questions about the validity of such parallels. If Bachmann equates women to Jews in these passages, then can the extermination of over six million victims murdered precisely for their alleged otherness within western European culture, a culture to which Bachmann belonged, be compared to a destructive relationship? Does this comparison not negate the significance of the human tragedy of the Holocaust? The specificity of such a collective and individual destruction becomes diminished, even loses its singularity, when linked to an interpersonal act of destruction, such as that between father and daughter, Franza and Jordan, Fanny and Marec.

Although the gas chamber dream sequences of *Malina* have traditionally been read as the female narrator identifying herself with a Jewish victim of the Holocaust, Bachmann does not specify who the dreamer is identifying with in the gas chamber. Bachmann, however, specifically refers to the murder of Jews within the italicized literary tale in *Malina, The Princess of Kagran*, in which the female narrator meets her savior twice and envisions their third encounter. In a dream sequence later in the novel the female narrator identifies herself as a Jewish woman who is waiting to be deported by truck in as a snow storm. It is here that she meets the Jewish stranger from the earlier tale for the third time.[31] After their brief reunion the stranger's transport falls into the Danube in which he drowns. The distraught female narrator is approached by an unidentified man with a message specifically for the Princess of Kagran, yet she wants nothing to do with it since the man "she loved more than life"has drowned. The hope that one day the message would arrive, coupled with the hope to someday be reunited with her "first love," has been shattered by his return to her and his consequent tragic death.

The gas chamber motifs in both *Malina* and *Franza's Case*, as well as certain references to the Holocaust found in *Franza's Case*, illustrate Bachmann's awareness of the machinery of the National Socialist regime. Franza's situation seems to be very closely related to the events of the Holocaust, in that she finds herself pulled into this fascist structure and machinery, one that destroys the qualities that would make her a fulfilled individual. Franza's psychiatrist husband Jordan, who has made her into one of his cases, is still part of the fascist structure in that he dominates and destroys her for her alleged otherness. Franza begins to understand the fascist structure behind her husband's actions, which are methodical and carefully planned to destroy her person, as she describes: "He must be crazy. And there is no one who acts more rational . . . . He tormented me so horribly, not spontaneously nor rarely, no, with reflection, everything was planned, tactics, tactics, how can one be so calculating?"[32]

The perspective shifts here, for now it is Franza who realizes Jordan's insanity. Whereas the narrator Martin often refers to his sister as crazy and Jordan notes down Franza's actions as mentally unstable in his "exploration"[33] of her, Franza is later aware of the patriarchal and fascistic structure to which these men belong and which makes them view her as insane. Jordan, having written a book entitled *Concerning Experiments on Female Prisoners, Concerning Later Injuries*,[34] continues to carry out experiments on his wife as he both creates and observes her mental unraveling. Franza's complicity in Jordan's project contributes greatly to her destruction: "Because of this I have also become ill."[35] It is due to her collaboration on Jordan's project that Franza recognizes Dr. Körner, to whom she has been referred in Egypt for medical attention, as one of the "Death Doctors" of the euthanasia program in Dachau and Hartheim.

In confronting Dr. Körner with his past, Franza positions herself as both judge and victim. In observing Dr. Körner's silence when confronted by her accusation, Franza recalls the reactions of silence during the Nuremberg trials of "Witness B", who is silenced when he is accused of the torturous sterilization of prisoners: "Witness B had faltered, no, moreover he seemed swallowed up by the paper and print on the page."[36] Franza becomes the silencing agent when confronting Dr. Körner with his past, for no sooner has she divulged his secrets than he leaves the area in fear: "Körner had really driven away, out of fear, because of her. Someone had been afraid of her, for the first time of her, and not she of someone else."[37]

Franza becomes empowered by her ability to silence the murderer. Franza, however, also identifies with the victims of this euthanasia program in that she desires to be eradicated by the fatal injection. She pleads with Dr. Körner: "I want you to do it again . . . Give me a shot . . . .How could she make it clear to him that she wanted him to eradicate her? Yes, eradicate, that was it."[38] Once again, Franza is classified as insane by yet another man, Dr. Körner, as he judges her: "You are insane."[39] Only Franza seems to realize the hypocracy of the situation: " . . . I ask him for something he had previously done voluntarily and without having been asked to do so, and now someone comes along and can't even beg or pay for it. What kind of a world is this?"[40]

Bachmann's detailed observations about the euthanasia program points out her knowledge and interest in how the mechanics of the program functioned and whom it was directed against. It has generally been assumed that Bachmann was writing exclusively about the extermination of Jews in her trilogy. It is my belief, however, that her discussion of the Holocaust pertains largely to crimes committed against the mentally insane, as documented in Mitscherlich's account of the Nuremberg Trials, *The Death Doctors*, published 1962, translated from *Medizin ohne Menschlichkeit* (1949). The tenth chapter entitled "Euthanasia Program" discusses these "mercy killings," the murders of the incurably insane, and the elimination of those declared to be "racially inferior" such as Poles, Russians, Jews and Gypsies.

The euthanasia program was first directed against the mentally ill and elderly who were confined to sanatoria and nursing homes throughout Germany. The euthanasia law, "to permit the extinction of lives not worth living," was decreed under Hitler as far back as 1932 and was ordered to be kept secret from the public. In this program the mentally ill were gassed and/or poisoned to death in the Grafeneck Castle and at Hadamar, directed by Dr. Schumann, as well as the Irrsee Institution, directed by Dr. Falklhauser. The mentally ill were transferred from sanatoria to "observation stations" such as Eichberg where most of the "patients" were killed within twenty–four hours. After each murder a letter was sent to the "patient's relatives, stating that he or she had died due to mysterious circumstances. The secret however did not last long; in fact, when the mentally ill arrived at Hadamar, local school children would even call out, "Here comes the murder truck again,"[41] or "There they go again for gassing."[42]

In the April issue of the National Socialist paper, *Volksdienst*, Professor Kranz wrote that the elimination of these "patients" was desired to reach the figure of one million.[43] Karl Brandt, the chief defendant in the Nuremberg trials, believed the number to be closer to three million. This euthanasia program is referred to throughout the trial as "14F13," although it is not clear from the text what this number specifically meant. From this fact, however, one can infer that this code number was meant to conceal the murder of the more than three million victims in the euthanasia program of the mentally insane.

It becomes clear that the method of the gas chamber was initially used for the mentally insane and was later extended to Jews, then to prisoners in work and concentration camps. Bachmann, who was well-read in historical details about procedures concerning the mentally ill, as well as historical facts concerning the Third Reich, was most likely aware of these gas chamber procedures. The gas chamber narratives in *Malina* and *Franza's Case* quite possibly illustrate the situation of women who have been labeled insane by the outside world and whose lives are, therefore, threatened by a fascistic patriarchal society.

Another supporting factor is that it was stated during the trials that the gas chambers at locations such as Hadamar and Schloß Grafeneck were of the same size and appearance as any other room in the institution, so that the "patient" would find the room familiar and would not be frightened to enter it. The patients were brought into the room naked and were then poisoned with carbon monoxide gas.[44] In the first dream sequence of the chapter "The Third Man" in *Malina,* the room in which the female narrator enters is described as follows: "The chamber is large and dark, no, it is a hall, with dirty walls, it could be in the Hohenstaufen castle in Apulia. For there are no windows and no doors."[45] The German term for "chamber" illustrates the small size of the room, as well as the narrator's initial response to the room as being "at home" and "homey," i.e., "familiar." The German word for "hall," typically used in describing a hospital or institution room or ward, signals its reference to a mental institution with which the female narrator also seems familiar. More importantly, though, is the description of the "Hohenstaufen castle in Apulia" – most likely a reference to one of the castles in Sicily once belonging to the German Staufen family whose homes Bachmann might have toured when she lived in Rome – which captures the image of a medieval castle such as Schloß Grafeneck. In the passage directly following the gassing scene, the narrator describes herself as being insane: "When it begins the world is already mixed up, and I know that I am crazy,"[46] after which she has a series of hallucinations in which her father torments her throughout. Again the narrator describes the world as one in which she is insane,[47] and where the world itself has come to an end. As the narrator comes out of her hallucinations she realizes that she has been given an electroshock treatment.[48]

In his testimony on January 17, 1947 under examination by Brandt's defense counsel, Dr. Mennecke participated in the following dialogue. When the judge asked Mennecke: "So at first it was a matter of people of unsound mind?" Mennecke answered, "It was a medical matter." To the next questions, "Then later it became a political and racial matter?" Mennecke only replied, "Yes . . . "[49] Hitler ordered the termination of the euthanasia procedures in the summer of 1941, but no one could attest to this fact at the trial. It is known that some of the gas chambers dismantled at Hadamar were re-erected in the eastern city of Lublin, where Polish Jews were murdered. "Idiotic and deformed children" were exterminated until the end of the war.

The leaders of the euthanasia program were tried at Nuremberg and many were sentenced to death. Because Hitler's orders were never mentioned in public, were not published anywhere, and because very few people had access to documents concerning these matters, it was unclear who was actually involved. Defendants were accused of not having resisted orders given by Viktor Brack, under Hitler's orders, February, 1940 in Berlin concerning the euthanasia program. Since there is no public access to Ingeborg Bachmann's extensive library now in Klagenfurt, it is unclear which books Bachmann specifically owned concerning the Holocaust and the euthanasia program. Bachmann's *Franza's Case* makes evident that the author had read detailed facts concerning both the euthanasia program in Austria and Germany during the Third Reich, as well as detailed information about the Nuremberg trials.

It becomes evident that Bachmann's primary concern was not only the plight of those murdered in the war, but the situation of psychiatric cases, as well as the mentally ill and the insane. Was Bachmann then referring to the position of female writers who were viewed as mentally ill by a conservative and traditional post-World-War-II society? Did Bachmann project her own fears onto her characters who were productive women authors during and after the Third Reich, a time when they might have been part of this euthanasia program, for criticizing the socio-political situation through their writings and for not conforming to society? Bachmann's gas chamber dreams can be read as narratives of fear in which a woman and independent writer is deemed unfit and insane by her patriarchal society. Is it then a Jewess being gassed by a Nazi in the *Malina* dream scene or rather a mentally ill "patient" who is being exterminated by her "doctor?" Perhaps both? The ultimate trust is broken in these scenes between two people, the "patient" and the doctor, as between the daughter and the father, wife and husband.

It has not been my wish merely to account for individual Holocaust elements within Bachmann's trilogy. Instead, I have attempted to demonstrate that Bachmann's narration of events during the

Third Reich shows an understanding of the cultural structures that allowed the Holocaust to take place, as well as her grave concern about the continuity of these structures in post-World-War-II society, as can be seen today in the frightening neo-Nazi movement in the western world. One might say that Bachmann's works can be read as a transcription of the code of historical writing into a more literary code.[50] Perhaps one of the most compelling arguments for the historical relevance of Bachmann's literary work is Hayden White's call for the representation of human truth:

> How else can any past, which by definition comprises events, processes, structures, and so forth, considered to be no longer perceivable, be represented in either consciousness or discourse except in an "imaginary" way? Is it not possible that the question of narrative in any discussion of historical theory is always finally about the function of imagination in the production of a specifically human truth?[51]

In conclusion, it becomes evident that Bachmann's writings illustrate the insistence of memory and how memory creates a narrative, therefore becoming history, in fact, her story.

Notes

1. Ingeborg Bachmann, *Werke* III, eds. Christine Koschel, Inge von Weidenbaum, and Clemens Münster (1978; München: Piper, 1993) 433.

2. Thomas Bernhard, *Heldenplatz* (1988; Frankfurt am Main: Suhrkamp, 1992) 159-165.

3. Gerhard Botz, "Historische Brüche und Kontinuitäten als Herausforderungen. Ingeborg Bachmann und post-katastrophische Geschichtsmentalitäten in Österreich," *Ingeborg Bachmann – Neue Beiträge zu ihrem Werk. Internationales Symposium Münster, 1991*, eds. Dirk Göttsche and Hubert Ohl (Würzburg: Königshausen & Neumann, 1993) 201. Peter Beicken also cites the Klagenfurt newspaper of March 15, 1938 which called Hitler's "Einmarsch" into Austria: "Austria's homecoming into its motherland." Peter Beicken, *Ingeborg Bachmann* (München: C.H. Beck, 1988) 29.

4. "There was a certain moment that destroyed my childhood. Hitler's troops marching into Klagenfurt. It was something so horrifying that my memory begins with this day: through a premature pain that I would probably never experience in the same way again . . . . But this terrible brutality which could be felt, this yelling, singing and marching – my first deathly fear. Ingeborg Bachmann, *Wir müssen wahre Sätze finden: Gespräche und Interviews*, eds. Christine Koschel and Inge von Weidenbaum (München: Piper, 1991) 111.

5. The process of coming to terms with the Nazi past was an important part of the literary program of writers born in Austria and Germany between 1920 and 1930 who were committed to a democratic future through their writings. The intellectual literary group *Group 47*, of whom Bachmann was a member, focused on much of the same anti-fascist programs of the Federal Republic of Germany. This included compensatory payments to victims of National Socialism and summary reparations to the state of Israel. In Ursula Mahlendorf, "Confronting the Fascist Past and Coming to Terms with It," *The American Journal of Social Psychiatry*, 2.2,

(1982) 30.

6. Mahlendorf, 31.

7. In May, 1952 Heinz Werner Richter invited Bachmann to read at the "Group 47" in Niendorf on the Baltic. The following year she won a prize for her work in Mainz.

8. In an interview on November 25, 1964, Bachmann stated: "I belong to Group 47, which is linked to all sorts of foolish legends for some strange reason. Lately I have been hearing, I take it from the newspapers, that the political activity, possibly the political power, of this group is said to be noteworthy. I have not yet noticed it. At most I have noticed that German writers, who are rumored to represent radical, dangerous ideas, in fact think so moderately that they would be guilty of not thinking enough in another country, as in Italy or France. Bachmann, *Wir müssen wahre Sätze finden,* 50.

9. Ibid., 42.

10. Ibid., 133.

11. James Young, *Writing and Rewriting the Holocaust* (1988: Bloomington: Indiana U. Press, 1990) 132.

12. Bachmann's library documenting Poland during WW II clearly shows her knowledge of the horrors that befell this country, as Peter Longerich reports: "Occupied Poland was not only that country which lost the most Jews through National Socialist genocide, but also the locus of the six death camps in which the systematic murder of the remaining European Jews was committed." Peter Longerich, ed. *Die Ermordung der europäischen Juden: Eine umfassende Dokumentation des Holocaust 1941-1945* (München: Piper, 1989) 188.

13. Otto Weininger, *Sex and Character*, n.t. (London: William Heinemann, 1975) 302.

14. Bachmann, *Werke* IV, 400.

15. Otto Rank, *Beyond Psychology* (New York: Dover Publications, 1958) 275.

16. Ibid., 287.

17. Ibid., 288.

18. Ibid., 287.

19. Ibid., 288.

20. Peter Beicken, *Ingeborg Bachmann* (München: C. H. Beck, 1988) 187.

21. Bachmann, *Wir müssen wahre Sätze finden*, 131.

22. Ibid., 142.

23. Ibid., 97.

24. The book is not only a voyage through an illness. Crimes also fall under styles of death. It is a book about a crime . . . . Yes, I claim and will now attempt to offer primary evidence that still today many people do not die, but are in fact murdered . . . . The crimes which demand spirit, touch our soul and less our senses, therefore those that touch us most deeply – no blood flows there, and the carnage takes place within the permitted and the customs, within a society where its weak nerves tremble before the bestialities." Bachmann, *Werke* III, 341-342.

25. "Society is the biggest murder scene of all." Bachmann, *Werke* III, 276.

26. Bachmann, *Wir müssen wahre Sätze finden*, 89.

27. Bachmann, *Werke* III, 403.

28. Bachmann, *Wir müssen wahre Sätze finden*, 144.

29. "My father calmly takes the first hose off the wall, I see a round hole through which it's blowing inside, and I duck down, my father walks on, taking down one hose after the other, and before I can scream I'm already inhaling the gas, more and more gas. I am in the gas chamber, that's what it is, the biggest gas chamber in the world, and in it I am alone. There's no defense against gas. My father has disappeared; he knew where the door was and didn't show me, and while I am dying my wish to see him once more and tell him just one thing dies as well." Bachmann, *Malina*, Transl. Philip Boehm (New York: Holmes & Meier, 1990) 114.

30. Bachmann, *Werke* III, 407.

31. " . . . I find him in the very last room, where he is waiting for me, exhausted, a bouquet of Turk's-cap lilies is standing next to him in the empty room, he is lying on the floor in his starry mantle, blacker than black, in which I saw him a thousand years ago." Bachmann, *Malina*, 126.

32. Bachmann, *Werke* III, 404.

33. Ibid., 383-384.

34. Ibid., 455.

35. Ibid., 456.

36. Ibid., 458.

37. Ibid., 464.

38. Ibid., 462.

39. Ibid.

40. Ibid.

41. A. Mitscherlich and F. Mielke, *The Death Doctors*, Transl. James Cleugh (London: Elek Books, 1962) 256.

42. Mitscherlich, 253.

43. Ibid., 255.

44. Ibid., 251.

45. Bachmann, *Malina*, 114.

46. Ibid., 114.

47. "It is the end of the world, catastrophic fall into nothingness, the world, in which I am crazy . . . . " Bachmann, *Malina*, 116.

48. Electroshock was a common treatment for depression and other mental illnesses when Bachmann wrote her novels in the 1960s. It is said to be painful and disorienting for the patient and now only used in very serious cases of mental illness, as described by the character Franza: " . . . I have small metal plates on my shaved head and look around me in shock . . . . They have given me electroshock." Bachmann, *Werke* III, 178.

49. Mitscherlich, 278-279.

50. Hayden White. *The Content of the Form: Narrative Discourse and Historical Representation* (Baltimore; Johns Hopkins University Press, 1987) 47.

51. White, 57.

Ingeborg Bachmann's Flight from Song: The Radio Play *The Cicadas*

Gudrun Brokoph-Mauch

The literary world accepted Ingeborg Bachmann's prose volume *The Thirtieth Year* (1961) with surprise and consternation; after all, the writer had been celebrated for her lyrical work. It is now apparent from her literary remains that she had been writing prose as well as poetry all along; but how could her audience have known that, since she never published any? Today, looking back from the totality of her published work, it is quite easy to see that this change from poetry to prose did not come altogether unannounced. Signs of a decision to leave a genre behind in which she had acquired mastery as well as fame and to develop another are apparent in her radio play *The Cicadas*, where the writer builds a linguistic as well as programmatic bridge from poetry to prose.

Postmodern linguistic philosophy postulates that the poem celebrates the loss of the primal unity and that every additional poem constitutes a compulsive repetition of this return to the threshold of the original trauma of separation between ego and self, ego and world.[1] If this is true, then Bachmann declares in *The Cicadas* her consent to step over the threshold of forgetting and to enter the realm of remembrance. This courageous act contains a farewell to the songs filled with longing and lament which threaten to lead to the loss of the human voice, to the "frenetic song" from "dried out throats" (I,268) and demonstrates her readiness to remember the "story." In this play she maintains that for those residing in the exile of language it can be fatal to give in to the longing for pure presence over a long period of time.

The polyphony of the monologues and dialogues of this radio play resounds once again with Bachmann's large repertoire of human longings and laments,[2] variations of the one great desire for the Other. They are screams out of the "big secret pain with which man before all other creatures is distinguished" (IV,275). Symptoms of psychic repression and regression become apparent, results of the flight from the symbolic into the imaginary order of things, nourished by the longing for pure presence, for dissolution of the chasm between inner and outer, between ego and self, between language and being. All persons reside on an island together but alone, refugees from the mainland, the land of social and communicative forces, "shipwrecks" within the net of symbolic order of language. For to step out of language means in this play as in the language philosophy of Lacan to step out of humanity and in the last analysis out of life itself. On the other hand the main figure's return to the mainland is the return into the captivity and power of language as an inescapable conditio humanae. For the author it means the entrance into the narrative restrictions of prose and to the confluence of narration and memory, the "step towards Gomorrah."

In spite of the programmatic renunciations the radio play contains all of the images and metaphors of Bachmann's lyrical writing that precedes and follows this play: images of the south, the ocean, the sun, the sky, the water, the boat, flight and return, the "borrowed time," the redemption, the music, and the tension between language and silence. To an even greater degree sound, rhythm, and structure of these dialogues and narrative commentaries are grounded in her lyrics. And it is because of this close relationship to her preceding and succeeding work in image, motif, and sound that the absence of one of Bachmann's big themes in her work is noticeable in this play: love. Did the author exclude this personally so important theme in *The Cicadas* in order to devote to it a separate radio play, *The Good God of Manhattan*, three years later?

The dramatic form and dialogue structure in *The Cicadas* is characterized by a strongly symmetrical arrangement of persons and narrative compositions as well as punctuating musical intervals. The symmetry observed here reflects the symmetry of object and mirror image whose borders are unrecognizable and whose identification therefore meaningless. This is particularly noticeable with the two main characters, Robinson and the prisoner, each one a mirror image of the other, whose conversations form beginning, middle, and end of the entire dialogues within the play. Between their conversations the other dialogues which have the same length and structure arrange themselves as variations of the main theme.

The symmetry corresponds to the Lacanian division of the ego into subject and object, into signifier and signified, occurring with the first spoken word. "I speak of myself as of one who is someone else," (I,241) the prisoner says and expresses herewith the primal experience of every speaker who through language is referred back again and again to the division of ego and self, while at the same time trying to overcome this division through his speech – an undertaking which, according to Lacan, is in vain since language belongs to the world of objects, the world of order and law, which reaches out for the subject at the very moment of his birth and traps him in its grasp irrevocably. For the ego which has been alienated from itself in this way, there is only the realm of the Imaginary, belonging to the realm of the subconscious, which, having been developed through language is, therefore, determined by it to a great measure, just as consciousness is. Consequently to live means to live in captivity, the captivity of language, the Symbolic Order of things, society, and the law. " . . . do you wish to escape the world and the proud captivity?" (I,267).

This is precisely what Robinson attempts to do, and he does it through the refusal of language. Every day he waits for the song of the cicadas in order to be touched by it like by a magic wand and be changed, to experience the same metamorphosis that made human beings into cicadas:

> Once upon a time the cicadas were human beings.
> They stopped eating, drinking and loving in order
> to be able to sing forever. Upon their flight into
> song they became thinner and smaller, and now
> they sing lost to their longing,– enchanted but
> also damned because their voices have become
> inhuman. (I,268)[3]

Robinson experiences life as synonymous with captivity and penalty, both of which he tries to elude, just like the cicadas, by forgetting and losing language. By relinquishing conversations and reading, by practicing forgetting, not thinking, not understanding, he hopes that a part of his brain will atrophy, that part "with which I have absorbed letters" (I,239). This is the preparation for total silence, the silence of death: "I want it finally to be still. I wished that the cicadas would stop singing, so that I would not ever have to hear them anymore" (I,260).

The prisoner on the other hand, his alter ego or mirror image – just escaped from the prison on the small island far away on the horizon – seeks life, wants to eat, drink, speak and return to the mainland with the next ship. Both are inhabitants of islands, one voluntary, the other involuntary, fugitives seeking refuge on the large island. But both islands, the large and the small, are "remnants of an illusion" (I, 263), the refuge which they offer to both is the refuge of "dreams" (I, 264) and of "redemption" (I, 223). Dreams belong to the Imaginary, lead out of the "order of things" (Foucault) and the intimated "redemption from evil" here consequently does not mean salvation from death but salvation from life. "Release me! I can no longer die," it says in the *Songs in Flight* (239). At this advanced state of regression which aims at loss of language, loss of ego, unity with the Other and death, the confrontation with the mirror image resembles a cognizant jolt (*Erkenntnisruck*) or an "aha experience" (Lacan)[4] halting the regressive movement and initiating a change of direction.

If Lacan is correct, then the confrontation with the mirror image is decisive for the development of the individual out of the infantile preverbal phase into the verbal phase, since it establishes the recognition of a double existence of ego and world.[5] This is the preparation for the experience of a final division into interior and exterior by the acquisition of language. In the play Robinson attempts to mend this division by his renunciation of language and his social isolation. The painful song of the cicadas who sacrificed their human existence echoes the longing for the Other, for the lost primal unity which is the basis for this process of regression. Even if – again according to Lacan – the process of identification with the mirror image results in an "illusionary identity"[6] and establishes a fictional ego, it is nevertheless an identity which leads to language and thereby to the Symbolic Order. In this play it leads out of the regressive infantile island existence to the restricted but also productive life on the mainland. "I am certain," says Bachmann in her important essay *Die Wahrheit ist dem Menschen zumutbar*, "that we must remain in the order, that there is no such thing as the exit out of society and that we have to prove ourselves to each other" (IV, 276).

Without the confrontation with the mirror image, Robinson would not have waved at the passing ship with its sail pointing toward the continent – as in the third song from *Songs in Flight*. Following this jolt of recognition through the meeting of his mirror image he begins to resume language as a preparation for the reconstitution of the external ego and reentry into the Symbolic Order. At first he speaks "hesitantly," reluctantly, "someone who does not wish to speak but who is glad to be able to speak" (I, 219). And, through the conversation with the invader who speaks freely and sometimes "loudly" (I, 220), sometimes seriously, sometimes ironically and often speaks for both, he becomes more relaxed, more courageous and even picks up the letter which had fallen to the ground before the visit. In anticipation of the song of the cicadas which puts an end to any attempt at communication, Robinson had dropped the letter: " . . . letters cannot be read any longer. The answer has to wait. It sounds as if I want to free myself from all embraces for a different kind of happiness" (1, 261). He now reads the "phrases" of affection with which the writer, his wife Anna, tries to capture and lure him back home.

Shortly before the knock on the door which returns both of them to where they came from, one to the prison and the other to the mainland, another type of prison, Robinson opens himself up to the visitor. His memories of life on the continent with its games and rituals form – in the exchange with the prisoner's responses – a kind of ritornello. And this ritornello acts as a metaphor for the suspension of the division into subject and object originally represented by the mirror image of both fugitives. The resulting "illusionary identity" in this conversation is, however, short lived and fragile, the fundamental division of ego and self is always present, as is expressed in a poem of the cycle *Songs in Flight*: "Ich bin es nicht/Ich bin es" (I, 146) ("I am not I./I am I.") Here it is the suit, requisite of the social order and mask of the objectified "moi" which distinguishes one from the other, and which the prisoner first requested and then rejected: "No. It cannot suit me. It is your suit" (I, 262).

The mirror image also becomes effective as a structuring element in the two letters which the boat on its daily route carries in two different mailbags to the two islands. They can be read like two strophes of one and the same poem whose language, images, sound patterns, metaphors, and messages are arranged in a chiasmic pattern, thereby formally demonstrating that in spite of their apparent differences in tone and literal meaning, they are the same. What makes them the same is most importantly the phrases (*Redensarten*) which belong to every situation which they constitute and by which they are constituted, with the result that meaning and situation determine each other. In the phrases of the letters and even more extremely in the Morse code within the prison walls, we witness the mutilation of language as a result of the disappearing subject. It is only the subject that can expand the limits of language and that can throw the ball across the playing field, as Bachmann expresses it in a commentary to her poem *The Great Freight*: "The playing field is the language and its borders are the borders of a world which is looked upon without questioning, which reveals itself and is reflected upon with exactitude and praised in happiness."[7]

Bachmann maintains that the stagnation of language in phrases can only be fought through a "moral, visionary jolt . . . and not through an attempt to renew the language itself."[8] The linguistic phrases also reflect most clearly the gap between wish and request or as Lacan states it between "need" and "demand," based upon the "primal repression" in the linguistic expression.[9] The stereotype quenches the individual and strengthens the symbolic.

Because of their parabolic function, Robinson and the prisoner, two sides of the same newly created mythic figure, have in contrast to the other persons in the play no contemporary names and no "story" which would have given them an individual fate. However the seemingly individual lives of the others are really only variations of the same Robinson theme: flight from the mainland and from the order of things. While Robinson returns to the world of phrases the others remain caught in this speculative state of the Imaginary and in the straitjacket of their neurosis. If, according to Lacan, the neurosis is "the captivity of the subject in the situation,"[10] then we see here six persons confronted with each other like mirror images representing six different kinds of neurotic rejections of the power of order. They try to bridge the abyss between need and demand by repetitive rituals both in action and in language. Captives at the threshold of a trauma which has thrown their ego out of the healthy balance between the Imaginary and the Symbolic[11] in favor of the Imaginary, compulsory activities or escape rituals hold them fast in the same spot. Mr. Brown's daily water skiing, Mrs. Brown's harpoon hunt as well as Jeanette's daily beauty bath are symptoms of a great loss which they cannot overcome or even accept: the loss of a newborn child, a grown-up son, a youthful appearance. Salvatore's alcoholism, Prince Ali's languishing in the coffee house over lemonade, and Stefano's running away from home on the other hand are rituals of escape from demands which they are not capable of fulfilling: the surpassing of mediocrity in the artistic endeavor, the paralysis of someone incapable of ruling a country as well as juvenile rebellion against parental discipline and power.

The linguistic rituals which accompany the compulsive actions reside in the realm of the fantastic and distinguish themselves from the three dialogues between Robinson and the prisoner by their musical, intoxicatingly hypnotic quality as well as their distinctive and parallel structure. Their relationship to the Robinson dialogues is that of variation and theme of a musical score,[12] and they all begin with the same three part refrain:

> Antonio.
> Yes, Mrs. Brown.
> It is good, Antonio. (I, 231)

The dialogue partner is in every case Antonio, the only young native of the island, who is at their disposal – for money – and to whom they all have an almost addictive dependent relationship. This relationship rests, like all forms of addiction, on a vague desire, which his presence evokes and transmits into language.[13] The fantasy images of the first three speakers are determined by a longing for a lost condition of happiness, for pure presence, while those of the other three speakers are determined by a struggle to conquer an inner and outer blockage. Antonio's rhythmic "yes," responding to the escalating fantasy images, gives permission to the speakers who hallucinate in a state of trance to travel far into the realm of fantasy. Up to the critical point where Antonio's "no" brings down the barrier between the border of fantasy and reality, the realm of the Imaginary and the Symbolic, and denies further advancement. Only in one case – with Stefano – does Antonio withhold his "yes," so that in its place, in spite of repeated pleas for agreement, Antonio's silence punctuates the long excursions into fantasy land. Apparently Antonio does not want the child to be among the fugitives on this island; for Stefano still has a chance to return into the world of order, a chance to be saved from enchantment and damnation by the flight into the Imaginary.

The effect of the musicality of language, structure, and rhythm of these "duets"[14] that hold the fugitive in a state of unfulfilled yearning, in conjunction with the suggestive, seductive "yes" of the accompanying "Ton" (sound)) the middle syllable of the name Antonio[15] – corresponds to the effect of lyrical poetry. And it is here that Bachmann's skepticism toward poetry and its escapism begins. This becomes evident in Antonio's new secularized role in the radio play, where he appears without a halo as in the cycle *Songs on an Island* (where the choir of the cicadas is also mentioned) (I,122),[16] as well as in his cooperation with his employer Benedict. Benedict, the editor of the island newspaper who engages Antonio as his voice and messenger, represents the poet Bachmann insofar as she engages her poetry as the awakener of the longing, the seductive echo of the lament, the intoxicating drug. He silences the unpleasant and only prints that which does not take the inhabitants of the island out of their dream world, just as if these people were not capable of bearing the truth. Benedict is also a fugitive who landed on this island as a political refugee. But although he could have returned to the mainland a long time ago, he remains in this self-chosen exile in order to prepare – just like the poet Bachmann – the drug for his co-refugees and co-sufferers, changing pain into enchantment and condemning these addicts who long for ever higher dosage to a cicada-like, death-oriented existence. In her acceptance speech for the Blind Veterans' Radio Play Prize Bachmann speaks resolutely against such an anesthetizing function of poetry and fiction: "It cannot be the task of the writer to deny pain, to wipe out its traces, to smooth it over. On the contrary he has to recognize it and make it come true once more in order for us to see" (IV, 275). Benedict does not receive a "no" from Antonio and thereby mirrors Stefano in an inverse pattern. Stefano does not receive a "yes," for he is a professional fugitive, more drug mixer than drug consumer: Orpheus with the lyre returning from the realm of death empty- handed, as Bachmann writes in her poem *Darkness Spoken*: "Like Orpheus I play/death on the strings of life" (*Songs in Flight*, 13).

Life in exile as a pose is a frequent occurrence in Bachmann's poems, particularly those written after this radio play and before the prose volume *The Thirtieth Year*: exile as metaphor for the homelessness in language:

> long since given up
> and provided with nothing
> Only with wind with time and with sound
> I who cannot live among humans
> (*Exile, Songs in Flight*, 285)[17]

To be at home in the language means in this poem to be without a house and a roof, even to be dead. But to be without language outside the symbolic order which is the order of language, means in this radio play to be equally death-bound. Bachmann's poetry and writing moves back and forth between sentences such as "Deliver me, my word!" (*Songs in Flight*, 181) and "The language is the punishment" (Speech for the Anton-Wildgans-Prize, IV, 295).[18] Even when she turns to prose the same tension between language and silence exists in the beginning as a task to be mastered and at the same time as a new breakthrough in the expansion of language. Bachmann knows about the hypnotic, paralyzing quality of the lyrical elixir and is ready) in contrast to her own figure Benedict – to tell the truth to her fellow men and women and to find a new language to do so.

In this connection it is interesting to note that the poem *No Delicacies,* which appeared in the same year (1961) as the prose volume *The Thirtieth Year*, is "associatively dangerous"[19] as the last poem in the *Werke* edition. It is a farewell to poetry. In its content and structure the poem is being dissected into its individual parts and then renounced.

> Nothing pleases me anymore.
> Should I fit out a metaphor
> with an almond blossom?
> crucify the syntax
> upon an effect of light?
> Who will rack their brains
> over such superfluous things)
>
> I have learned an insight
> with words that exist (for the lowest class)

Then the strophe breaks into individual negative language pieces:

> Hunger
>   Shame
>   Tears
>   End
> and
>   Darkness

and finally the rejection:

> (Should? The others should.)

> My part, it shall be lost. (*Songs in Flight*, 321-323)

In this poem we see the execution of what is announced in *The Cicadas*: the rejection of the lyrical word, the flight from song.

Although word and world, the Imaginary and the Symbolic impregnate and modify each other in their mutual interaction, the radio play takes on the task of revealing the illusion to which people at certain times are subject: that things of the external world change in their forceful reality and presence. In this way the "monotonous tormenting noise" of the song of the cicadas works together with the "nebulousness of high noon" (I, 262) to seemingly dissolve the exterior world for the inhabitants of the island. Robert Musil's "day-bright mysticism" (*taghelle Mystik*) comes to mind here, the experience of "the other state" (*der andere Zustand*) i.e., the world with a different composition. But here this different world condition does not form the basis for a new moral scrutiny of the world but only leads to a loss of world. Just as the dissolution of space in the bright sunshine leads to no actual modification of the world, so does the cessation of time at high noon not bring the experience of pure presence, at least not in life but only in death. This apparent dissolution of space and time, incidentally, stands in stark contrast to the world of the prison with its rigid spatial and temporal borders, representing the world of the Symbolic. As Funke has pointed out, the danger of the illusion of a transformation of time and space at high noon is recognized and expressed by the prisoner.[20] At one point the prisoner engages in an imaginary dialogue with Robinson while examining two hypotheses: the things change or I change.

> . . . my intestines burn, but I desire different nourishment.
> I cannot use knife and fork, for they are not what they
> are, just as the pan with the fried fish is what it is."
> "They are fork and knife. Which metamorphosis are you
> alluding to?"
> "Then it is happening, and I am lost, my God. It is my own
> metamorphosis. (I,241)

The great "revelation" is the consciousness of his own transformation, the process of atrophy through the rejection of the world and the flight from the "proud captivity" of which the song of the cicadas warns. The insight "I am lost" is the call of awakening which forces Robinson and the prisoner to turn back.

A reviewer of the year in which the radio play appears wants to see in Bachmann the young writer who in *The Cicadas* describes a danger "with the coolly distancing probe of her generation"[21] to which her elder colleagues succumb in their escape from reality, without herself being confounded by this danger. He is obviously not acquainted with her lyrical writing. From today's perspective we see here a decision to change direction in her published work. And it is exactly the recognition and acknowledgment of her own participation in this escapism and this lament which motivate Bachmann to perfect her prose writing skills in order to move away from the island and establish a home on the mainland. Like Robinson, Bachmann has waved to the passing ship:

> White rescuers, the ships,
> – oh lonesome sailor's hand! –
> they point, before they sink,
> back towards the land. (*Songs in Flight*, 225)

This brings us back to our thesis at the beginning of this essay that the radio play *The Cicadas* forms a bridge from Bachmann's poetry to her prose in content and form. Although conceived as a drama in which the dominant form is the dialogue, it contains strong lyrical as well as narrative elements which point in both directions to the genealogy of Bachmann's work. On the one hand, we have the poetic density of the language, the strong rhythm and rich imagery, the cryptic allusions, and musical cadence. In addition, we find a tendency toward the monologue within the dialogue and the lyrical ritornello as well as the dialogue within the monologue, all typical elements of poetry.[22] On the other hand, alongside these characteristics which connect the radio play with the poems, we find the narrator's comments displaying a distinct tendency towards the epic, a tendency to which the author will yield during the following years. These lyrical and epic characteristics within a dramatic-acoustic work lead to a mixture of genres which typically denotes a passage from one important phase in Bachmann's writing to another.[23]

Thus it is not surprising that Bachmann's first prose volume *The Thirtieth Year* is still embedded in the lyrical language, most noticeably in *Undine geht*, a monologue narration which not only ends in a strophe but whose sentences are strongly rhythmic and whose language is rich in poetic density. Hartung has quoted several examples of explicitly lyrical prose in which "an exclamation or an image reaches all that in one single leap which otherwise can only be arrived at step by step."[24] Bachmann herself said in this regard: "This first prose still partially stems from the condition of writing poems. It still contains many attempts to escalate the sentence to a point where no narration is possible anymore."[25]

All in all Hartung only permits the connotation "story" for two of the seven short stories; the others he claims are too strongly structured by the closed form of the poem.[26] To strengthen his judgment he also draws on the predominantly subjective expressions and the omission of all that which does not support the construction of the experience narrated. The reason for this condensed and economical form is the fact that in this prose volume as well as in *The Cicadas* what is at stake is always the whole, "*Alles* (everything) as the short and suggestive title of her best story reveals."[27] Bienek's claim that these seven stories are never about just one life or one action but always about everything concerning man, truth, love, desperation,[28] is not just applicable to this prose volume, but also to the two radio plays *The Cicadas* and *The Good God of Manhattan*.

Moreover, in addition to the urgency and finality which the radio play *The Cicadas* has in common with her poetry, both forms utilize simliar themes which they also share with her first prose volume. Gone are the images and sounds of the south, but retained are the themes of new beginning, negation of the status quo, search for the absolute and above all, the theme of language: Creation of language combined with creation of world, loss of language as rejection of conventions and norms, and in the end resignation and return to the scorned language; return with a glimmer of hope that one can still do something about it, along the lines of the well known motto: "In the interplay of the impossible with the possible we expand our possibilities" (IV, 276). The fight for language as expansion of possibilities proves to be the most consistent and most urgent theme in her work and will also be carried out in her second prose volume *Simultan* as well as the novel *Malina*.

Notes

Quotations from *Die Zikaden (The Cicadas)* in Ingeborg Bachmann, *Werke vol. I* (Zürich: Piper, 1978) (English translation is my own.)

1. Richard Wollheim, "The Cabinet of Dr. Lacan," *The New York Review of Books, Vol. XXV, No. 21-22* (January 25, 1979) 36-45.

2. See Manfred Jurgensen, *Ingeborg Bachmann, Die neue Sprache* (Bern: Lang, 1981).

3. Horst Günter Funke, *Ingeborg Bachmann. Zwei Hörspiele* (München: Oldenburg, 1973) 20-27.

4. Jacques Lacan, "Das Spiegelstadium als Bildner der Ichfunktion," *Schriften* (Olten: Walter, 1973-1975) I, 63.

5. See Saskia Schottelius, *Das imaginäre Ich* (Bern: Peter Lang, 1990) 16-27.

6. Lacan, I, 67.

7. Bachmann, *Werke*, vol. 4, 304, quoted by Friedrich Wallner, "Die Grenzen der Sprache als Grenzen der Welt. Wittgensteins Bedeutung für die moderne österreichische Dichtung (demonstriert am Beispiel Ingeborg Bachmann), *Österreich in Geschichte und Literatur*, Vol. 25, No. 2 (1981) 81.

8. *Werke*, vol. 4, 102.

9. Jacques Lacan, "Die Bedeutung des Phallus," *Schriften*, II, 126.

10. Lacan, I, 70.

11. Frederic Jameson, "Imaginary and Symbolic in Lacan: Marxism, Psychoanalytic Criticism and the Problem of the Subject," *Yale French Studies*, Nos. 55-56 (1977) 338-395.

12. Funke, 50.

13. According to Lacan the alienated relationship of need and demand depends on the existence of the father, the phallus, the Third, which dissolve the primal unity of mother-child-world-ego and at the same time produces language and the subconscious. The fact that every demand misses the need depends upon this primal

separation which introduces a desire for the ..... which can never be fulfilled.

14. Karen Achberger, *Understanding Ingeborg Bachmann* (Columbia, S. C. : University of South Carolina Press, 1995) 35.

15. Ibid., 37.

16. See the interpretation: Walter Muth, "Einmal mu8 das Fest ja kommen." Aus dem Zyklus *Lieder von einer Insel, Interpretationen zu Ingeborg Bachmann* (München: Oldenburg, 1975) 73-89.

17. *Songs in Flight. The Collected Poems of Ingeborg Bachmann* Transl. Peter Filkins (New York: Marsilio, 1994).

18. Quoted from Jurgensen, 61.

19. Ute Maria Oelmann, "Lyrisches Sprechen und narratives Sprechen im Werk der Ingeborg Bachmann," *Ingeborg Bachmann. Neue Beiträge zu ihrem Werk. Internationales Symposium Münster 1991* (Würzburg: Königshausen & Neumann, 1993) 57.

20. Funke, 48-50

21. Claus-Henning Bachmann, "Warnender Gesang," *Frankfurter Hefte*, vol. 10 (1955) 587.

22. Dieter Lamping, *Das lyrische Gedicht* (Göttingen, 1989) 64f., quoted from Oelmann, 62.

23. See Oelmann, 62, who speaks of "Gattungszwittern" at important stations in Bachmann's works.

24. Rudolf Hartung, "Vom Vers zur Prosa. Zu Ingeborg Bachmanns *Das dreißigste Jahr*," . . . *Kein objektives Urteil – nur ein lebendiges. Texte zum Werk von Ingeborg Bachmann.* Eds. Christine Koschel/Inge von Weidenbaum (München: Piper, 1989) 61.

25. Oelmann, 58.

26. Hartung, 58-60.

27. Horst Bienek, "Immer geht es um: Alles," *Kein objektives Urteil – nur ein lebendiges*, 63.

28. Ibid.

Ingeborg Bachmann's Poetry:
A Sense of Passing.

Reingard Nethersole

Ingeborg Bachmann's poetical oeuvre, when compared to that of her friend, Paul Celan, for instance, is not extensive. It consists of two volumes, *Borrowed Time (Die gestundete Zeit)* and *Invocation of the Great Bear (Die Anrufung des großen Bären)*, which appeared in 1953 and 1956, respectively. In addition to these slim collections and translations of selected poems by Giuseppe Ungaretti, published initially in 1961, *Werke* in four volumes of 1978[1] contain a mere further forty poems written between 1942 and 1967.[2] Bachmann's lyrical voice, thus, at once saturnine, celebratory and questioning is sedimented in less than a hundred poems composed mainly in the fifties. Ceasing altogether five years before her untimely death, it is not as prolific as that of many other poets of the postwar period.

Yet her fame as a leading postwar writer was founded upon poetry. When Hans Werner Richter, the organizer and father figure of the influential *Gruppe 47,* discovered some of her poems "by chance" in 1952[3] and invited the then twenty-five-year-old scriptwriter of the Austrian Broadcasting Corporation, *Sender Rot-Weiß-Rot,* and author of the radio play *Ein Geschäft mit Träumen* to the Group's meetings,[4] he provided a much sought after platform for the young Doctor of Philosophy from Klagenfurt. Bachmann who had published in the Viennese journal *Lynkeus* among others since 1948, seemed to have thrived in the ambience of these gatherings. In a draft essay on the *Gruppe 47* (IV:323-332) echoing her impressions of the Group's tenth meeting at Niendorf on the Baltic Sea in May 1952, she describes her first encounter with the Group as a never ending series of laughter, fun, talks, and a "brief spell of youth" (324) away from the war-induced hardships and the closed literary circle of regional Vienna: an initiation onto the big stage of German literature. Invited by her fellow writers to read "a few poems" (325), among them the rhyming poem *The Heavy Cargo* and the free-verse lyrics *Wood and Shavings* and *Night Flight* which form part of *Borrowed Time,* she, Paul Celan, and Ilse Aichinger were, according to Bartsch,[5] the Group's "great discovery" of that year. Remembering this and other early readings, Joachim Kaiser says of the writer's verses: "This tone, this distance, this daring and tender inexorability belong solely to her; they are the highlights of German poetry which find their continuation here."[6] And when the coveted Prize of the *Gruppe 47* was awarded to Ingeborg Bach-mann in 1953, an event which prompted the news magazine *Spiegel* to devote a feature article to her, she had arrived on the German-speaking literary scene almost overnight, as it seemed.

However, the very same literary establishment which engineered her meteoric rise, alluded to disparagingly in the drafts of the Malina-figure (III:527-554), not only rejected Bachmann's novelistic work but slammed her poetry as untimely celebration of an "aimless ambivalence of signs."[7] Increasingly dominated by a younger generation of writers and literary scholars in the late sixties, the new arbiters of literary taste accused earlier critics of an overenthusiastic, undifferentiated view[8] of her lyrical oeuvre. "Poetry like bread," albeit "sharp with cognition and bitter with longing" (IV:197), arising from a deeply wounded lyrical subject,[9] utterly "pierced" by "sorrow" (*Leave, Thought, SF*:293), yet continually demanding "See to it that you remain vigilant" in the face of false political promises (*Wood and Shavings, SF*:29), was no longer called for in the post-Adenauer era. With the formation

of the Grand Coalition between Christian Democrats and Socialists in West Germany in 1966, a "New Left" and with it most
writers and intellectuals, including Bachmann's composer friend
Hans Werner Henze,[10] whom she had met in Niendorf in 1952, increasingly recognized non-aestheticised revolutionary change as
the artist's obligation to society. Not only was the political impact
of literature subjected to renewed examination but a poetry of
"magic realism" which Richter had advocated as early as 1947[11]
seemed out of place in a venue where Brecht's succes-sors felt any
"discourse on trees" to be irrelevant "because it masks too many
crimes."[12] Thus Bachmann's "beautiful language" in which
"appears pure being" (*Of a Land, a River and Lakes*, *SF*:115),
wrought from the malady of distress brought on by "the devastated
world" (*My Bird*, *SF*:139) seemed suddenly out of place. The fact
that "yesterday's henchmen" were again "drinking from golden
goblets" (*Early Noon*, *SF*:37), a veiled reference to the continuation of fascist thought in politics, needed to be spelled out in more
direct and unadorned language. And a melancholy voice speaking
from a position of solitude (*Night Flight*, *SF*:53), deeply skeptical
of history and "With a sharp ear for the fall" (*Great Landscape
near Vienna*, *SF*:67), appeared irrelevant where political experiments with communism, for instance in Cuba,[13] seemed to promise
collective social change for the better. That the poet's embrace of
"the most transitory moment" in time and the fleeting appearance
of "beauty" (ibid.), was purchased with an extreme struggle for
artistic articulation within the framework of debased language
escaped critics concerned with social relevance.

Ingeborg Bachmann, although engaging with political activities,[14] distanced herself from the then fashionable committed literature and rejected "the idiotic talk about the role of the writer" in
her acceptance speech for the Anton-Wildgans-Prize in 1972 (IV:
296). Convinced that "writers have no power, and no influence"
(IV:297), the author insisted that the first duties of a writer are to
writing and not to the delivery of public statements. Although no
longer believing in the space of song and deeply aware of "the
language of the subalterns," namely "hunger/ shame /tears/ and/

darkness,"[15] she still struggled for the "kristallinischen Worte," those special and irretrievable words Bachmann says are the object of the writer's wretched work. Thus she remained unfashionably faithful to a multivalent language consonant with a fluid lyrical sensitivity which make even her novelistic work like *Malina* appear metaphoric rather than metonymic. Something contemporary critics were quick to notice and condemn in the early seventies.[16] And although the lyrical oeuvre bears many resemblances to *Malina*,[17] most strikingly perhaps in *A Type of Loss*, *SF*:317), broadcast by the BBC in 1967, the author had already distanced herself from her earlier evocative style to which she refers in the poem *No Delicacies* (*SF*:321) as "contrived word operas" as early as 1963. As she grew increasingly aware of the impossibility of commanding the "grace of breath and sound" and the "redeeming word" (*Spoken and Rumored*, *SF*:179) as well as a reconciliation between world and self in the beauty and fragile musicality of the poem, Bachmann's later verses became more sparse and brittle. With the short poem *Enigma* (*SF*:319), consisting largely of "borrowed words" and not of the in-spirational "fire" to which Myshkin alludes in the *Ballet Pantomime The Idiot* (*SF*:73), Bachmann's poetry ends in 1967. The last lines of *A Type of Loss* (*SF*:317), probably written around the same time, speak of the "loss of the world." While Peter Mayer suggests the poet chose silence because "a metaphoricity implying that truth can crack the wall and free from the chains" was no longer in demand,[18] Rita Svandrlik[19] explains the author's "turn to prose" as arising from her growing concern with writerly processes.

However, the literary establishment remained largely deaf to her preoccupation with prose, or what she called in an interview in 1962 a conscious "relocation" from the poetic domain to that of the narrative,[20] until critical re-evaluation of Bachmann's novelistic work at the hands of largely feminist literary critics began to emerge from the early eighties onwards.

When the German literary scene of the fifties enthusiastically embraced Bachmann's poetry, it flirted with Existentialism, Surrealism, and every other diction perceived to be authentic, heroic, new, and different to the drab and hackneyed propaganda verses (cf.*Wood and Shavings*, *SF*:29) of the Third Reich. During the heyday of *werkimmanente*, formal and immanent criticism, reminiscent of the American New Criticism, furthermore, poetry, seen since Romanticism as the pinnacle of writing, enjoyed a special status. During that era in which central Europe emerged from the devastation wrought by fascism and five years of destructive warfare, which had shaped the teenage years of Bachmann's generation, lines like "We, arrested in time and expelled from space/ we, aviators through night and vertigo" from *Night Flight* (*SF*:53), read at a broadcasting session in Hamburg in 1952, seemingly encapsulate a *Zeitgeist* ready to celebrate a *Journey Out (Ausfahrt)* (*SF*:5) or rather a departure for new shores.

To read such an embarkation also as an allegorical representation of the particular logic which rules the writer's lyric is possible, perhaps, but only from a position of the nineties. It is this logic postulating the contradictory interdependence of two forces, namely the drive to flight and the desire for arrival at an utopian destination, whereby transience marks the writerly process and arrival inscribed in the texts as "land" signifies the space of the poem.

> Smoke rises from the land.
> Remember the tiny fishing huts,
> because the sun will sink
> before you've set ten miles behind you.
> The dark water, thousand-eyed,
> pens its white-foamed lashes,
> studying you, deep and long,
> thirty days long.
>
> Even when the ship pitches hard
> and makes each step uncertain,
> stand calm on deck.
>
> At the table they eat
> the heavily smoked fish;
> then the men will kneel
> and mend the nets,

though nightly each will sleep
an hour or two
and their hands will soften,
free from salt and oil,
soft as the bread of the dream
from which they break.

The first wave of night hits the shore,
the second already reaches you.
But if you stare sharply yonder,
you can still see the tree
which defiantly lifts an arm
– the wind has already knocked one off
– and you think: how much longer,
how much longer
will the twisted timber withstand the weather?
Of land there's nothing more to be seen.
With your hand you should have dug into the sandbank
or tied yourself to the cliff with a strand of hair.

Blowing into conches, sea monsters float
on the crests of waves, they ride and slice
the day to pieces with bright sabers; a red trail
remains in the water, where sleep takes hold of you
for the rest of your hours,
your senses spinning.

But then something happens with the ropes,
you are called and you are happy
that you are needed. Best of all
tis the work on ships

that sail far away,
the knotting of ropes, the bailing of water,
the caulking of leaks, the guarding of freight.
Best to be tired and at evening
to collapse. Best in the morning
to awaken clear to the first light,
to rise up beneath the immovable sky,
to ignore the impassable water,
and to lift the ship over the waves
towards the forever recurring shore of the sun.

Journey Out has its source, like many other poems of *Borrowed*

Time, in the journey to England and France which Bachmann undertook in the winter of 1950-51. It was originally conceived of as a cycle or series of five poems,[21] before it became the opening poem of *Borrowed Time.* Seemingly indicating a new beginning after the *Kahlschlag,* or the apparent zero hour of German writing after the Nazi period, *Journey Out,* void of an expressive "I" and addressed to a characteristically ambiguous "you" which might be that of the reader as well as that of the lyrical self's Other, typically combines direct, unadorned poetic diction with seemingly hermetic metaphoric constructions. These often echo the work of the classical tradition as do the final lines of the last stanza, expressing a defiant stance in the face of a godforsaken world by accepting mundane, everyday tasks which recall Goethe's *Prometheus.*[22] Other lines like the opening ones of the famous *Great Landscape near Vienna* (*SF*:67) with their breathtaking imagery of a view across the Danube valley, set in elegiac dactylic meter, recall Hölderlin's verses describing the rivers Rhine and Neckar.

While essentially sharing Hölderlin's nostalgic sense of dispossession in an age of crisis, *Journey Out,* like all Bachmann's poetry, is not one of reminiscence. It is rather a lyric of transience in which a nomadic subject allows herself to be carried with the flow, forever passing through time and from one territory to another. Hence the respite mentioned in the title poem of *Borrowed Time* (*SF*:23) not only demands a departure from the "land" and a shelter, however poor, but time passing also obscures the vision of the "land" (line 31) during the uncertain boat ride. You could have clung to "the sandbank" or to "the cliff," suggests the poem in subjunctive mood (lines 32-33). Yet any clinging gesture is denied here and elsewhere even when the relentless "first wave of the night saps the shore" and "the second already reaches you" (lines 22-23). This inevitable drift requires almost inhuman strength in order to secure the subject for which the heroic, personified tree becomes the symbol, signifying "obstinate" resistance (line 26) despite mutilating injury by the elements (lines 25-30).

Although time might be arrested in the repetitive tasks of daily existence (lines 54-58) or elsewhere during heightened moments of love, an end is always already contained at the start of a journey out. Thus *Songs in Flight* (*SF*:223), the last cycle of poems in *Invocation of the Great Bear*, describing watery "waves/ which fleeing/ deliver the vanishing/ from the next destination" concludes:

> Love has its triumph and death has one,
> in time and the time beyond us.
> We have none.
> Only the sinking of stars. Silence and reflection.
> Yet the song beyond the dust thereafter
> will transcend us.

While time triumphs inevitably, it is the hope for "always returning shores of the sun" (line 53), that celebrated element of life and inspirational energy conjured in the poem *To the Sun* (*SF*:219), or the promise of sublimating the experience of love into song which sustain the subject "in flight."

Time as "the murderer" (*Scream*, *SF*:291), the universal destroyer forms the warp of Bachmann's poetry into whose texture is stitched the weft of an incessant longing for meaning and dialogue. Time's destruction is articulated among others in *Great Landscape near Vienna* and *Fall Down Heart* (*SF*:11), where the sense of passing is captured in the notion of relentless tumble.[23] For in an age in which "Our deity,/history, has prepared a grave for us/ from which resurrection is impossible," as stated in *Message* (*SF*:47), the "heart" is commanded to "fall off the tree of time," mindful of the "wound" inflicted by events, in order to "oscillate between yesterday and tomorrow" in the timelessness of verbal creation. "We are not forced to stay" because "we earned our farewell," says an untitled early poem published in *Lynkeus* in 1948-49 (*SF*:247).

Yet in order to return in "ever new farewell shape" (cf. *Great Landscape near Vienna*), the exiled[24] subject not only needs to "flow away, knowingly" (ibid.), but it also has to, like the sailors in *Journey Out* (lines 16-21), partake in the nocturnal mystery of communion, nourished by the "bread of dreams."[25] While the nocturnal realm and especially the orphic domain of death[26] and sleep (line 37) constitute the space of Bachmann's poetry, the relentless passing of time denotes its limitation: a limitation that knows passing and never forgets it but, without being blinded to its transience, counts on a new departure, on a renewal of the self and a transformation into song.

In *Journey Out* temporality is marked by the one or two hours sleep at night (lines 15 and 16) and the narrative episode which introduces the last stanza (line 40). The latter is characteristic of the cyclic compositions like *Psalm* (*SF*:57), "Of a Land, a River and Lakes" which, incidentally, repeats the idea of the respite from *Borrowed Time* (*SF*:23), and the *Songs in Flight*. Most importantly, though, *Journey Out* associates the passing of time with *Schlagen*. Schlagen in German, of course, refers to the beating of time as well as it does to hitting. In Bachmann's semantic field it appears also as "the word with which you beat me" ([*At the Hoofbeat of Night*], *SF*:257),[27] and it defines living and especially the communicative relation between two people as "Wundenschlagen" in the late poem *Brotherhood* (*SF*:279). "Schlagen" appears three times in the German *Ausfahrt* (lines 22, 27, and 36). Time, therefore, even if it drives life in the direction of a utopia,[28] the *non*-place of "immerwiederkehrende Sonnenufer" entails abject suffering which is invoked by the "red trace," sign of blood, "remaining in the water" (lines 36 and 37). Elsewhere a "meadow threshold glistens with my blood" (*The Way Home*, *SF*:153), and the poem *After Many Years* (*SF*:211) offers the image of the sea as "Meer verwöhnt und glanzerfahren,/ erhöhts den Spiegel fhr die Handvoll Blut," while the subject, identifying with Orpheus, speaks of "a string of silence/ stretched across the wave of blood" (*Darkness Spoken*, *SF*:13).

Taking poetry as self-expression, critics like Manfred Jurgensen and Susanne Bothner[29] have searched for sources of this suffering in Bachmann's life. And while such investigations might throw light on the personality of the author one can never assign an agent distinct from the subject of the text. For although *The Writing Self* (IV:237) "lives" no matter if it has been "beaten and bruised, amputated, and in doubt about itself," it "becomes itself only in the act of writing." "The ball," says the poet in a little essay, entitled by the editors of *Werke*: "Wozu Gedichte?" (What Good Are Poems) (IV:304) cannot be

> thrown outside the limits of the playing field:
> This playing field is language, and its limits are
> the limits of the unquestionably revealed and
> unmasked world, thought about in an exact
> fashion; the world experienced in sorrow and
> praised in happiness.

There is no doubt that the lyrical subject has "received the word ... / from the hand of mourning," as Myshkin says in the *Ballet Pantomime "The Idiot"*, (*SF*:73) and "the conditions of possibility for which we have to testify for creation" (ibid.) lie in the sorrow as source for all art as the late poem *Bohemia Lies by the Sea* (*SF*:311) shows. There the idea of reaching land after having been aground in the sea not only echoes the position of the subject in *Journey Out*, written some twelve years earlier, but also the last verses refer to the life of a "vagrant," in search of the "chosen land." Without possession other than the seer's gift the nomadic self envisages this to be the domain of art and poetry where paroxysmal sadness reverses into mystical jubilation.

Bachmann's poetic project is a dual one: the celebration of the heightened moment in which it becomes possible that the lyrical subject, "fired by the night," creates sparks from within itself (*My Bird, SF*:139), usually associated with an erotic encounter as in *Tell Me, Love* (*SF*:165), and a critique of the presence which the subject sees beyond repair and without solace. The latter is often linked to the burden of having to speak in everyday debased language (*Literatur als Utopie*, IV:270) which conjures up the idea of truth and promises solutions to all the world's ills. What this language is capable of and where it fails is thematized by the poem *Advertisement* (*SF*:175) from *Invocation of the Great Bear*. It first appeared in *Jahresring* 1956-57:

> But where are we going
> *carefree be carefree*

when it is dark and when it grows cold
be carefree
but
with music
what should we do
cheerful and with music
and think
cheerful
in facing the end
with music
and to where do we carry
best of all
our questions and the dread of all the years
to the dream laundry carefree be carefree
but what happens
best of all
when dead silence
sets in

The poem based on a question and answer dynamic intercepts two discourses, namely one of a search for meaning and another, printed in italics, belonging to the world of advertising. The former asks the ancient question "where to" when "it is dark and cold," obviously implying an unconsoled presence and a dreaded, insignificant end in the face of death. To these epistemological and existential questions the latter provides the soothing, repetitive and well worn assurances of commercialism: "don't worry, be happy" and enjoy the "music." However, these "quick-fix" promises of the advertising world evaporate in the deathly silence of an essentially unutterable end, which the poem "shows"[30] rather than articulates in the penultimate empty verse line. Death like jouissance in the erotic encounter defies verbalization, the erasure of the subject in the final passing of death as well as in the temporal transience of bliss are inaccessible to speech and representation. The poet, nevertheless, sees her task as one of "exerting herself within the orbit of the given, corrupt language in order to reach a language which has not yet ruled, but which governs our presentiment, a presentiment which we have to reflect" (*Literatur als Utopie*, IV:271).

Keeping watch "in the darkness" and looking after truth, "turned towards the unknown exit" of death (*What's True*, *SF*:183), the lyrical subject wrestles with the "word." This orphic word, though, seemingly necessary but unsustainable in the fast-living, murderous world described in the Büchner-Prize acceptance speech, "Ein Ort für Zufälle" (IV:278f.), is always in danger of failing the writer. Could I only command "the word" despite "deadly terror," is the poet's desire in *Curriculum Vitae* (*SF*::145). The 1964 poem *Truly* (*SF*:309) again alludes to the difficulty of having to communicate in a utilitarian language which instrumentalizes the world and humankind. Yet "To make one sentence stand/ and to endure amidst the ding-dong of words" in the face of high-sounding verbiage becomes practically impossible.

Where "words only always connect to other words" and the "image in the web of dust" appears as "a vacuous rolling over of syllables and words for death," always already spoken as in the poem *You Words* (*SF*:303), consolation with the help of the orphic word of the lyric, that most fragile of all art forms, is no longer possible. "To write poems," Bachmann said in 1952 (IV:523),

> seems to me to be the most difficult undertaking because the problem of form, theme and expression has to be tackled all at once; because poems have to obey the rhythm of the age as well as encapsulate the plenitude of old and new within the circumference of our heart in which past, present and future are contained.

"The art of poetry," states Julia Kri-- .va with regard to Gérard de Nerval,[31] "asserts itself as the memory of a posthumous harmony, but also through a Pythagorean resonance, as the metaphor of universal harmony." Yet, where this "universal harmony" is denied because a reconciliation between Self and Other, self and world is renounced, as in *Undine geht* and *Malina,* the orphic word is disavowed. To be sure, the writer has to continue with "an extirpation of slogans, "as Bachmann says in the acceptance speech of the Anton-Wildgans prize (IV:297) in 1972, but the scene of poetry, dependant upon a "staging" of the orphic word,[32] is vacated. As the saturnine poem *Love: The Dark Continent* (*SF*:295), published in the Italian multilingual literary magazine *Bottege Oscure in 1957* shows, the price extracted from the female subject seems too great:

> The black king holds aloft the panther's claws
> and chases ten pale moons around like prey;
> commanding great tropical rain that begins to fall.
> The world is looking at you in a different way!
> [from its other end]
>
> You are drawn across the sea and to those coasts
> of gold and ivory, and onward towards his mouth,
> but there you always fall upon your knees;
> for he chooses and rejects you without grounds.
>
> Yet he's the one who orders the day to change.
> The air shatters, pieces of green and blue glass,
> as the hot sun boils the fish in shallow water,
> and around the buffalo herd it burns the grass.
>
> He, hairy, brightly colored, is by your side;
> he snatches you up, throws over you his snare.
> Soon long liana ropes will bind your hips,
> your throat is ruffled with a lush fern collar.
>
> From every jungle recess: sighs and screams.
> He lifts the fetish. You have no reply.
> Sweet wooden sticks begin to beat dark drums.
> You stare transfixed, seeing where you will die.
>
> Look, gazelles are floating on the breeze,
> halfway down bends the date's ripe swarm!
> Everything is taboo: earth, fruit, streams...
> The [chrome] snake hangs shimmering upon your arm.
>
> He gives to you insignia from his hands.
> Wear the corals, walk in deluded raiment!
> You can deprive the kingdom of its king,
> for it's you who, secretly, has seen his secret.
>
> On the equator all barriers are lowered.
> The panther lives alone by love's own laws.

> He crosses over from the valley of death,
> trailing the heaven's fabric in his claws.

It seems as if the torrent of passion, bearing in its beguiling, compounded, violent images an almost hysterical effect, overflows the soothed composition of the constraining rhyming couplets. Reminiscent of *Songs in Flight* the nine stanzas seemingly narrate the passage through the inferno of desire to the utopian realm of the "Liebesraum" (line 30). This passing entails the gaze of a reversed world upon the subject (line 4) at its beginning and, having surmounted despair in the "valley of death" (line 31), ends after the typical traversal of a watery realm (line 5) at those familiar Beaudelairean "azure shores," hinted at already in the final line of *Journey Out.* And although sounds spring forth (line 23) there is no "song" as in the last stanza of *Songs in Flight* which will surpass a collective subject. To be sure, a musicalization and resensualization of the familiar signs of jouissance or erotic bliss which is ultimately beyond speech have been achieved, but the poem strains against consolation. Instead of such "Syllables in oleander, /words in acacia green, / cascades from the wall." which fill "the basins,/ turbulent and clear,/with music." sighs and screams fill the audible domain of the jungle, proverbial heart of darkness. Despite the glistening sunny setting, recalling the poem *The Native Land* in the South (*SF*:185) as well as Ungaretti's beloved Africa, this "dark continent" marks a descent into hell from which Orpheus will not return. For *Dir entfällt das Wort (The Word Escapes You)*, sign of paroxysmal melancholia, when the black king "lifts his fetish" (line 18).) The text, here, plays on the opposition of raise and fall, creating a causal interdependence between the two. Bereft of the word (line 18) "you" are left with nothing other than a petrified gaze upon the *Todesort* (Place of Death) (line 20) without any hope of resurrection. The leap from "the valley of death" to the edge of the sky (lines 31-32) is reserved solely for the (male) "panther."

The link of *eros* and *thanatos* traverses and shapes the representation of this shattering erotic encounter as does the sense of passing, including the suffering engendered by it in the "welts" in the "red sand" in line 16. Yet unlike *Songs in Flight* this poem refuses to bond the lovers in a collective plural "us," however tenuously and transiently. Instead the subjects of the utterance, a masculine master and a female second person singular, identified as such by the biblical attribute of the snake "on your arm" (line 24) remain separated despite the tight mesh around *her* whole body by vegetation generated by *him* (lines 14-16).

The symbolism of fecundity in the image of "tropical rain" (line 3), "fire" (lines 12 and 16) "worlds, fruits, streams ... " (line 23) as well as the magical hour of the "Mittagswende" (line 9)[33] and the absorption of boundaries which open the space for love (lines 29-30) promise the gift of inspiration (lines 25-26) and aesthetic fiction. In both cases, the subject drawn to the object of desire imagines and constructs the beloved or the fiction for itself, and Bachmann's texts usually associate them with change in everyday existence as in *Tell Me, Love*. There nature and self are magically transformed and even "a stone knows how to move another stone." Love, furthermore, usually dispels darkness and despair however temporally as, for instance in the poem *Hotel de la Paix* (*SF*:283) where the erotic encounter secures a "hatch in front of [the door] of death." And although at the equator, the meeting point of two hemispheres, all "barriers fall" (line 29), it is the animal image of the "panther," black like the "king" of the opening line which, without another is able to take the leap into the heavenly realm, that glorious domain of the aesthetic (lines 31-32). The "you," however, is merely advised to utilize her knowledge of *his* "secret" which, grasped fully, could topple masculine rule (lines 27-28).

The gaze of the impersonal speaker of the poem gathers a multitude of things, as is common in Bachmann's poetry, where numerous seemingly disjointed images are joined semantically rather than syntactically. Usually this wandering gaze comes to rest either in the expiry of love, after which the orphic word emerges (cf. *Songs in Flight*) or in sadness (cf. *Reigen, SF*:19 or *Black Waltz*, 209). Neither is the case, though, with *Love: The Dark Continent* where the gaze fixes a masculine *er* and a feminine *du* as subjects of the utterance. Here a *he* occupies a position of agency and the *you* that of object. *He* chases time, commands nature (lines 1-3) and bestows attributes of esteem and precious decorative items (lines 25-26). Driven to *him* and *his* "mouth" across seas and shores (lines 5-6) by an unconscious desire (*es*), the female subject succumbs submissively "on its knees" (line 7). Placed at opposite ends of the hemispheres – the "world" views the feminine subject "vom andren Ende" (line 4) – a *he* commands an empire in which the *du* is merely in the position of receiving object. Possessive (cf. lines 19-20) and domineering, the masculine subject constitutes the "law" in the Lacanian sense, for the "fetish" is his (line 18). While stereotyped images usually provide jungle kings with fetishes, this symbol of power could be seen here as being itself a "fetish" for it marks the sign of the "secret" alluded to in line 28. This is the fetish of the symbolic order which places power and plenitude with the male subject, leaving the feminine in a permanent state of lack; even if she now carries a snake fashioned in chrome, that very metal which has become the sign for the modern age [in the sixties]. Access to the "worlds, fruits, and streams" is possible solely through him, they are "taboo" to her (line 23). Yet the feminine subject also holds a "secret" (line 28) albeit an oppressed one: After all, according to Freud woman *is* the "dark continent" and love, as the poem's title seems to suggest, is *her* enigmatic territory. This realm of the "heart" often referred to in Bachmann texts is invisible but from it emerges all longing for a utopia, the non-place represented in the recurring images of land-taking or *Settlement* (*SF*:143).

Love, a *dis*position rather than a position, a libidinal current, free to roam through time and space without regard for possession, usually demands submission in Bachmann's texts. Yet in the epiphany of love it is a sign of equality whereby the partners mutually "raise each other," as stated in *Rome at Night* (*SF*:203). No matter that this epiphany is transient and purchased with pain and despair, it nevertheless marks a productive state, for "the mouth imbibes a new language" (*Tell Me, Love, SF*:165). However in *Love: The Dark Continent* a female subject, denigrated (line 8)

and disavowed, is transfixed upon a "place of death," that murderous scene of which *Malina* speaks, condemned to silence.

Written not long after *Songs in Flight,* which constitute its
binary opposite, this poem about the triumph of male dominance
in a patriarchal order – even in the realm of art[34] – might hold the
key to Bachmann's rejection of an aesthetic form with which she
once sought to seduce the reader. In an illuminating fragment
entitled *Das Gedicht an den Leser (The Poem for the Reader)*
(IV:307), found posthumously, the writer courts the reader to
whom she offers the poem as gift in return for his/her submission.
This is a poem which is crafted "of the aura of all things [*Stoffe*]"
and which will "rapture the reader "when the black blaze of
mortality engulfs him/her. Pretending not to know what the reader
wants, the poet says she is incapable of offering "songs for
winning battles" or for succeeding in business. Instead she wants
to move the reader to tears and, with a covert reference to Celan,
wishes to "make the stone bloom" (ibid. 308). However, such
lyrics, both cathartic and utopian, become obsolete when the
woman poet recognizes their inevitable complicity with harmony.
A harmony furthermore, which is always on the side of the "king"
and where any meaningful communication appears constantly
threatened. An early untitled poem published in *Lynkeus* in 1948
(I:12), still speaking in the collective "we," anticipates this fundamental lack of dialogue and the erasure of the female voice,
thematized in Bachmann's later prose work:

> It could mean so much: we cease to exist,
> that we arrive unmasked and then must yield.
> That we speak, and yet misunderstanding persists,
> and not for a moment is another's hand held,
>
> destroys so much:
> we shall not survive.
> Even strange signs forbid what we hold devout,
> and the need for introspection that's still alive
> a cross severs, as alone we're canceled out.

Notes

1. In the following, references to Bachmann's work used in the text will be given in brackets, denoted by Roman numerals I to IV, indicating the volume of *Werke*. (München: Piper, 1978), followed by page numbers. Wherever possible, as in the case with poems, translations refer to *Songs of Flight. The Collected Poems of Ingeborg Bachmann*. Transl. Peter Filkins (New York: Marsilio, 1994), indicated as *SF* followed by page numbers.

2. Of these, seven are marked as "Jugendgedichte," fifteen others appeared prior to the collection *Borrowed Time*, containing twenty-three pieces together with *A Monologue of Prince Myshkin to the Ballet Pantomime "The Idiot,"* while the thirty-one titles of *Invocation of the Great Bear* are complemented by a further eighteen poems written between 1957 and 1967.

3. Hans Werner Richter, "Wie entstand und was war die *Gruppe 47? Hans Werner Richter und die Gruppe 47*. Ed. Hans A. Neunzig (München: Nymphenburger, 1979) 104. An interesting survey of German literature during the halcyon days of this informal association of writers and critics is provided in Hans Werner Richter's *Almanach der Gruppe 47 1947-1962* (Reinbek bei Hamburg: Rohwolt, 1962).

4. Richter apparently read "six or seven type written poems" on Bachmann's desk in her office while waiting for an interview with Weigel, taking an immediate liking to them (ibid. 107). Upon Bachmann's instigation, Richter also invited "a friend from Paris, who is very poor, unknown like herself, who writes very good poems, much better than she.... His name: Paul Celan." (ibid. 106)

5. Cf. Kurt Bartsch, *Ingeborg Bachmann* (Stuttgart: Metzler 1988; Sammlung Metzler 242) 178. Bartsch also partly explains the "aura of the exceptional" surrounding the *Gruppe 47* and in particular the personality of the poet as an "auratic appearance in post-auratic times." (ibid. 2f.)

6. Joachim Kaiser, *Ingeborg Bachmann. Eine Einführung.* 2nd., expanded edition, 1968, cited in *Der Georg Büchner Preis 1951-1978. Eine Ausstellung des Deutschen Literaturarchivs Marbach*

und der deutschen Akademie für Sprache und Dichtung (Darmstadt) (Marbach am Neckar:1978) 174ff.

7. Cf. Christa Bürger, "Ich und wir. Ingeborg Bachmanns Austritt aus der ästhetischen Moderne" (Text+Kritik, 1984) 10.

8. Cf. the assessment of Peter Conradi, "Fragwürdige Lobrednerei," which surveys the Bachmann criticism of the fifties in the earlier *Text+Kritik* Heft 6 (1971) 48ff.

9. Speaking as an injured self reminds the reader not only of Celan and Nelly Sachs but especially of Sylvia Plath (1932-1963), on whose *Bell Jar* Bachmann wrote a short, insightful essay (IV: 558f.) in 1968.

10. The importance of the artistic cooperation between Bachmann and Henze, reflected in the concluding lyrics of *Borrowed Time* and numerous other evidence, not least the libretto for *Der junge Lord* (1964-65), can not be overestimated (cf. also Hans Werner Henze, *Musik und Politik. Schriften und Gespräche 1955-1984* (München: DTV, 1984). Henze, fired by anti-Vietnam sentiments, embraced the Cuban revolution and East Germany, and even abandoned his earlier style of composition from 1968 onwards.

11. Hans Werner Richter coined the term "magischer Realismus" as far back as 1947 in "Literatur im Interregnum" in his journal *Der Ruf* 1 (1947) No. 15. In conscious opposition to the apolitical writings of "Naturmagie," Richter advocated a combination of political awareness with aestheticism. Christa Bürger (op. cit. p.15), a left-wing, progressive critic, is of the opinion that it is the diffuse feeling engenderd by magic realism that appealed to the immediate post-war reading public.

12. Brecht's lines are repeated by Bachmann in that part of her Frankfurt lectures entitled "Über Gedichte" (IV:215). Celan quotes the same lines in a poem "A leaf, treeless – for Bertolt Brecht..." in *Schneepart*.

13. It was the time in which Enzensberger, for example, whose poetry *Die Verteidigung der Wölfe,"* 1957, Bachmann had singled out as exemplary in her Frankfurt lectures (cf. IV:209f.), depicted the Cuban revolution favorably in *Das Verhör in Habana*.

14. As Otto Bareiss' "Vita Ingeborg Bachmann" (Text+Kritik, 1984) 184f. shows, the writer publicly objected to nuclear testing and signed a petition against the Vietnam War in the sixties.

15. Cf. the poem *No Delicacies* (*SF:*321).

16. Cf. Walter Helmut Fritz und Helmut Heißenbüttel, "Über Ingeborg Bachmanns *Malina,*" *Text+Kritik*, 6 (1971) 21-27, who remark on the "lyricisms" and a lack of plot, which they consider inappropriate for the "social reality" of the times. Of interest here, too, are Bartsch's (op. cit., 11f.) observations concerning the unease with which male critics responded to what they considered feminine issues in the novel.

17. Cf. also *The Blue Hour* (*SF:*161), *Letters in Two Drafts* (*SF:*199) and especially *What's True* (*SF:*183).

18. Peter Mayer "Zeit zum Schweigen?" *Text+Kritik* (1971) op. cit. 17, refers here to the poem *What's True* (*SF:*183).

19. Cf. "Ästhetisierung und Ästhetikkritik in der Lyrik Ingeborg Bachmann's *Text+Kritik* (1984 op. cit.) 28.

20. In an interview with the poet, editor and later organizer of the Berliner Literarisches Colloquium, Walter Höllerer, in 1962 Bachmann explains her preoccupation with prose as a conscious "relocation" (Ingeborg Bachmann, *Wir müssen wahre Sätze finden. Gespräche und Interviews.* (München: Piper, 1983) 38.

21. These include "[The World is Far and Wide]," which did not find its way into *Borrowed Time, Departure from England* (*SF:*9), *Wie Orpheus*, entitled *Darkness Spoken* in this Collection (*SF:*13), and *Paris* (15). This cycle was read for a broadcast at the NWDR in Hamburg on 27 May, 1952, immediately after the Niendorf meeting. The cyclic composition is typical for Bachmann.

22. Many critics have remarked on the recurrence of traditional expressions as well as phrases from contemporary poetry in Bachmann's lyrical work. Thus Ulrich Thiem's doctoral thesis, *Die Bildsprache der Lyrik Ingeborg Bachmanns* (Köln: Philosophische Fakultät, 1972) for instance, which concentrates on what he calls "Zentrale Bildkomplexe" 46f., devotes a whole chapter, albeit restricted to German examples, to what would rightfully be called intertextual references today. He refers to *Journey Out* only as a

prelude to later "island imagery" without recognizing in the apparently "embarrassing message" of the last stanza the Prometheus resonance.

23. Cf. here Hölderlin's final lines in his *Hyperions Schicksalslied* which speak of man's fate as one of restlessness, suffering, and blind descent into uncertainty.

24. Cf. the poem *Exile*. (*SF*:285)

25. This genitive metaphor like the daring personifications are typical of poetic productions under Surrealist influence at the time.

26. Cf. the first and last stanzas of the poem *Darkness Spoken*: Like Orpheus I play death on the strings [the lyre] of life. Like Orpheus I recognize life on the side of death.

27. Cf. also *Curriculum Vitae*, which repeats the image (I;102).

28. In an essay on Musil's *Man without Qualities* "Ins tausendjährige Reich,"(IV:27) Bachmann speaks of a utopia as "direction" and not "as destination," and describes utopian thinking in association with Musil as a non-teleological process capable of subverting the ruling order of the world.

29. Cf. Manfred Jurgensen, *Ingeborg Bachmann, Die neue Sprache* (Bern, Frankfurt am Main, New York: Peter Lang, 1981) and Susanne Bothner, *Ingeborg Bachmann: Der janusköpfige Tod. Versuch der literaturpsychologischen Deutung eines Grenz-gebiets der Lyrik unter Einbeziehung des Nachlasses* (Bern, Frankfurt am Main, New York: Peter Lang, 1986).

30. Bachman's high regard for Wittgenstein's philosophy seems evident here. The 1953 radio essay on Wittgenstein, *Sagbares und Unsagbares – Die Philosophie Ludwig Wittgensteins* (VI:119), suggests that, where no questions remain, life's problems seem solved. In the face of a transgression of boundaries like death or "mystical experiences of the heart" (120) we can only be silent. Such transgressions, however "show" themselves.

31. Cf. "Gérard de Nerval, the Disinherited Poet" *Black Sun* Trans. from the French by Leon S. Roudiez (New York: Columbia University Press, 1989) 150.

32. Cf. here the interview of 23 March 1972 in *Wir müssen wahre Sätze finden*, op. cit. 78.

33. Traditionally, this is the hour of the appearance of Pan, the ancient god associated with eroticism and art. Nietzsche was fond of this image.

34. The poem contains a great number of intertextual references to German poetry which can not be fully described here but which support my reading of the poem as being critical of the masculine voice in art. It is also noteworthy in this connection that all examples mentioned in the Frankfurt lectures on poetry with the exception of Nelly Sachs are by male authors.

Female Subjectivity and the Repression of the Feminine in Ingeborg Bachmann's *Malina*

Bachmann's discussion on contemporary poetry in the opening lecture of the *Frankfurter Vorlesungen* begins with an observation that suggests an epistemological shift which dislodges the subject of discourse from its central position: "The concepts of time and space have disintegrated, reality continues to await a new defini-tion because the sciences have reduced all of it to a series of abstract formulas. The relationship of trust between subject, lan-guage, and object has been seriously undermined."[1]

As the conceptual constructs of time and space are called into question, both the signified and the subject lose their predominant position. This gives way to a literary discourse in which the signi-fier gains the upper hand and the subject, as the central entity generating meaning, all but disappears from the text.

In the lecture entitled *Das schreibende Ich* Bachmann's analytic glance shifts to the pronoun I, the linguistic marker of the subject. She begins her analysis from the position of lecturer speaking to an audience of scholars and students. Even in such simple declarative statements as "I am telling you," Bachmann reasons, the I becomes uncertain the moment it is spoken. He [sic] who speaks it can no longer be sure whether he can articulate a relationship for this I on the tip of his tongue, whether he can guarantee it" (FV 41). Within the framework of these speculations, the speaking subject cannot be reduced to a fixed content of consciousness. The very act of enunciation introduces a breach between speaker and pronoun, so that the audience receives only a rhetorical I, which in turn becomes the subject of a sentence cut off from its speaker. "Ich ohne Gewähr" (FV 42), Bachmann puns; however, it is a pun we are meant to take seriously. The acoustically ambiguous "Gewähr"[2] redefines the traditional subject within the space of a single term: it tells us that the modern subject is in no way guaranteed, that it does not endure beyond the moment of enunciation, and that it cannot presume the phallic authority it had once taken for granted. The autonomous subject proves to be an illusion or a mere posture without any substantive quality.[3]

Although the subject's former position in discourse is greatly compromised, it does not disappear altogether from the literary text. Its function is simply redefined. The subject as a unified autonomous entity in control of the production of meaning is displaced by the subject as the "site of the human voice" (FV 61).

It is no coincidence that Bachmann's theory of the subject strongly resembles that of post-structuralist thought. Sigrid Weigel's illuminating essay, *Ein Ende mit der Schrift, ein anderer Anfang: Zur Entwicklung zu Ingeborg Bachmanns Schreibweise*, calls attention to Bachmann's essentially Lacanian, psychoanalytic understanding of language, as well as to her conception of writing as a cultural process inscribing and encircling the subject, much as it is later elaborated in Derrida's *Grammatology*.[4]

While Bachmann uses the *Frankfurter Vorlesungen* as a forum for thinking through her theoretical position by analyzing the texts of various twentieth-century authors, it is her own prose fiction that will become the testing ground which applies this theory to a social context. The narrative *Everything* of *The Thirtieth Year,* for example, explores the possibility of effecting changes by stepping outside the given sociosymbolic order. Here the narrator pins his hopes for changing society on his new-born son, Fipps, whom he has chosen to become the first member of a renewed, enlightened human race. The father naively assumes that he can shield his son from normative social inscription by teaching him the language of the shadows, stones and water. The language of nature, so the reasoning goes, will displace the conventional linguistic system along with its implicit mental constructs and perceptual modes. The present sociosymbolic order is thought to be a deviant form of a former, more "authentic" signifying system, one that has presumably been corrupted by culture and civilization. The narrator clearly believes it must be possible to return to this more natural state of being by exchanging the linguistic system founded on arbitrary signs for a more "authentic" one grounded in the body and other natural phenomena.

While the narrator's vision may be clouded by romantic notions of "origin" and "authenticity," Bachmann's is not. In the essay *Dem Menschen ist die Wahrheit zumutbar*, she argues that our perception is renewed by the interplay of the possible with the impossible, but at the same time acknowledges that we are confined by the linguistic and cultural norms in which we live. Quite predictably, then, the narrator of *Everything* will run up against the linguistic/cultural barrier, and will ultimately become aware of the foolishness of his enterprise.[5] As he tries to educate his son, he soon realizes that he knows nothing about the language of nature, nor do his attempts to invent "pure games" and "other fairy tales than the familiar ones" (Bachmann, *Everything,* 66) result in anything but imitations.[6] Fipps grows up to be just another enterprizing, rowdy little boy who, "was capable of anything, only not of breaking through the hellish circle" (65, translation changed). And how could it be otherwise? The subject as "site of the human voice" necessarily speaks and performs the culture in which it is embedded.

In *Malina* the focus shifts from the male to the female subject. What are the social and psychic forces that construct it? What is its place in the Symbolic? And how can the female assert her place as a subject of discourse in patriarchal culture? These are just some of the questions underpinning this novel or, more precisely, they are the questions the text generates for me, as I work my way through its multiple complex layers.

The female narrator of Bachmann's *Malina* speaks in the unstable voice of the *Ich* invoked in the *Frankfurter Vorlesungen*. As a sign of this subjective lack of stability and coherence, the narrator neither has a name nor seems to have a specific profession. She always signs her letters "an unknown woman," and when Ivan writes to her, he signs his name but omits the salutation. In the rare moments when Ivan speaks to her, he uses the familiar *du* but fails to address her by name; on one occasion, when the narrator finally summons the courage to relate some of her personal thoughts and feelings, Ivan pays little attention and casually dismisses her remarks with the questionable term of endearment, "my sweet little lunatic" *(Malina* 184).[7] With this gender specific designation, the narrator is classified as a woman, but continues to remain nameless and we learn that she is a writer only by way of several seemingly insignificant incidents: one day Ivan discovers some scraps of paper inscribed with the titles of present and future Bachmann works *(Deathstyles, Three Murderers, Darkness in Egypt* [30]), Fräulein Jellinek occasionally comes by to type the professional correspondence, and a reporter interviews the narrator for a literary magazine.

In Lacanian terms, this want of an autonomous identity signifies the lack defining the female subject in patriarchal culture.[8] The new-born infant begins the development toward becoming fully human "the moment he [sic] enters into a symbolic relationship," that is to say, the moment he/she receives a name (Lacan quoted by Jameson, 362).[9] "The name alone" Bachmann states, "suffices to place one in the world" (quoted by Achberger 123; my translation).[10] If the proper name is the mark of the individual's membership in the Symbolic, its lack necessarily denotes her exclusion. And indeed, Franza's psychic destruction in *The Franza Case*, her social exclusion, begins with the elimination of her name from the manuscript on which she and her psychiatrist husband had been working together. In addition, Jordan begins to take notes on Franza's behavior. With these two gestures, he effectively reduces Franza from the status of autonomous individual participating in public discourse, to an object of scientific observation or to a psychoanalytic case study.

In *Malina* the narrator's marginal position in the Symbolic is spatially represented by an imaginary geography of desire: "an intoxicated country containing only two houses" (13; translation changed). This imaginary space, intended to safeguard the narrator from violence and aggression, will, however, soon be violated itself by the narrator's involuntary memories translated into psychosomatic symptoms: "I'd like to – no I don't want to know who did this to you, this wincing, this jerking and shaking your head, this turning your head away" (26; translation changed). In other words, the boundary separating inside from out is transgressed by the invasive force of external reality, which enters the imaginary, protective space via the memories of the female narrator herself. Elizabeth Boa provides a very insightful theoretical formulation of this inside/outside continuum between psychic content and social reality and the conflicts it encloses when she defines the subject as "the intersection between many power relations" (Boa, *Schwierigkeiten* 128; my translation).[11]

If we read the female narrator's namelessness as the lack endemic to female subjectivity, then her desperate, if not pathological, desire for Ivan comes as no surprise. No less than her very existence as a human being is at stake. Her self-affirmation depends on Ivan's desire for her to the extent that a casual rejection has the power to transform an ordinary telephone receiver into a lethal weapon: "So, Ivan has no time. The receiver feels ice cold, not made of plastic but of metal; as I hear him hang up, it slides up to my temple and I wish that this sound were a shot, brief and quick so that it might all be over…" (23; translation changed).

In the beginning of the novel the narrator tells us there are two stories, her own "unavoidable dark story," and Malina's "bright, clear story" (8-9; translation changed). The center of the obscure story harbors the repressed memories of present and past events which the narrator must remember and recount if she is to recover her lost self and assume her rightful place in the Symbolic as a subject of discourse. "I must talk," she insists, "I will talk.

There is nothing more to disturb my remembering" (9; translation changed).

She begins by remembering various people from Klagenfurt, the city of her childhood, some incidents from her school days along with the first kiss and, most importantly, her first encounter with masculine brutality: "It was my first slap in the face, and my first awareness of the deep satisfaction that comes from hitting someone" (10; translation changed). Unlike the preceding, this last recollection almost brings memory to a halt.

Although the most painful memories will never rise to the level of full conscious recollection, their presence in the narrator's unconscious produces "gloomy frightening images" (14; translation changed) and involuntary physical responses to every abrupt movement. And in the second chapter, "The Third Man," the emotional energy stored in these repressed memories will translate into the manifest content of the nightmarish dreams.

In *Happy with Ivan* the female narrator is modeled on conventional femininity as it is constructed by patriarchal culture. This means that within normative male/female dynamics, the female assumes the passive, narcissistic role of desiring to be desired. Within this schema, being desired by the male constitutes the very core of feminine identity and sexuality. Without male confirmation, the female lacks self-definition and access to power in the Symbolic.

The narrator of *Malina* seems to be perfectly aware of the role into which she has been cast. As she looks at herself in the mirror while putting on makeup she comments, "A composition is in the making. Its goal is to create a woman..." (86; translation changed). Despite this lucidity, the narrator is unable to cast off the gender role which makes her totally dependent on the male object of desire to rescue her from the condition of namelessness or non-being into which she has fallen. She believes that Ivan will protect her from the world in which she habitually lives "in perpetual panic, with a dry mouth, with the noose around... my neck... "(13; translation changed). Ever since I have been able to dial this number, my life has finally stopped taking turns for the worse, I'm no longer crushed by its weight..."(13; translation changed). Ivan is the antidote "against the slow decay inside and against being devoured outside..." (15; translation changed). Most importantly, Ivan will uncover the narrator's former, buried self, and will restore her lost voice: "He has come to secure the consonants and to make them tangible again, and to unlock the vowels, so that words may once more issue from my lips" (15; translation changed).

The recovery of the lost voice is particularly important in Bachmann's theoretical framework in that, like Lacan, she links the constitution of the subject to the discursive act of speaking and/or writing. In *Three Paths to the Lake*, Bachmann dramatizes this link by having Elizabeth exclaim, "What have you done to me and to so many others, ... hasn't it ever occurred to anyone that you kill people when you deprive them of the power of speech and with it the power to experience and to think?"(*Three Paths* 173).[12] This exclamatory question is bound to produce what Bachmann, in speaking of her expectations for modern literature, calls a "shock of recognition" (FV 34) among female readers in that it crystalizes the complex psychological issues involved in the feminist debate on the silencing of women.

In *Malina*, the success or failure of the love relationship between the narrator and Ivan depends on Ivan's willingness to meet the narrator's desperate need to articulate the frightful images of her past: "I simply have to talk, talk without stopping, in order to save myself" (128). The actual communication between the two, however, does not begin to measure up: "I still don't know whether you could say today we're able to talk and converse with one another like most people" (18). The relationship never moves beyond fragmentary exchanges; the need to communicate seems to be strictly one-sided. Ivan is quite content to occasionally telephone, to now and then spend the night, to drink his whiskey, and to play chess. All this generates only minimal forms of communication which the narrator on one occasion calls "head-sentences, ... telephone sentences, chess sentences" (26) and on another" swearing sentences," such as "You're a little beast," "You're too dumb," or "you don't understand anything" (52) and shortly before the end, time sentences – "no time," "less and less time," "the pressure of time" (150), on the part of Ivan. Meaningful communication between men and women, it seems, becomes possible only in the realm of fairy tales: "The princess and the stranger began to talk as of yore and when one spoke, the other smiled. They told each other bright things and dark" (40).

These fragmentary verbal exchanges prove to be poor substitutes for that full recovery of her voice the narrator had envisioned. Ivan, acting out stereotypical masculinity, apparently has little need to communicate, at least not with a woman, in order to confirm his identity and assert his subject position in the Symbolic. Posturing as a self-assured male ("only Ivan is totally absorbed by his name" [52 translation changed]), he suffers no lack (or at least thinks he does not) and therefore has no desire to go beyond a playful physical relationship involving only casual verbal exchanges, suspecting, no doubt, that anything more complicated might lead to the "entrapment" he apparently fears.

Among the different groups of sentences the narrator lists, those expressing feelings remain conspicuously absent; only once does the narrator summon enough courage to say "I am happy" (34), but then at a moment when the car radio and the traffic noise are loud enough to keep her voice from reaching Ivan's ear. How-ever, the one sentence for which she silently waits, hopes, begs – the "I need you," which would secure her selfhood in this world will never be pronounced at all: "one sentence keeps me insured and nothing else. No policy in the world can cover me…" (46).

In the title story of *The Thirtieth Year* the introspective narrator reflects on the complex psychic structure of the self: "I, this bundle of reflexes and a well-educated will. I, fed on the refuse of history, of drives and instincts. I, with one foot in the wilderness and with the other on the road to everlasting civilization" (*The Thirtieth Year* 20-21; translation changed).[13]

In Lacanian terms, this interplay of conscious and unconscious elements, of cultural conditioning and libidinal impulses constitutes the subject and positions it in the Symbolic. The second chapter of *Malina*, "The Third Man," based on the psychoanalytic model of the narration of dreams and their analysis, takes us behind the scenes, to the psychic space or to the Other of patriarchal culture: "It is a place called Everywhere and Nowhere. ... Time no longer exists at all, because it could have been yesterday, it could have been long ago, it could be again, it could continually be, some things will have never been" (113).

Fundamental to the organization of this timeless space is the Lacanian symbolic father representing the paternal law. Earlier, in her interview with Herr Mühlbauer, the narrator refers to the pervasive, invisible, frightening presence of the paternal law when she tries to explain why she abandoned her legal studies after only three semesters: "Excuse me, Herr Mühlbauer, what would you have done in my place, since we all live in a law that no one understands, since we are incapable of conceiving *how frightening this law really is*..."(55; translation changed; emphasis added).

In the nightmarish dreams of "The Third Man" the symbolic father takes the form of a fascist, demonic, libidinally-charged father figure, who feeds on acts of brutality, sexual abuse, and aggression, especially directed against the daughter. "He knows how closely cruelty is bound with lust" (138). Scenes of torture ranging from imprisonment, to rape, to abandonment on an island – from being locked in a gas chamber, to being turned into an ice statue – together with the repeated invocation of the cemetery of the murdered daughters symbolize the daughter's psychic destruction, and her ultimate loss of self: "I try to explain to him how sick he has made me... with difficulty I count the hospitals I have been in" (124).

Significantly, the rape/incest scenes of the nightmares are often coupled with the stifling or loss of the daughter's voice (stuttering, inability to speak, tearing out the daughter's tongue), the destruction of her books, the order to take away her writing materials, and the prohibition against mailing her letters. All of these paternal assaults are directed at the potential threats to the sadomasochistic balance of power, which structures the father/daughter relationship. Normative patriarchal socialization of the daughter demands her dutiful submission to the paternal law, which governs the entire social order, including language and knowledge.[14] The daughter's attempt to appropriate these represents a transgression into masculine domains, hence a threat to masculine power.

The father figure is also the key player in the development of the daughter's sexuality, which, in keeping with her subordinate position, takes the form of a masochistic attachment. Despite all the atrocities committed against her, the daughter repeatedly refuses to renounce her father; she does not allow Malina to save her from the abuse she suffers; she complies with her father's wishes to perform nude in a film directed by him; and finally submits to sexual intercourse and to having his child. After an orgy of drunkenness, she lies down beside him, "for my place is here, next to him" (134). More than once the dreamer exclaims, "Incest, it's unmistakable. I know what that means" (146; translation changed), or "Yes, that's what it was, he was the one, it was incest" (118; translation changed). And we can never be certain whether this represents the daughter's actual victimization, her fear of sexual aggression, or her own repressed incestuous desires.

It is on this level, on the level of desire, that the father figure of the dreams intersects with the lover in real life. This begins with the episode in which the father appears half naked, wearing only pajama pants. While the daughter responds with confusion, disdain, and embarrassment, "I hate him, I can't look at him, I pretend to be busy with my suitcases" (147), her body speaks a different language: she begins a rhythmic movement, a dance and calls out Ivan's name. Somewhat later in the same episode, a letter in her handwriting reads: "My beloved father, you have broken my heart ... I want Ivan, I mean Ivan, I love Ivan, my beloved father" (148).

As the narrator analyzes her dreams through the lucid intervention of Malina, her rational Other, she begins to make connections between dream content and lived experience. "I know who you are. I have understood everything" (154). Gradually she comes to understand that the brutal acts committed by the father figure are linked to the schoolgirl memory of the first slap in the face, and to the later war-time memory of being buried under a pile of rubble during a low-flying aircraft attack. These memory traces in turn are re-inscribed when Ivan "raises his hand in jest, ... the fear returns, I say to him, choking: Please don't, not my head" (*Malina* 46). And the parallels multiply.

The daughter asks her father for a ring as a mark of his affection and she silently begs for a verbal sign from Ivan. The father stifles the daughter's voice, takes away her writing material and forbids her to mail her letters. Ivan belittles her work: "Merrily he takes one [a page] and reads DEATH STYLES" and then dismisses this and the other titles as "loathsome" and criticizes her "obsession" with this "gloom" (30). The daughter stutters in the presence of her father and, at one point, intends to confront him with, "My father, this time you are going to talk to me and answer my questions" (153), and already in the early stages of her relationship with Ivan, the narrator finds it impossible to talk to him about herself and later imagines asking him, "Why don't you ever let me talk?" (184). The actual confrontations, however, never take place, neither in the dream nor in the lived experience.

To be silenced, Bachmann tells us in *Three Paths to the Lake*, is to be annihilated. And at the end of "The Third Man," the narrator concludes: "It's not my father. It's my murderer" (154); yet she insists: "I am alive, I will live, I claim my right to live" (152; translation changed). Live! Yes, but how?

Malina provides the answer. In telling the narrator to kill him (Ivan), he urges her to destroy her feminine self, that masochistic side of her psychic being subordinate and submissive to the symbolic father and to all his manifestations in empirical reality.[15] Once it becomes clear that the relationship with Ivan, her "continuous, soft, painful crucifixion" (112), merely repeats the oppressive paternal order, the narrator begins to understand the complicitous role she has been playing in her own oppression. The feminine self that has put her back in touch with her body is also that psychic impulse which is sustained by subordination and repression. All forms of active resistance lie beyond the realm of its connotative signification that the only possible means of escape is total self-effacement: "There you will be yourself to the point that you can give up your self" (208).

The elimination of feminine complicity, according to Malina, will momentarily stall the patriarchal power machine: "It will be the first place where someone has healed the world" (208). Just as the "sovereign" subject maintains its mastery by dismissing and repressing all psychic impulses that tend to interfere, so the oppressive social order needs the oppressed in order to maintain its operation.

Through the dream work the narrator learns that she has become an unwitting accomplice in her own oppression. "Maybe you didn't know," Malina says, "but you were in agreement" (145). Translating this subliminal awareness into active resistance, however, becomes virtually impossible, in that within the confines of patriarchal structure the female libidinal economy is organized around submission to the male. In the case of the narrator, this submission, albeit lucid, borders on self-annihilation: "I will submit. I can do that on occasion. And this is not the result of any rational deliberation. It stems from either affinity or aversion" (163), and "I cannot extricate myself from it, for it happened with my body against all reason" (112; translation changed). Reason and desire are at odds; for the moment the latter holds sway.

Before the dreams, the narrator's desire for resistance to the loss of self translates into psychosomatic symptoms in the form of ever-increasing anxiety attacks, as the suspicion of becoming the prisoner of a repressive relationship becomes more intense. Like the dreams, these symptoms function as points of convergence, reducing present and past to a continuous today. While their origin must be sought in earlier traumatic events, the actual manifestation of the symptoms is triggered by present experiences. Although the narrator suspects that there may be several forces at work – "But it may not be Ivan alone, perhaps something greater has conquered me, it must be something greater, since everything is driving us to one destiny"(166) – the awareness of their connections, however, does not become explicit until the manifest content of the dreams has been worked through. Once this has been accomplished, the present self-destructive relationship and those of her past converge into a single monumental timeless event: "What are you really thinking about? About Marcel, or still about the same One thing, or about everything which has helped nail you to the cross?"(175; translation changed).[16] Until the time of this recognition, Malina, "the Other in me" (88; translation changed), is kept at bay, and the narrator unquestioningly performs her gender according to cultural expectations: she caters to Ivan's whims, cooks for him, waits for him, waits on him, spends endless hours waiting for the telephone to ring, listens to him, lets him win at chess, tolerates his refusal to let her speak and buys a new dress to please him: "A composition is in the making. Its goal is to create a woman..."(86; translation changed).

The drama of the dreams, played out within the space of the war metaphor, attempts to draw the battle lines between the law/symbolic father, violence and victimized daughter, only to reveal that oppressor and oppressed are not as neatly separated as the dreamer had supposed. In response to her "I don't want to talk, everything in my memories disturbs me" (11) in the very beginning of the novel, long before the dream chapter, Malina responds: "For the time being. But there is another recollection disturbing you" (11; translation changed). This other memory might well be the unconscious knowledge of the narrator's unwitting collaboration with a social order that defines and maintains itself by dominating and repressing those groups and psychic impulses which figure as potential threats to its conception of society, culture and order.

The protagonist (and I use the term to include both the narrator and Malina) bears the double and necessarily conflicting inscription of the paternal law. In terms of the perception of reality this means that the masculine persona associated with the Symbolic (order, reason, logic, analytic thought, linear conceptions of time, etc.) conflicts with the non-linear dream logic, and strong visual, tactile and acoustic images of the Imaginary associated with the feminine. The difference between the two perceptions of reality is the difference between pondering the problems of economic exchange upon hearing the word schilling and perceiving it as a physical entity. "I suddenly have a schilling in my mouth, light, cold, round, so irritating that it makes me want to spit it out" (215;

translation changed).

Within the imaginary, the distance between signifier and signified tends to collapse, and seeing becomes a physical act in which the observer and observed momentarily merge in bond of mutual modification. By contrast, in the Symbolic, the distance between signifier and signified is maintained and seeing becomes appropriation through the act of classifying and naming. With the latter, we associate reason, mastery, self assertion and knowledge,[17] while the former is connected to imagination, emotion, compassion and creativity. One set of attributes is coded masculine, the other feminine – the basic hierarchical binary structure that sets up all of Western thought with its resulting conflict between men and women: "Something must have gone wrong with the primates, at the latest with the hominoids. A man, a woman ... strange words, strange madness!" (220; translation changed). It also sets up the inner conflict of the protagonist. In the last chapter, the battle waged between the father figure and the daughter is reproduced in the opposition between the female narrator and Malina. This extends the historical, social, and political conflict between men and women to the two opposing forces comprising the individual psyche.[18] Perhaps this is what Malina means when he says: "It's war. And you are the war. You yourself"(21), a variant of Bachmann's reflection that the I no longer resides in history, but that history resides in the I (FV 54).

From this perspective, the protagonist (narrator and Malina combined) becomes more than unwitting collaborator in the destruction of the feminine, she/he becomes both master and slave, oppressor and oppressed. The resolution of the masculine-feminine binary bind begins with a dress rehearsal before the final elimination of the feminine. Of the two black dresses remaining in the empty closet, the Ivan dress and the Malina dress, the narrator chooses the latter. To heighten the toxic effect of her "Nessus-garment" (213), she sits down to read a philosophical text while waiting for Ivan. The next morning (or what seems like the next morning) the erasure of the feminine is completed. Wearing Malina's robe, the narrator disappears in the crack of the wall facing

Malina silently standing by.

In this intra-psychic battle, the triumph of the masculine seems complete.[19] Just as the father figure of the dreams takes away the daughter's letters and words, so Malina will take over the narrator's stories and the telling of them. "Go ahead and take over all the stories which make up history. Take them all away from me" (221). This means that we can expect the scattered scraps of paper and discontinuous episodes to be homogenized and synthesized into a continuous piece of narrative prose, structured on the basis of temporal progression, cause and effect, and fully developed characters to become yet another shield forged to protect the "author," or the "sovereign" subject, that "illusory essence, designating an illusory identity."

In the final telephone conversation, Malina's complete, self-assured, properly punctuated sentences, displace the short phrases and elliptic fragments of the preceding ones. The speaking subject now has a stated identity: a name, a profession and a specific place in the sociosymbolic order. The triumph of the masculine over the feminine seems complete.

In the final analysis, the protagonist of *Malina* can no more escape the paternal law than the narrator of *Everything* can step outside the sociosymbolic. But neither can the paternal law completely erase the feminine. Malina might well break the narrator's glasses, throw away her coffee cup, letters and glass cube; the feminine, however, remains. Just as the blank space on the temple wall recalls queen Hatschepsut's name in *The Franza Case*,[20] so the crack in the wall facing Malina will continue to trace the repression of the feminine; but at the same time it will call attention to the everlasting possibility of its return, if not as a subject of discourse in the Symbolic, then as a relentless force of resistance to it.

Notes

1. *Frankfurter Vorlesungen* (München, Zürich: Piper, 1989) 12. All quotations from the *Frankfurter Vorlesungen* are my translations and will henceforth be cited as FV in the body of the text.

2. *Gewähr* means guarantee but we also hear *Gewehr* meaning rifle.

3. Paul Smith has this to say about posturing: "Psychoanalysis has shown that the privilege granted to the knowledgeable subject is misplaced and that the hold of the ego is not only precarious but also indefensibly and complexly tied to structures of misrecognition and repression" *Discerning the Subject* (Minneapolis: University of Minnesota Press, 1988) 78.

4. Sigrid Weigel, "Ein Ende mit der Schrift. Ein anderer Anfang. Zur Entwicklung von Ingeborg Bachmanns Schreibweise." *Kein Objecktives Urteil) Nur ein Lebendiges*. Eds. Christine Koschel and Inge von Weidenbaum (München: Piper, 1989) 265-310.

5. Sigrid Weigel comes to the same conclusion. Furthermore, she points out that critics have repeatedly taken the phrase, "no new world without a new language," from *The Thirtieth Year* to substantiate the claim that Bachmann argues for a new language (281). In taking this sentence out of context this argument misses the point. Bachmann's fiction illustrates the impossibility of founding a new language leading to a new society and not the reverse.

6. Ingeborg Bachmann, *Everything. The Thirtieth Year*. Transl. Michael Bullock (New York, London: Holmes & Meier, 1989) 62-82.

7. All quotations from *Malina* are based on the Philip Boehm translation (New York, London: Holmes & Meier 1990).

8. Sigrid Weigel points out that the narrator refers to herself as "disinherited" (289).

9. Frederic Jameson, "Imaginary and Symbolic in Lacan: Marxism, Psychoanalytic Criticism, and the Problem of the Subject." *Literature and Psychoanalysis* (Baltimore and London: Johns Hopkins University Press, 1982) 338-395.

10. Karen Achberger, "Bachmann und die Bibel." *Der dunkle Schatten dem ich schon seit Anfang folge.* Ed. Hans Hüller (Wien, München, Kleinenzersdorf: Löcker, 1982) 85-95.

11. Elizabeth Boa, "Schwierigkeiten mit der ersten Person: Ingeborg Bachmanns *Malina* und Monika Marons *Flugschale. Die Überläuferin und stille Zeile sechs.*" *Kritische Wege der Landnahme.* Eds. Robert Pichl und Alexander Stillmark (Wien: Hora Verlag, 1994) 135-145.

12. *Three Paths to the Lake.* Transl. Mary Fran Gilbert (New York/London: Holmes & Meier 1989) 117-212. In *Voraussetzungen einer Erzählung: Kassandra*, Frankfurter Poetik Vorlesungen (München: DTB Verlag, 1993) Christa Wolf asks a similar question. "The faded Syrian women, dressed in pitch black, without a moment's hesitation obeying the slightest gestures of their husbands. Cassandra could have resembled one of them, one of the younger ones. None of them, however, could speak today as she did so many centuries ago. What have they done to them in the meantime?" (15, my translation).

13. Ingeborg Bachmann, *The Thirtieth Year.* Transl. Michael Bullock (New York, London: Holmes & Meier, 1989) 62-82.

14. Brigit Vanderbeke calls attention to the phallic signification of the staff of the University of Vienna to which the narrator recollects swearing allegiance after passing her doctoral examination. "Kein Recht auf Sprache" *Text und Kritik, Sonderband, Ingeborg Bachmann.* Ed. Heinz Ludwig Arnold (München: Edition Text + Kritik GmbH, 1984) 114.

15. Elizabeth Boa comes to the same conclusion: "In order to emancipate themselves from conventional femininity, women must conduct themselves like men (133-134). "Women Writing about Women Writing and Ingeborg Bachman's *Malina.*" *New Ways in Germanistik.* Ed. Richard Sheppard (New York, Oxford, München: Berg Publ. Ltd., St. Martin's Press, 1990) 324-335.

16. The image of the cross recurs in *Word for Word.* Here language itself becomes the social force that has "crucified" the female protagonist.

17. In one of the dreams the daughter literally fights with the

father to gain control of the golden staff, the staff of the University of Vienna (187).

18. In relationship to the inner conflict which reproduces the difficulties of binary thinking, Elizabeth Boa has this to say: "This does not mean that Ich is the true feminine self and Malina a false masculine persona. Rather, it conveys how intellectual curiosity, practical rationality and emotional needs are constructed in ways which lead to conflict within individuals and between the sexes through a culture which splits such qualities along gender lines and through the division between the public and the private." "Unnatural Causes: Modes of Death in Christa Wolf's "Nach-denken über Christa T." and Ingeborg Bachmann's *Malina*." *German Literature at a Time of Change*. Ed. Arthur Williams (Bern: Peter Lang, 1989-1990) 144-145.

19. "Only the rational, productive, masculine side, Malina, is able to survive in this society" (27, my translation). Angelika Rauch. "Sprache, Weiblichkeit und Utopie." *Modern Austrian Literature* 18, 3/4 (1985) 21-38.

20. This scene is cited by Andreas Hapkemeyer, *Ingeborg Bachmann, Bilder aus ihrem Leben* (München, Zürich: Piper: 1983) 111.

The Development and Ultimate Cessation of Ingeborg Bachmann's Lyric Voice

Amy Kepple Strawser

Ingeborg Bachmann dealt with the possibilities and limitations of language throughout her career, particularly in her later poems. Despite her concern with the inadequacies of verbal expression, Bachmann wrote prolifically. Despite her seeming preoccupation with language barriers and word-obstacles, she nonetheless sought and found manifestation of her thoughts, ideas and images in written form. Despite her continual questioning of silence and its ramifications, she did not cease to communicate through written symbols.

Bachmann triumphed in the sense that she did not, like other contemporary poets, fall victim to wordlessness during her lifetime. Nor did she, as did others such as Paul Celan, Sylvia Plath, and Anne Sexton, retreat willfully to death as the silencing solution. In her development as a writer, however, Bachmann did indeed succumb to silence in the genre of poetry. What caused the poet to abandon the lyric form? What factors contributed to her choice of literary modes other than lyric poetry after 1967? One of Ingeborg Bachmann's last poems, *No Delicacies*, exemplifies the impending cessation of her participation in the lyric form: "My share, it should be dispersed."[1] The final line of this poem could serve as the closing statement to her poetry. Shortly thereafter her poetic voice becomes silent.

Bachmann poses a number of questions in this poem to depict extreme frustration and doubt in the writing of poetry; more specifically, in the dubious relation between poet, concept, object and the poetic devices of language. Bachmann is questioning the value of capturing thoughts and images in metaphors, in the well-turned phrases of a poem.

No Delicacies provides the epitaph for Bachmann's poetry, a final utterance of the poetic voice. The poem closes one phase in the development of the writer and opens the door to the realm of prose. Yet in this defiant statement against the lyrical form, Bachmann has nonetheless used a poem (albeit an abstract one) to accomplish her goal. As Christa Wolf says of the piece in her Büchner-prize acceptance speech: "Metaphors are rejected by a metaphor, . . . The poem that disowns art must paradoxically be a work of art."[2] The destructive impulse toward the artistic products demonstrated by the words *rip apart, sweep away*, and *destroying* in the poem seems a necessary step in the author's progression beyond the lyric genre, while not abandoning the literary sphere altogether. Christa Wolf affirms this continuation of the now-relinquished aesthetic form: "One who expresses herself completely does not cancel herself out: the wish for obliteration remains as a witness. Her part will not vanish."[3] What is it about this literary form that drove Bachmann to retreat from it? Through a survey of her poetry, I intend to point out several features which contribute significantly to the extinguishing of Bachmann's poetic voice.

Bachmann's poetry demonstrates stylistic features shared by other German poets of her time, in keeping with the tradition of modern lyric verse. Noteworthy among the frequent appearances of metaphor in general is the occurrence of many genitive metaphor constructions. Bachmann, in this sense, is writing quite conventionally, in the tradition of twentieth-century lyric poetry, the foundations of which are built on dissonant constructions.

The use of genitive metaphors is characteristic of Bachmann's early poems, such as *In the Storm of Roses*, but is not typical of her later, more abstract poems, such as *No Delicacies* – a fact which indicates a change in her poetry over the years. Also, in contrast to her final poems, in *In the Storm of Roses*, for example, Bachmann uses the more general pronoun *we* instead of the specific poetic voice *I*. Avoiding the *I* seems to allow her a freer, non-subjective expression of a universal voice: "Wherever we turn in the storm of roses,/thorns illuminate the night. And the thunder/of a thousand leaves, once so quiet on the bushes,/is right at our heels"/(67).

A look at Bachmann's use of pronouns in poems from various time periods proves insightful. Beginning with the later poems, grouped in her collected works from 1957 to 1961 and 1964 to 1967, one finds most frequently the pronoun *I*. For example, in the poems *Exile*, *After This Deluge*, *Stream*, *Truly*, and *No Delicacies*, this *I* does not impress one as a universal lyrical voice, but rather as that of the poet: self-conscious, speaking personally, and from her own experience. In *Stream*, she writes: "So far in life and so close to death, /that I shall litigate no more./ From the earth I rip my part;" (165). And in *Exile*: "I who cannot live among people/ I with the German language/ this cloud about me/ that I keep as a house/ drive through all languages" (161). The lyrical voice here is not claiming to speak for the reader, but instead is setting forth the subjectivity of the poet. This personal *I* is often interwoven with images concrete and abstract, as in *Stream*:

> into the still ocean, into its heart
> I plunge my green wedge and
> wash myself onshore.
> Tin birds rise up and cinnamon smell!
> With my murderer time I am alone. (165)

The pronouns in a sampling of poems from the collection *Invocation of the Great Bear* (1956) are more diverse. In the poems *Stay*, *That Which is True (Was wahr ist)*, and *Hill of Shards (Scherbenhügel)*, Bachmann employs the unspecified second-person familiar singular, *you (du)*, a technique also found frequently in Paul Celan's poetry. Here, the poetic voice gives the impression of greater confidence in its declarations because the use of the subjective *I* is avoided. The use of *you* creates a more inclusive plea to the reader, for, although it is possible that the author intended to address herself or someone else in these poems, one nonetheless does not feel excluded; the lines are written to be potentially applicable to all:

> That which is true does not throw sand in your eyes,
> That which is true is an apology to you by
> sleep and death... [4]

Two other poems from *Invocation of the Great Bear – Land of Fog* and *The Blue Hour (Die blaue Stunde)*) offer unusual treatments of the poetic voice. In *Land of Fog* the *I* is a male persona who describes his "beloved," who changes forms metaphorically in nature: she is with the animals of the wood, a tree among trees, and in the water among the fish. Bachmann has here assumed the traditional male voice in an effort to write a convincing poem. She has not, whether consciously or sub-consciously, tried to integrate her voice as a woman writer.

> In winter my love
> is among the beasts of the forest.
> The vixen knows
> I must be back before morning
> and she laughs. . . .
> In winter my love
> is a tree among trees
> and invites the hapless crows
> to nest in her beautiful boughs. . . .
>
> In winter my love
> is among the fish and cannot speak.
> A slave to the waters her fins
> stroke from within, . . . (101)

In contrast, *The Blue Hour* is composed of three stanzas, the first with an old man, the second a young man, addressing the same girl as *you*. Both men are placing their expectations and demands on the young woman. In the third stanza, she answers them in a forceful response proclaiming potential or longed-for mythical powers:

> You gentlemen, put the sword in my hand,
> and Joan of Arc will save the fatherland.
> Friends, we will bring the ship through the ice,
> I am holding the course, which no one knows. . . .
> From the high trapeze in the circus tent
> I jump through the world's rings of fire,
> I give myself into the hands of my master,
> and he graciously gives me the evening star.(117-118)

One could read in these lines the awakening of a female voice in Bachmann's lyrics. The girl in the poem is aware of the requirements placed on her by the masculine world, but she demands control, the ability (as bestowed by the male figures, who would give her the symbolically phallic sword) to take the situation into her own hands and to lead things successfully. However, this is only in cooperation with her male counterparts, as in the give-and-take expressed in the final two lines. This imagery could represent Bachmann's desire to be an acclaimed and accomplished writer, yet remain herself, a woman, in a patriarchal world. Without losing her identity in men, she would rather gain power and recognition as an individual with their support. In the context of the poem these lines express the unreal fantasies of the girl.

In two of Bachmann's earliest poems, *Behind the Wall* (*Hinter der Wand*) and *What Shall I Call Myself?* (*Wie soll ich mich nennen?*), the pronoun *I* predominates. However, this *I* is different from the subjective *I* of the later poems; the voice here is a being or force in close metaphorical contact with nature. In *Behind the Wall*, she writes:

> I hang as snow from the branches
> in the spring of the valley,
> as a cold spring I drive in the wind,
> damp I fall into the blossoms
> as a raindrop (25)

And in *What Shall I Call Myself?*: "Once I was a tree and bound,/ then I escaped as a bird and was free" (30).

The *I* of these two poems is not at all limiting. In fact, this poetic voice is quite distant from any individuality of the author, who is acting solely as a medium in transmitting the impressions of some universal power. The mysterious *I* then identifies itself directly in "Behind the Wall": "I am the child of the great world fear, /. . . / I am the always-thinking-about-death " (25).

The self-assertion of this voice convinces us of a significance in the poem which is larger than life: our simultaneous fear of and fascination with death and dying. This statement transcends the realm of the author-specific *I* because it speaks to and for that which is shared by everyone, our human mortality.

In contrast, the *I* of *What Shall I Call Myself?* appears to be the seed of life, which has existed in myriad different forms and which has undergone countless metamorphoses of being:

> How do I act? I have forgotten,
> where I come from and where I am going,
> I am possessed by many shapes,
> a sharp thorn and a fleeing deer. (30)

This *I* recalls the nameless power in Dylan Thomas's poem, *The force that through the green fuse drives the flower*[5]: that is, the abstract, but universally real, dynamic energy of nature. Like Thomas, Bachmann is unable to give a name to this force (hence the title), for the poem ends with the lines: "A word is lacking! What shall I call myself, / without using another language" (30). Here too Bachmann introduces the problem of language, a topic which demands the attention of anyone reading her work.

The pronoun *we* is used in two other early poems by Bachmann, *We go, our hearts in the dust* (*Wir gehen, die Herzen im Staub*), and *Message*. Both works deal with the common postwar theme of coming to terms with the past *(Vergangenheitsbewältigung)*. This topic occupied many of Bachmann's predecessors and contemporaries, particularly the Jewish German poet Nelly Sachs. The first poem uses the pronoun *we* in connection with dust imagery, a technique also prevalent in Sachs's poems. "We go, our hearts in the dust,/ and for a long while close to failure./ We are just not heard, they are too deaf/ to lament the groaning in the dust" (21).

The poem *Message* presents the existential problems of the immediate past and the difficulty in reconciling the fact that so many people's lives were sacrificed. Bachmann depicts how history has killed many human beings and how our worship of it has destroyed the hope of the survivors: "... Our godhead, / History, has reserved us a grave / from which there is no resurrection" (55). The poet's choice of pronoun in these poems is appropriate and effective for her purpose. She speaks not only for herself as a poet and individual here, but functions also as a spokesperson for her society.

To review a general usage of pronouns in Bachmann's poetry, let us summarize chronologically: 1) a collective *we* is used in several early poems to confront the horrors of the immediate past; 2) a cosmic *I* speaks in several other early poems to communicate concepts of death and existence through nature images; 3) in one poem, the *I* is a male persona; in another, two males address a young woman as *you*, who in turn responds to them with lines which use the only appearance of the first-person pronoun *I* in the poem; 4) the unspecified *you* is found in several poems from about midway in Bachmann's poetic career, a pronoun, which, by avoiding precise address, speaks to a broader (and thus more ambiguous) audience; and finally, 5) the subjective *I* of the author appears frequently in the later poems).

Although this examination has analyzed a selection of Bachmann's poetry, the examples chosen can be considered representative and therefore illustrate the following point. Through a look at the pronouns, we can observe a steadily more subjective, individualistic lyrical voice in Bachmann. In view of other aspects of these poems, too, Bachmann's lyrical works become progressively more unconventional over the years. As she abandons the traditional (male) *I* of the poems, the poet proceeds to the use of the second-person pronoun for the purpose of objectification. Bachmann then leaves the *you*-form to return to the first person. However, this *I* is not that of a collective voice; rather, the *I* in the last poems is finally the identifiable voice of the female poet. Thus I hypothesize that the discovery of her subjective voice contributed to Bachmann's desertion of the lyric form. In other words, Bachmann's poems become less traditional over the years, while simultaneously the themes of language and silence appear in them more and more frequently. This phenomenon is almost certainly related to the growing awareness of herself as a woman writer, both within and beyond the bounds of the lyric form. In the essay *Music and Poetry (Musik und Dichtung)*, Bachmann writes: "We, engaged in language, have experienced what speechlessness and muteness are – our, if you will, purest conditions! – , and have returned from the no man's land with language, which we will pursue, as long as life is our pursuit."[6]

We can see here how Bachmann addressed the juxtaposed problems of speech and speechlessness in her expository prose as well as in her poems. This quote expresses that she has experienced the threat of silence through a self-conscious concern with language, yet this statement also affirms the poet's optimistic, hopeful return from the void in order to carry on her work with language. Bachmann stresses in these lines the prerequisites of life and the pursuit of it for the ability to produce literature, be it prose or poetry. However, as an Austrian woman writer in the 1960s, the development of a more subjective, yet also more limiting lyric voice signals the burgeoning of a feminist consciousness in Bachmann's work. As with many female authors in German-speaking countries in the past thirty years, Bachmann turned to prose as the arena for grappling with the difficult issues of gender identity and violence against women,[7] themes she struggled with in the novel *Malina* (1971) and the novel fragment *Franza's Case (Der Fall Franza* 1979).

Notes

1. Ingeborg Bachmann, *No Delicacies*, *In the Storm of Roses: Selected Poems by Ingeborg Bachmann*, edited, translated, and introduced by Mark Anderson (Princeton: Princeton University Press, 1986) 187. All further references to Bachmann's translated poems are from this edition and will be cited parenthetically in the text.

2. Christa Wolf, "Shall I Garnish a Metaphor with an Almond Blossom? Büchner-Prize Acceptance Speech," Transl. Henry J. Schmidt, *New German Critique* 23 (1981) 10.

3. Wolf, 10.

4. Bachmann, "Was wahr ist," *Sämtliche Gedichte* (München: Piper, 1983) 128. All further references to Bachmann's poems in German will refer to this edition. The translations are mine.

5. Dylan Thomas, *The force that through the green fuse drives the flower*, *The Poems of Dylan Thomas*, ed. Daniel Jones (New York: New Directions, 1971) 77.

6. Bachmann, "Musik und Dichtung," *Werke*, eds. Christine Koschel et al., vol. 4 (München: Piper, 1978) 60.

7. As Sigrid Weigel notes, in German women's literature, "...prose represents the forum in which the development of theory, topoi, themes and perspectives of female culture expresses itself most significantly." This is not necessarily the case, however, for English-speaking women writers, for whom poetry has served as a vital genre in the development of feminist discourse. See Weigel, "Overcoming Absence: Contemporary German Women's Literature," Transl. Amy Kepple, *New German Critique* 32 (1984) 20.

"Monuments looking out upon Utopia": *The Thirtieth Year* by Ingeborg Bachmann – a Reading

Kathleen Thorpe

> A thought contains the possibility of the situation of which it is the thought. What is thinkable is possible too. *Ludwig Wittgenstein. Tractatus Logico-Philosophicus.* 3.02

Failure to achieve aims such as truth, a new language, and harmony between the sexes in Ingeborg Bachmann's *The Thirtieth Year*[1] should not be seen so much as failures than as experiments that have not had a positive outcome. Constantly running at, and colliding with, the limits of language is not a fruitless exercise but an attempt to extend the range of language and thus perhaps shift the boundaries of the "sayable" in the sense of Wittgenstein. The seven stories comprising *The Thirtieth Year* (1961) explore different aspects of this endeavor. Indeed, the concept of resistance, the need to have something to resist is integral to Bachmann's prose work, of which *The Thirtieth Year* is the first attempt since voluntarily stepping off her pedestal as the most revered female lyric poet of the post-1945 period in German language literature. Bachmann explores the "sayable," and thoughts that can be expressed in language have the potential for one day becoming reality. Facticity merely represents the boundaries of the world at present and should not be confused with the truth residing beyond articulation in the Absolute. Wittgenstein, of course, does not deny the existence of "the mystical"[2] but merely points to its inexpressibility, so any attempt at transgressing the border between what can and what cannot be expressed in language must be viewed as an attempt to gain ground and thus venture into the realm of the Absolute.

Pushing against these boundaries is perhaps the prime motivation for Bachmann's "descent" from the lofty realms of poetry to the more mundane sphere of prose writing. The fact that Bachmann's life and works have assumed the character of the legendary should not color an evaluation of her prose work either. Contrary to how it may now appear, i.e., that her poetry and prose flow into each other, as well as a renewed interest in her prose works in recent years, should not gloss over[3] the difficulties facing her short stories in gaining the acceptance of critics. It is true that Bachmann did receive a prize for *The Thirtieth Year* in the year of its publication, but these stories also encountered resistance from those critics who viewed her new prose writing as a debasement of her talent.[4] However, Bachmann herself said:

> I have nothing against poems, but you have to imagine that one can suddenly have everything against them, against any coercion to allow phrases to string together, against this absolutely felicitous appearance of words and images. That one would like to stifle it so that one can check it once again, what it is about and what it should be.[5]

This seems to be uncanny unison with her Austrian compatriot Thomas Bernhard who also stated: "The most dreadful thing for me is writing prose. . . But I wanted this enormous resistance, and through this I write prose."[6]

The means by which Ingeborg Bachmann gathers material to push against the boundaries of the sayable is *Recollection*. In addition, *Recollection*, as Andrea Stoll remarks, is perhaps the "decisive quality of the poetic I . . .The ability to remember assists the epic I to achieve a new way of dealing with time."[7] It is not something that arises spontaneously, but rather occurs as a result of a process set in motion and maintained effort. Recollecting, gathering and reviewing, thinking through the past results not only in a crisis in awareness, but in an awareness of crisis that will project into the future. None of the seven stories comprising *The Thirtieth Year* has a final resolution of conflict as a conclusion. Life goes on, but in a heightened state of awareness of the nature of an ongoing crisis. Thus a constant source of resistance is maintained.

While Bachmann's prose contains elements already known from her poetry, her prose should rather be viewed as rhythmic prose in the tradition of Hölderlin, for example, than as erred poetry. This is particularly the case of the first story of the collection *Youth in an Austrian Town*. A refusal to judge these stories on their merits and to accept that the effort of consistently refusing to give up the attempt at gaining ground on "the mystical" will lead to an interpretation of the stories as demonstrations of the "senselessness of any kind of rebellion, every hope of renewal."[8]

The seven stories of *The Thirtieth Year* are not randomly selected texts, but movements in a decidedly musical composition,[9] with an evocatively visual element – in short, a type of opera. The title story is the starting point from which all the other stories fan out and for this reason will form the main focus of this essay. The individual stories may be self-contained and be individually structured, but taken as parts of the whole, provide a panoramic sweep of experience activated by the device of memory. Opening with *Youth in an Austrian Town* ...mory is activated. "Monuments looking out upon Utopia"(11) are brought into focus by the lighting of a ceremonial torch, illuminating the theater of language and imagination: "Only when the tree outside the theater works the miracle, when the torch burns, do I manage to see everything mingled, like the waters in the sea" (11). This overture celebrates language, the vehicle of memory, as a gift, "like a torch dropped by an angel" that is impervious to the destructive natural elements which cannot extinguish this eternal light:

> Who, faced with this tree is going to talk to me
> about falling leaves and the white death? Who
> will prevent me from holding it with my eyes and
> believing that it will always glow before me as it
> does at this moment and that it is not subject to
> the laws of the world? (1)

Writing thus becomes an act of faith and the creative act itself, that of finding expression, trying out a voice long kept in oppressive silence, is like children shouting loudly in the attic, and exercising the first cries of opposition to the status quo. The expressions of dissent commence in *The Thirtieth Year* as "little low cries of rebellion" (5) here and swell later to the commanding and strident tones of "Think! Be! Speak out!" (175) in the final story *Undine Goes*, only to fade out on the yearning notes of "Come. Just once./ Come" (181).

The title story, the lengthiest of the collection, is by contrast, subdued in tone: "his shout does not become audible" (12); uncertain and anguished, the nameless protagonist "crashes down into a fathomless abyss, until his senses fade away, until everything which he thought he was has been dissolved, extinguished and destroyed" (12). To denigrate this story, narrated, it is true, in "feverish in disjointedness" and, therefore, find it "artistically unconvincing"[10] is to overlook the internal structuring of *The Thirtieth Year* in which disjointedness effectively reflects the agitation of the protagonist. The existential crisis, inherent in the title of the story, is experienced by the protagonist in his fall into the abyss of uncertainty, recovering consciousness in the miraculous discovery of his "ability to remember"(12-13). Two contrasting images are evoked in the "painful compulsion"(13) with which he reviews his life. The expansive gesture of casting a net contracts and expands once more in the transcending of time and place:

> He casts the net of memory, casts it over himself
> and draws himself, catcher and caught in one
> person, over the threshold of time, over the
> threshold of place, to see who he was and who he
> has become.(13)

The rhythm of nature in the time-honored structuring device of the seasons to reflect the stages of human development is exploited, too, in the expansion and contraction that govern the narrative rhythm of the entire text. The overture is characterized by restless activity. In playing through his naive early faith in himself and the limitless possibilities he saw in his future, the language tone and rhythm move from the grandiose and expansive: "A great man, a beacon, a philosopher," through the clipped tones of the strong, silent man of action – "in khaki drill"– escalating into the devil-may-care revolutionary, torching the "rotten wooden floor of society"(13), suffering, failing and finally triumphing, carried on by a wave of enthusiasm, through to the contemplative, self-indulgent "idler out of wisdom"(13). Feverish activity while borne aloft on a cloud of oblivion without awareness of limits or finality: "He felt that he could give the world notice, that he could give himself notice"(14) preludes the conclusion of the overture in the first moment of awareness of existential crisis in the theatrical image of the curtain rising and the drama of his life beginning in earnest in the year prior to that fateful thirtieth birthday, marking his maturity and signaling that he has been given his cue. Disillusion is the consequence of this realization.

The protagonist's mood of depression gives way in the first movement to restless physical activity, marking a break with the past: "He has to be free this year, to give up everything" (15). Divesting himself of his mementos of the past, freeing himself from people, places and possessions, he makes a type of pilgrim-age to Rome in the hope of being able to reveal his true self. However, in Rome he is merely trapped in the "straitjacket" (16) of the identity he had chosen to assume there many years before. Initial protest subsides in the despairing realization that "He will never . . . be able to free himself, to begin from the beginning" (16). Accosted by the ubiquitous Moll, the minor key dominating the everyday, who casts shadow over all of his activities, symptomatic of the wearing demands of quotidian existence, he expresses disgust at the "monstrous affront that is life" (19).

This leads, as the year progresses through to autumn, to a desperate attempt at regaining a hold on life through the senses: "August was full of panic, full of the compulsion to snatch at life and hurry to start living" (19). The tempo of the language reflects the his desperate agitation: "he sauntered to and fro between the sea and the city," the summer weather cruelly driving his desperation: "The melons ripened; he tore them to pieces . . . He loved a myriad women, all at the same time and without distinction" (20). He is insatiable in his desperation to lay in a stock of living before the winter.

All the while his devotion to physical sensation is a flight from the "mind which my flesh houses" (20), which ultimately catches up with him. Despite his efforts at escaping self-awareness, the protagonist is ultimately confronted with his "I" and the knowledge of its paradoxical, fragmented and essentially ephemeral identity:

> I, this bundle of reflexes and a well-educated will. I, fed on the refuse of history, refuse of impulse and instinct, *I* with one foot in the wilderness and the other on the high road to everlasting civilization. *I impenetrable*, a mixture of all materials, matted, insoluble and yet capable of being extinguished by a blow on the back of the head. Silenced *I of silence* ....(20)

The concluding silence is the ultimate protest against this state of affairs.[11] This knowledge then fuels his helpless desire for some sort of compensatory originality and individual creativity. He comes to acknowledge that hedonism was only a futile attempt at avoidance of confessing his awareness that

> I am an abandoned instrument upon which someone, a long time ago, struck a few notes on which I helplessly produce variations, out of which I try furiously to make a piece of sound that bears my handwriting. (21)

This crisis of awareness of his own impotence requires isolation from others, "Keep your distance from me, or I shall die" (22), in order to ponder and work through his anger at human beings and their inability to end the agonizing uncertainty of existence. Silence remains the only appropriate answer.

Late autumn appears as an intermezzo, bringing some respite from his anger. This is a period of recovery, narrated in a calmer tempo. Commencing with an invocation: "Come, lovely autumn. In this October of the last roses . . . " out of which an idyll of a Greek island "in the Aegean, on which there are only flowers and stone lions" (23) rises. This dreamlike invocation leads into an expansive attitude toward time and adopting a habitual way of life, distancing himself from social ties, enjoying, not merely using his time. With this pause comes firstly the desire to become integrated into society: "He sought a duty, he wanted to serve" (24); and secondly, in the activation of memory, the rediscovery of his first existential crisis, which he seems to have forgotten, and the timely recollection of which at the outset, would have saved him much suffering.

The central passage of the entire story recalls his first existential crisis, some ten years previously. In his experience of a type of euphoric "satori" in the National Library in Vienna when, "he was pursuing a problem of knowledge and all concepts lay loose and handy in his head" (25) and, being overcome by a "a feeling of happiness," as if he were on the verge of a breakthrough, he experienced the limit of his capacity to think and therefore, articulate his discovery: "He had exceeded his capacity for thinking" (25) and was brought down to earth like Icarus for his audacity. His knowledge that he would never again be able to "touch the logic upon which the world is suspended" (26) nevertheless leaves him longing for the utopian:

> He would like to have set himself up outside, to have looked over the frontier and from over there back upon himself and the world and language and every proviso. He would like to have come back with another language that would have been capable of expressing the secret the had discovered.(26)

This desire for a new language, Bachmann's stock-in-trade, as the only means of renewing the world, is echoed increasingly as the story progresses. Generating resistance to the status quo is Moll's language, the "thieves' cant"[12] of common currency, a constant reminder of man's separation from the Divine.

Recollection of the past also activates the protagonist's memory of past guilt seen in the image of his exploitation of a girl, at Moll's instigation. Knowledge of Man's separation from the Divine, therefore, does not mean the abandoning of all ethical considerations. Indeed, both this and the following brief movements or adagios are devoted to the question of how to live with the knowledge of having been "thrown" into the world" (Heidegger). The Faustian "Walpurgisnacht" just mentioned, the memory of the "giggling of witches" (29), provided no relief, and the second of these two adagios concerns itself with the problem of how to live in the present, "when religion has been hung up with one's Sunday suit, when a man has fallen into the pit he dug for another, when the proverbial has been fulfilled" (29). In the knowledge of his own ignorance, the protagonist confronts himself with a "stubborn, sticky mush of old questions" (30) of moral responsibility and, in a lengthy series of elliptical sentences, ponders his concerns regarding a new order, a utopian future for society. These thoughts gather momentum through their cumulative effect and the searching tone gives way to a desire for action in the transformation of himself as the only means of changing the world: "Then be different, so that the world shall change, so that it shall change direction, at last!" (32).

This burst of enthusiastic energy again subsides into inactivity,

> winter comes, when a peg of ice holds November
> and December together and his heart freezes, he
> falls asleep over his agonies. . . . To hibernate
> with his thoughts and feelings. To remain silent
> with a shriveling mouth. (32)

In entering the cycle of nature with images of roots buried in the frozen earth, the protagonist is subsequently projected into spring and new growth: "And suddenly he is holding in his hands the snowdrops that he didn't want to buy" (33). His awakening is a precipitation into "the unbelievable love" (33) which is, paradoxically, inimical to life, as was previously portrayed in Bachmann's radio play *Der gute Gott von Manhattan*.[13] This love, with "the rites of death and the ritual pains," is almost abstract, "he couldn't speak her name because she had none," in short:

> Love was unbearable. It expected nothing, demanded nothing and gave nothing. It did not allow itself to be fenced in, cultivated, and planted with feelings, but stepped over all boundaries and smashed down all feelings. (33)

In its all-consuming nature this searing love motivates him to flee: "He packed his bags, because he realized instinctively that even the first hour of love had already been too much" (34). In this flight from absolute love, the protagonist enters into the final stages of his purgatory: "Before the summer! Then he would have atoned for this year, and everything which he was later able to prepare from the material of thirty years promised to become ordinary" (35).

The final stretch of the protagonist's journey of self-discovery is marked by a type of regression in his acknowledgment of family ties and dependence on others. Travel now assumes a slower, almost drifting pace, and he enters a realm of light in Venice: "Light, bright luminosity, far from the rabble. He drifted through like a phantom" (35). His view of paradise now resides in the beautiful, which is simultaneously acknowledged as being only a temporary refuge: "I promise not to waste time over it, for beauty is disreputable, no protection any more, and the pains are already taking a different course" (36).

As he nears the end of this year of expiation he wishes to return to his starting point, Vienna. However, this first attempt at a return is marred by incertitudes. As a tourist in his own city he is again assailed by Moll, his "system" and the "thieves' cant," (39) showing off "with a thousand peacock's feathers from other languages" (40) and who, with his "*Allora, dasvedanya*" (39) and handshake, finally has to be acknowledged as a fact of life, but from which the protagonist will try to distance himself. Nonetheless, by being part of the everyday world, he lapses into the very use of language he despises in Moll.

On his subsequent journey away from Vienna, an entire section is devoted to a gathering up of the protagonist's memories of the city. Staccato-like exclamations alternate with lengthier recollections of Vienna, its history and atmosphere. Ambivalence marks his attitude. In conjuring up the spirit of the city: "Let me sweep out something of your good spirit from the dust and surrender your evil spirit to the dusty! Then may the wind come and sweep away a heart that was proud and offended here!" (45), he finds the city both cruel and beautiful. Vienna is not only the "City of the Turkish moon! City of the barricades! ... terminal city!" (45) and "City of silence! ... Plague city with the smell of death!" (46), but also the city of resurrection and beauty: "Let me think of the radiance of a day that I have also seen, green and white and sober" (46). The structure of this section prefigures that of *Undine Goes* in its diatribe-like stance, softening at the conclusion. The journey ends provisionally in Rome. Love and sensuality remain for him an essentially life-threatening experience. Nevertheless, he is drawn to it by the spirit of adventure, repeating his experiences: "He had always loved the absolute and setting off towards it..., when it was near enough to touch, he became prey to a fever, lost his speech, was consumed with the desire to find the language for it" (47-48), but now he is constantly called back to life by the demands of the everyday and again, agitatedly and impatiently longing for peace and quiet in which to contemplate. Inserted as an intermezzo is a brief credo, presented as extracts from the protagonist's diary. He has no answer as to precisely why he wishes to show himself and partake in the life of society, beyond the fact that he is alive. His concern with ethics, freedom and prejudice again finds expression in his desire for a moral world order. However, the utopian aspects of such desiderata as the freedom from injustice and oppression, are demonstrated in his insight that the "disgraces" are inherent in the "continued existence of the words (50). Therefore, he draws the conclusion: "No new world without a new language" (50).

The final movement of the story commences in spring, but on a subdued note of submission and resignation. In entering into a contract of employment, a contract with the wider world is indicated, but it is one concluded without joy or urgency. Continuing with the topos of the journey, the protagonist's re-entry into the social order is brought to an abrupt halt by a motorcar accident – he is hurled against a wall. The image of the wall is analogous to the sensation experienced in the protagonist's quasi "illumination" in the library. His subsequent recuperation provides him with a breathing space in which to recover: "This year had broken his bones" (53).

In May, at the height of spring, he finally regains his life and is ready to live in a spirit of self-confidence. His new-found equanimity restores his faith in language in the face of a reality that obscured much for him. He accepts his first white hair as the badge of a hard-won maturity that has removed his fear of the existential "process that is being made physically visible" (55) to him. *The Thirtieth Year*, in its concluding affirmation of life, trumpets out a command against disability and hopelessness: "I say unto thee: Rise up and walk! None of your bones is broken" (55). However, in echoing Christ's words, not only is a utopian vision affirmed, thus denying the ultimate triumph of the world, but the price to be paid for such a vision is contained in it, too, as Peter Mayer comments: "As if a Redeemer had spoken these words from the Bible. He who once spoke thus – as a Redeemer – sacrificed himself. A new Kingdom was founded on him."[14]

Bachmann's intense title story provides the themes for the remaining five shorter prose pieces, such as the utopian new language, relationships between men and women, individual and social ethics and responsibility, the search for the truth. The symmetrically structured story "Everything" is elegaic in tone and functions as a type of requiem for the utopian dream of a new language to change the world. The death of a child on which utopian dreams had been fixed by the narrator/father commences with an image of all-encompassing pain and existential loneliness: "I feel our mourning like a bow stretching from one end of the world to the other – that is to say, from Hanna to me – and to the bent bow is fitted an arrow that must strike the impassive sky in the heart" (56). This state of affairs is the end result of a failed attempt at reaching beyond the limits of human language, attaching messianic hopes that he could preserve his son "from our language until he had established a new one and could introduce a new era." (62). His attempt at teaching his son the "language of shadows" (63), a language which is not human, is doomed to failure on account of the narrator's own human limitations: "But since I knew and found no word of such languages, had only my own language and could not pass beyond its frontiers, I carried him up and down the paths in silence, and back home, where he learned to form sentences and walked into the trap" (63). Whereas the child's mother, Hanna, attempts the possible in her social education of her child to the extent of initiating him into religion, the narrator sees her efforts as a similar betrayal to his own retreat into silence: "We were both delivering him up, each in his own way" (66): Having attracted guilt by his attitude to his son, "I couldn't be friendly to him because I went too far with him" (76), the narrator essentially acknowledges that his wife did all she could and that is perhaps the most viable attitude of living in the world. In admitting that there is much that his wife could teach him, he simultaneously acknowledges the perhaps unbridgeable divide between male and female attitudes to life: "For time without end, where for me there is a minefield, there will be a garden for Hanna" (76), once again returning to the starting point of the story: "Don't go too far. First learn to walk forward. Learn it yourself. But first one has to be able to tear to pieces the bow of sorrow that leads from a man to a woman" (76).

Among Murderers and Madmen is perhaps the least musically constructed of the seven texts of the collection, but it is nevertheless significant for its treatment of the individual in society and the humanizing aspect of individual responsibility. The story, based on character portraits, commences on a relaxed note, evoking a certain coziness: "Men are on the way to themselves when they get together in the evening, drink and talk and express opinions" (77). The historical relevance of this story, indeed its contribution to *Overcoming the Past* is made clear in the specificity of time and place: "We are in Vienna, more than ten years after the war" (77), and the aura of the evasion of intimacy between the sexes is portrayed in the description of the men's ritual participation in the traditional "men's circle" (78), while their neglected wives, also described as victims of the order of society that condemns women to waiting while the men go to war, lie alone in bed where they imagine revenge and weep bitter tears "over their husbands who had gone out, ridden out, never come home and finally they wept over themselves. They had come to their truest tears (78-79.) In this third paragraph of the story, the main themes have been introduced: the divide between men and women, personal responsibility, the feelings of victims and the stifled ones of the perpetrators and lack of sincerity, or rather, unwillingness to squarely face the past, in postwar Austria.

The result of all this is a life suspended in a kind of schizophrenic existence, operating "in two worlds and were different in the two worlds, divided and never united egos which were never allowed to meet" (89). The men of the story are, therefore, fragmented identities with the existential identity crying out for release. The pain can be only temporarily assuaged by the "civilian egos, the loving social egos that had wives and jobs, rivalries and needs of all kinds" (90). This "civilian I" is, there-fore, seen as a soothing mask, hiding the loss of an elusive spirit or dream, without whose unifying force the characters of Bachmann's story are condemned to a life in fragmentation and a distorted perception of reality: "And they hunted the blue deer which early on had emerged from their one ego and never come back, and so long as it did not come back the world remained a madness" (90).

The only way out of this dilemma of living with a split identity is seen in a type of communal healing: "But we all need one another, if anything is ever to become good and whole" (92). Exacerbating the situation are the avoidance tactics adopted in relation to the Nazi past; while some "felt embarrassed ... most of them denied and covered up" and others merely distance themselves physically: "I shall never set foot in that country again. I shall never walk among murderers" (94). The matter is problematized by Bachmann in a discussion concerning the victims. To dwell on the victims alone seems a fruitless exercise without taking the perpetrators of violence into consideration: "The victims, ... don't show us any way at all. And for the murderers times change. The victims are the victims" (95).

In the shape of a "stranger" who joins the group, the matter of personal responsibility for one's actions is introduced. The would-be-murderer highlights the problem of the anonymity of the mass murder of the Jews and other persecuted groups during the Nazi era and, in a bizarre inversion, i.e., his desire to be personally responsible for murdering an individual, simultaneously attacks the inhuman language practice of mass killing. He could not hide behind the "slang talk" (101), a synonym for the "thieves' cant" in this context, in its denigration and dehumanization of people: "the names the others gave people in their slang talk – Polacks, Yanks, Niggers" (101) and shoot them. He did not wish to be a player on a "murder-field," as he explains: " 'I was just a simple murderer, I had no excuse, and my language was clear, not flowery like the others. 'Wipe out' 'rub out' 'smoke out' such expressions were unthinkable to me, they revolted me" (101). He wants personally to murder another human being. He is murdered in turn, and his blood brings the narrator to his senses in the face of an individual death: "It was as if through the blood I had received protection, not to become invulnerable, but so that the effluvium of my despair, my desire for vengeance, my rage could not force its way out of me" (104). The conclusion, however, remains essentially open-ended.

A Step Towards Gomorrah shifts again to the problem of dominance in interpersonal relationships. Not only is this problem approached from the point of view of heterosexual relationships, but it is also further problematized by the exploration of the controversial issue of a lesbian relationship. The lesbian relationship is ultimately rejected or rather passed up with regret as a utopian moment for gaining different knowledge. The deciding factor, however, in rejecting a lesbian relationship between the pianist Charlotte and Mara is Charlotte's realization that, despite the shortcomings in her relationship with her husband Franz, she is able to find a viable mode of existence within the institution of marriage. Through her experience with Milan, she had tasted "ecstasy, intoxication, depth, surrender, delight," but in order to live in the world she had settled for the socially sanctioned struc- ture of marriage with Franz "on the basis of kindness, being in love, benevolence, care, dependence, security, protection, of all sorts of admirable things which did not remain mere projects but could actually be lived" (125).

The commencement of the story is vivid and dramatic: "The last guests had left. Only the girl in the black sweater and red skirt was still sitting there" (105), thus reviving the idea of the torch flame in *Youth in an Austrian Town*. Indeed, the color red with its connotations of passion and danger, is clearly intended to dominate in the reader's imagination; the girl's hair shines with a reddish glint, her skirt is red, the lampshade is red, the backs of books in the room are red, in fact, "just for once the world was in red" (106). The girl Mara represents a dividing line between the familiar and the foreign – she is "from the border" (106) and the transgression of borders is the main issue in this story, beckoning Charlotte into "a great temptation" (123). However, although Charlotte is attracted by the idea of a risky adventure, she withdraws from it in the realization that the promise of a new beginning with Mara would catapult her out of the "lucid order that belonged to Franz" (119) and into a confrontation with her own femininity, molded by the subordination imposed by a patriarchal society: "So that was what her own lips were like, this was how they met as man, thin almost unresisting, almost without muscles – a little muzzle, not to be taken seriously" (114).

Charlotte recognizes a repetition of her own language usage in her relationship with men as well. In Mara she hears the "intona- tion," the "sing-song full of ignorance," indeed, "She had acted out the same weakness that Mara was acting out to her ... blackmailed tenderness" (117). Charlotte also recognizes that a relationship with Mara would merely duplicate the structure of domination and subordination of patriarchal hegemony, as Mara's weakness "demands this role from her" (123). With Mara as her "creature" (123), she would dominate language: "Then she would have to make the choice regarding the home, regarding the ebb and flow, the language" (124). She does not wish to make the language of women the norm. This she finds to be worse, "undignified" (127) even, than that of men. Charlotte hopes for a new realm of language. This realm, however, in its messianic promise is, of course, utopian in dimension: "Her kingdom would come and when it came she would no longer be measurable, no longer estimable by an alien measure" (126). In recognition of her desire to transcend established borders into this new kingdom – "Not the kingdom of men and not that of women" (130) – symbolized by Mara's skirt, "the red cloth," dragging on the floor, an inversion of the myth of Bluebeard enters her mind: Mara would merely be subjected to the fate of the "husbands" of Charlotte/Bluebeard, as she alone would hold the key. In Mara's expression of fatigue, "I'm dead" (131), Charlotte recognizes that the moment for the great "change of shift" (130) had passed and the discarded red skirt lies like an extinguished torch.

The rhythmic language of *A Step Towards Gomorrah* with its pauses and ellipses gives way to a more insistently searching tone in *A Wildermuth*. The first sentence, "A Wildermuth always chooses the truth" (133), provides the opening phrase for the story, in which the judge Anton Wildermuth, whose task it is to establish the truth, but who, within the parameters of Bachmann's works, will ultimately fail. As in *The Thirtieth Year*, for instance, Wildermuth's wife speaks the language of social convention, "at the expense of the truth" (133). He, however, had made the early discovery that the articulation and narration of events merely removes the speaker further from the truth. Wildermuth's aim, to establish truth and bring it into harmony with his physical existence is, of course, doomed to failure: "I should like to bring my spirit and my flesh into harmony, and because I cannot force this harmony, cannot achieve it, I shall cry out" (156). His wife Gerda, with her "flowery language" (163), has established a form of communication, but this, in Wildermuth's eyes, is merely an "emergency bridge" (164) enabling them to live together. This story once again demonstrates Bachmann's concern with the unattainable utopia of the identity of language with the Absolute.

Concluding the collection, the well-known diatribe *Undine Goes* gives voice to the eternal search for the truth in language, which would bridge the divide between men and women in their perception of reality. From the outset Undine's recollections[15] with their structuring review of her life with "Hans" project her desires into the realm of the utopian. As the elemental water nymph of myth, Undine, in her diatribe against "Hans," the generic term for men, searches for a place where it would be possible to meet him and speak the language of love, devoid of domination, where, as Manfred Jurgensen puts it, "a powerful knowledge ... would be exchanged between the sexes."[16] The ambivalence of Undine's stance, alternately longing and loathing, determines the rhythm of this text, which fades out in the yearning tones of Undine being yet again called from the water in answer to the unfulfilled desires of men.

In constantly exploring, searching, failing and beginning again, Ingeborg Bachmann's refusal to resign keeps alive the productive elements of utopian thinking. As such, the collection *The Thirtieth Year* stands as the product of a reflective process, a thought-provoking monument to the productivity of memory and utopian thinking, perhaps most succinctly encapsulated in her posthumously published poem

> *Bohemia is at the Sea*
> And if you should err a hundred times,
> as I erred and did not pass the tests,
> yet I passed them time and time again.
> Like Bohemia passed them and one fine day
> was granted as a favor to the sea and is
> now situated at the water.[17]

Notes

1. Ingeborg Bachmann, *The Thirtieth Year*, Stories by Ingeborg Bachmann. Transl. Michael Bullock. (New York: Holmes and Meier, 1987) (Original German: *Das dreißigste Jahr*. Erzählungen. 1961). All quotations from this collection will be acknowledged by the page number in brackets.

2. Ludwig Wittgenstein, *Tractatus logico-philosophicus,* The German text of Ludwig Wittgenstein's *Logisch Philosophische Abhandlung* with a new transl. by D.F. Pears and P.F. McGuinness (London: Routledge and Kegan Paul, New York: The Humanities Press, 1961) 6.522. 151.

3. An example of this is the Introduction to the translation of *Das dreißigste Jahr* into English, where Karen Achberger seems to have lost sight of the problematic reception of Bachmann's prose stories, remarking, for example: "*The Thirtieth Year* was widely reviewed and acclaimed ... Beyond the positive critical reception of her works, Bachmann's life is and was a legend ... the talented, intelligent woman in largely male circles." *The Thirtieth Year.* Stories by Ingeborg Bachmann. Transl. Michael Bullock. viii and ix respectively. See note 1.

4. Cf. Andrea Stoll's observations: "Kritik und Leser verzeihen Ingeborg Bachmann ihre Abkehr vom lyrischen Schaffen über viele Jahre nicht. Die mutwillige Zerstörung des schönen Bildes von der jungen Lyrikerin, die sich bruchlos in die Tradition der literarischen Moderne einfügte, nahm die (vorwiegend männliche) Kritik, wie viele Rezensionen belegen, äußerst übel." Andrea Stoll: "Grenzerfahrungen der poetischen Existenz. Ingeborg Bachmann 1926-1973. Ein Porträt," Gisela Brinker-Gabler, *Deutsche Literatur von Frauen.* 2 vols. *19. und 20.* Jahrhundert (München: C.H. Beck, 1988) 440-441.

5. Ingeborg Bachmann quoted by Brinker-Gabler 440. Translation K. T.

6. Thomas Bernhard, "Drei Tage," *Der Italiener* (München: DTV. sr. 122, 1973) 85-86. Translation K. T.

7. Ibid., 440. Translation K. T.

8. G. He, "Das dreißigste Jahr" *Kindlers Literaturlexikon* vol. *7* (München: DTV, 1974) 2869. Translation K. T.

9. Cf. Andrea Stoll, "Die stakkatohaften Rhythmen kurzer Aussagesätze unterbrechen abrupt den steigernden Erzählfluß langer Satzreihen. Mit dem Erzählprinzip der Motivwiederholung und Variation transportiert Bachmann musikalische Strukturelemente in ihre Prosa." ibid. 442.

10. G. He, ibid., 2868.

11. Ingeborg Bachmann herself mentions these exact words, i.e., "Schweigen als Protest" at the "Ignoranz gegenüber der ganzen Wirklichkeit" in her essay: "Sagbares und Unsagbares – Die Philosophie Ludwig Wittgensteins," *Ingeborg Bachmann. Werke. Essays, Reden, vermischte Schriften, Anhang*, eds. Christine Koschel, Inge Weidenbaum, Clemens Münster (München/Zürich: Piper, 1978) 126.

12. See Hans Bender, "Ingeborg Bachmann hat den Begriff der 'Gaunersprache' geprägt. Eine Sprache is damit gemeint, die ungeprüft und gedankenlos übernommen wird. Sprache wie Mobiliar, Sprache der Meinungslosigkeit und Lüge." "Über Ingeborg Bachmann. Versuch eines Porträts." *Ingeborg Bachmann. Text + Kritik*, vol. 6, ed. Heinz Ludwig Arnold (München: 1976).

13. Ingeborg Bachmann, *Der gute Gott von Manhattan*, radio play (1958) (Stuttgart: Reclam, 1981). See, for example, Jennifer's statement: "Ich liebe. Und ich bin außer mir." ("I love. And I am beside myself") 69.

14. Peter Mayer, "Zeit zum Schweigen?" *Ingeborg Bachmann. Text+Kritik, vol. 6*, 13. Translation K. T.

15. Cf. Andrea Stoll: "Erinnerung ist als poetische Kraft im Bachmannschen Sinne niemals auf plumpe Weise autobiographisch zu verstehen. Erinnerung liefert das poetische Strukturmodell für ein geistiges Prinzip. Die Vorstellung von Autobiographie ist – wenn überhaupt – nur in dieser Weise anzuwenden. Erinnerung erweist sich als die eigentliche subversive Macht der Bachmannschen Prosa." Ibid., 442.

16. Manfred Jurgensen, *Ingeborg Bachmann. Die neue Sprache* (Bern/Frankfurt am Main/Las Vegas: Lang, 1981) 35. Translation K. T.

17. In: *Ingeborg Bachmann. Werke I. Gedichte Hörspiele Libretti Übersetzungen* 167-168. Translation K. T.

Bibliography of Cited Works

Works by Ingeborg Bachmann

Der gute Gott von Manhattan. Hörspiel. Stuttgart: Reclam, 1981.

Die Wahrheit ist dem Menschen zumutbar: Essays, Reden, Kleinere Schriften. München, Zürich: Piper, 1981.

"Die Zikaden." *Werke.* Ed. Christine Koschel et al. vol. 1. Zürich: Piper, 1978.

Eyes to Wonder, Three Paths to the Lake: Stories by Ingeborg Bachmann. Transl. Mary Fran Gilbert. New York: Holmes & Meier, 1989.

Frankfurter Vorlesungen. München, Zürich: Piper, 1989.

Malina. München: Kuchenreuther Filmproduktion GmbH; Wien: Neue Studio Film GmbH, 1990.

Malina. Transl. Philip Boehm. New York, London: Holmes & Meier 1990.

"Musik und Dichtung. "*Werke.* Ed. Christine Koschel et al. vol. 4 München: Piper, 1978.

No Delicacies. The Storm of Roses: Selected Poems by Ingeborg Bachmann. Ed., Transl., and Intro. Mark Anderson. Princeton, NJ: Princeton University Press, 1986.

Requiem für Fanny Goldmann. Frankfurt am Main: Suhrkamp, 1979.

Songs of Flight: The Collected Poems of Ingeborg Bachmann. Transl. Peter Filkins. New York: Marsilio, 1994.

The Thirtieth Year. Transl. Michael Bullock. New York: Holmes & Meier, 1987.

Three Paths to the Lake. Stories. Transl. Mary Fran Gilbert, Intro. Mark Anderson. New York, London: Holmes & Meier, 1989.

Was wahr ist. Sämtliche Gedichte München: Piper, 1983.

Wir müssen wahre Sätze finden: Gespräche und Interviews. Eds. Christine Koschel und Inge von Weidenbaum. München, Zürich: Piper, 1983-1991.

Secondary Literature Quoted in this Volume

Achberger, Karen. "Beyond Patriarchy: Ingeborg Bachmann and Fairy Tales." *Modern Austrian Literature, 18, Nos. 3/4,* 1985.

——. "Bachmann und die Bibel." *Der dunkle Schatten dem ich schon seit Anfang folge.* Ed. Hans Höller. Wien, München, Kleinenzersdorf: Löcker, 1982.

——. *Understanding Ingeborg Bachmann.* Columbia: University of South Carolina Press, 1995.

Arendt, Hannah. "What is Freedom?" *Between Past and Future. Eight Exercises in Political Thought.* New York: Penguin, 1993.

Bachmann, Claus-Henning. "Warnender Gesang," *Frankfurter Hefte,* vol. 10, 1955.

Bail, Gabriele. *Weibliche Identität: Ingeborg Bachmanns Malina.* Göttingen: Edition Herodot, 1984.

Bareiss, Otto. "Vita Ingeborg Bachmann." *Text+Kritik,* 1984.

Bärnthaler, Irmgard. *Die Vaterländische Front: Geschichte und Organisation.* Wien: Europa Verlag, 1971.

Bartsch, Kurt. "Es war Mord": Anmerkungen zur Mann-Frau-Beziehung in Bachmanns Roman *Malina.*" *Acta Neophilologica,* 17, 1984.

——. "'Mord' oder Selbstvernichtung? Zu Werner Schroeters filmischer *Malina-Interpretation,*" John Patillo-Hess & Wilhelm Petrasch, *Ingeborg Bachmann: Die Schwarzkunst der Worte.* Wien: Verein Volksbildungshaus Wiener Urania, 1993.

Ingeborg Bachmann, Sammlung Metzler, vol. 242. Stuttgart: J. B. Metzlersche Verlagsbuchhandlung, 1988.

Beicken, Peter. *Ingeborg Bachmann*. München: Verlag C. H. Beck, 1988.

Bender, Hans. *Ingeborg Bachmann*. *Text + Kritik*. vol. 6. München: Heinz Ludwig Arnold, 1976.

Bernhard, Thomas. *Heldenplatz*. Frankfurt am Main: Suhrkamp, 1992.

——. "Drei Tage," *Der Italiener*. München: 1971.

Bienek, Horst. "Immer geht es um: Alles," *Kein objektives Urteil – nur ein lebendiges*. Eds. Koschel, Weidenbaum. München: Piper, 1989.

Boa, Elizabeth. "Schwierigkeiten mit der ersten Person: Ingeborg Bachmanns *Malina* und Monika Marons *Flugschale*. Die Überläuferin und stille Zeile sechs." *Kritische Wege der Landnahme*. Eds. Robert Pichl and Alexander Stillmark. Wien: Hora-Verlag, 1994.

Bothner, Susanne. *Ingeborg Bachmann: Der janusköpfige Tod. Versuch der literaturpsychologischen Deutung eines Grenzgebiets der Lyrik unter Einbeziehung des Nachlasses*. Bern, Frankfurt am Main, New York: Peter Lang, 1986.

Botz, Gerhard. "Historische Brüche und Kontinuitäten als Herausforderungen. Ingeborg Bachmann und postkatastrophische Geschichtsmentalitäten in Österreich." *Ingeborg Bachmann – Neue Beiträge zu ihrem Werk. Internationales Symposium Münster, 1991*. Eds. Dirk Göttsche and Hubert Ohl. Würzburg: Königshausen & Neumann, 1993.

Brinker-Gabler, Gisela. *Deutsche Literatur von Frauen. vol. 2, 19. und 20. Jahrhundert*. München: Verlag C. H. Beck, 1988.

Broda, Martine. *Dans la main de personne. Essai sur Paul Celan*. Paris: Editions du Cerf, 1986.

Bürger, Christa. "Ich und wir. Ingeborg Bachmanns Austritt aus der ästhetischen Moderne." *Text+Kritik*, 1984.

Cixous, Hélène. "The Laugh of the Medusa." Transl. Keith Cohen and Paula Cohen. *The Signs Reader: Women, Gender & Scholarship*. Eds. Elizabeth Abel and Emily K. Abel. Chicago: University of Chicago Press, 1983.

Conradi, Peter. "Fragwürdige Lobrednerei." A survey of the Bachmann-criticism of the fifties in the earlier *Text+Kritik*, vol. 6, 1971.

Culture, Science and Education: Austria's Cooperation with the United States. *Österreichischer Akademischer Aus tausch-dienst Kooperationen*. Ed. Wien: ÖAA, 1994.

Dassanowsky, Robert von. "A Destiny of Guilt: The Crisis of Post-imperial Austrian Identity and the Anschluss in Alexander Lernet-Holenia's *Der Graf von Saint-Germain*." *Germanic Review*, 69 (1994) 154-166.

Derrida, Jacques. "Heidegger's Ear. Philopolemology." John S allis, ed. *Reading Heidegger, Commemorations*. Blooming-ton: Indiana University Press, 1993.

Dollfuß, Eva. *Mein Vater: Hitlers erstes Opfer*. Wien: Amalthea, 1994.

Gölz, Sabine I. "One Must Go Quickly from One Light into Another: Between Ingeborg Bachmann and Jacques Der-rida. Ed." Margaret R. Higonnet. *Borderwork: Feminist Engagements with Comparative Literature*. Ithaca: Cornell University Press, 1994.

———. Legenda Feminia. Ingeborg Bachmanns verschwindende Poetik. Diss. Ithaca: Cornell University Press, 1987.

Griesser, Hermann A. *Konfisziert: Österreichs Unrecht am Hause Habsburg*. Wien: Amalthea, 1986.

Groddeck, Georg. *Vom Sehen, von der Welt des Auges und vom Sehen ohne Augen, Psychoanalytische Schriften zur Psycho-somatik*. Ed. Günther Clauser. Wiesbaden: Limes Verlag, 1966.

———. Das Es und die Psychoanalyse, *Verdrängen und Heilen: Aufsätze zur Psychoanalyse und zur psychosomatischen Medizin*. Frankfurt am Main: Fischer Taschenbuch Verlag, 1988.

Groddeck, Georg and Sigmund Freud, *Briefwechsel*. Wiesbaden: Limes Verlag, 1970.

Grossman, Carl M. and Sylvia Grossman. *The Wild Analyst: The Life and Work of Georg Groddeck*. New York: George Braziller, Inc., 1965.

Gürtler, Christa. *Schreiben Frauen anders? Untersuchungen zu Ingeborg Bachmann und Barbara Frischmuth*. Eds. U. Müller, F. Hundsnurscher and C. Sommer. Stuttgart: Hans-Dieter Heinz: Akademischer Verlag, 1985.

Halverson, Brigitte. "The Importance of Horatio," *Hamlet Studies*, vol. 16, 1 and 2, 1994.

Handbuch des österreichischen Rechtsextremismus, Dokumentationsarchiv des österreichischen Widerstands, 2 ed. Wien: Deuticke, 1993.

Hapkemeyer, Andreas. "Ingeborg Bachmann: Entwicklungslinien im Werk und Leben." *Österreichische Akademie der Wissenschaften Philosophisch-Historische Klasse Sitzungsberichte, vol. 560.* Wien: Verlag der Österreichischen Akademie der Wissenschaften, 1990.

———. Ingeborg Bachmann, *Bilder aus ihrem Leben*. München, Zürich: Piper, 1983.

Härtling, Peter. *Du bist Orplid, mein Land. Texte von Eduard Mörike und Ludwig Bauer.* Darmstadt: Luchterhand, 1982.

Hartung, Rudolf. "Vom Vers zur Prosa, zu Ingeborg Bachmanns *Das dreißigste Jahr.*" *...Kein objektives Urteil– nur ein lebendiges. Texte zum Werk von Ingeborg Bachmann.* Ed. Koschel, Weidenbaum. München: Piper, 1989.

Henze, Hans Werner. *Musik und Politik. Schriften und Gespräche 1955-1984.* München: DTV, 1984.

Hofmannsthal, Hugo von. *Andreas oder die Vereinigten.* Frankfurt am Main: Fischer, 1961.

———. "Die österreichische Idee." *Gesammelte Werke in Einzelausgaben.* Prosa III. Frankfurt am Main: Fischer, 1952.

Holeschofsky, Irene. "Bewußtseinsdarstellung und Ironie in Ingeborg Bachmanns Erzählung *Simultan.*" *Sprachkunst: Beiträge zur Literaturwissenschaft,* 11,1, 1980.

Jameson, Frederic. "Imaginary and Symbolic in Lacan: Marxism, Psychoanalytic Criticism, and the Problem of the Subject." *Literature and Psychoanalysis.* Baltimore, London: Johns

Hopkins UP, 1982.

Jens, Walter. "Laudito auf Nelly Sachs." *Das Buch der Nelly Sachs*. Ed. Bengt Holmqvist. Frankfurt am Main: Suhrkamp, 1968.

Jurgensen, Manfred. *Ingeborg Bachmann. Die neue Sprache.* Bern: Peter Lang, 1981.

Kaiser, Joachim. *Ingeborg Bachmann. Eine Einfhhrung.* 2. erw. Aufl. 1968, cited in *Der Georg Büchner Preis 1951-1978. Eine Ausstellung des Deutschen Literaturarchivs Marbach und der deutschen Akademie für Sprache und Dichtung.* Darmstadt, Marbach am Neckar: 1978.

Kindlers Neues Literaturlexikon, 1992.

Kleist, Heinrich von. *Briefe 1805-1811, Lebenstafel, Personenregister*. München: DTV, 1964.

Klüger, Ruth. *Weiterleben: Eine Jugend.* Göttingen: Wallstein, 1992.

———. *Katastrophen: Über deutsche Literatur.* Göttingen: Wallstein, 1994.

Komar, Kathleen. "The Murder of Ingeborg Bachmann," *Modern Austrian Literature,* 27, 2, 1994.

Krusche, Dieter. *Reclams Filmführer.* Stuttgart: Philipp Reclam jun., 1993.

Lamping, Dieter. *Das lyrische Gedicht.* Göttingen: Vandenhoeck & Ruprecht, 1989.

Lennox, Sara. "The Cemetery of the Murdered Daughters: Ingeborg Bachmann's *Malina*." *Studies in Twentieth Century Literature*, 5, 1980.

———. "The Feminist Reception of Ingeborg Bachmann." *Women in German Yearbook, 8*, 1993.

———. "Geschlecht, Rasse und Geschichte in *Der Fall Franza*." *Text + Kritik Sonderband: Ingeborg Bachmann.* Ed. Heinz Ludwig Arnold. München: Edition Text + Kritik, 1984.

Leonhard, Sigrun D.. "Doppelte Spaltung: Zur Problematik des Ich in Ingeborg Bachmanns *Malina*." Gudrun Brokoph-Mauch & Annette Daigger, eds. *Ingeborg Bachmann.*

Neue Richtungen in der Forschung? Internationales Kolloquium, Saranac Lake, 6.-9. Juni 1991. St. Ingbert: Röhrich, 1995.

Lernet-Holenia, Alexander. "Der Graf von Saint-Germain." *The Germanic Review*, Fall, 1994.

Löffler, Sigrid. "Undine kehrt zurück." *Der Spiegel,* 46, 1995.

Longerich, Peter. Ed., *Die Ermordung der europäischen Juden: Eine Umfassende Dokumentation des Holocaust 1941-1945.* München: Piper, 1989.

Luza, Radomar. *Austro-German Relations in the Anschluss Era.* Princeton: Princeton UP, 1975.

Mahlendorf, Ursula. "Confronting the Fascist Past and Coming to Terms with It." *The American Journal of Social Psychiatry,* 2, 2, 1982.

Malina: Ein Filmbuch von Elfriede Jelinek nach dem Roman von Ingeborg Bachmann. Frankfurt am Main: Suhrkamp, 1991.

Mauch, Gudrun. "Ingeborg Bachmanns Erzählband *Simultan.*" *Modern Austrian Literature,* 12, 3-4, 1979.

Mayer, Peter. "Ästhetisierung und Ästhetikkritik in der Lyrik Ingeborg Bachmanns. *Text+Kritik,* 1984.

——. "Zeit zum Schweigen?" *Ingeborg Bachmann.* Edition *Text+Kritik*, 6, 1971.

——. "Ästhetisierung und Ästhetikkritik in der Lyrik Ingeborg Bachmanns. *Text+Kritik,* 1984.

McAuley, James. "Against the Dark." *Surprises of the Sun.* Sydney, 1969.

McVeigh, Joseph. *Kontinuität und Vergangenheitsbewältigung in der österreichischen Literatur nach 1945.* Wien: Braumüller, 1988.

Meise, Helga. "Topographien: Lekthrevorschläge." *Ingeborg Bachmann.* Ed. Heinz Ludwig Arnold. München: Edition *Text + Kritik*, 1984.

Mitscherlich, A. and F. Mielke. *The Death Doctors.* Transl. James Cleugh. London: Elek Books, 1962.

Monas, Sidney. Transl. *Osip Mandelstam: Selected Essays.*

Austin: University of Texas Press, 1977.

Musil, Robert. *The Man without Qualities.* Transl. Sophie Wilkins and Burton Pike. New York: Knopf, 1995.

Oelmann, Ute Maria. Lyrisches Sprechen und narratives Sprechen im Werk der Ingeborg Bachmann." *Ingeborg Bachmann. Neue Beiträge zu ihrem Werk. Internationales Symposium Münster 1991.* Würzburg: Königshausen & Neumann, 1993.

Patillo-Hess, John & Wilhelm Petrasch. *Ingeborg Bachmann: Die Schwarzkunst der Worte.* Wien: Verein Volksbildungshaus Wiener Urania, 1993.

Pausch, Holger. "Ingeborg Bachmann." *Köpfe des XX. Jahrhunderts,* vol. 81. Berlin: Colloquium Verlag, 1975.

Pichl, Robert. "Rhetorisches bei Ingeborg Bachmann: Zu den 'redenden Namen' im *Simultan*-Zyklus." *Jahrbuch für Internationale Germanistik,* 8.2, 1980.

Rank, Otto. *Beyond Psychology.* New York: Dover Publications, 1958.

Rauch, Angelika. "Sprache, Weiblichkeit und Utopie." *Modern Austrian Literature,* 18, 1985.

Reich-Ranicki, Marcel. "Die Dichterin wechselt das Repertoire." Christine Koschel and Inge von Weidenbaum. *Kein objektives Urteil– Nur ein lebendiges: Texte zum Werk von Ingeborg Bachmann.* München: Piper, 1989.

Schacht, Lore. Ed. *Vision, the World of the Eye, and Seeing without the Eye, The Meaning of Illness: Selected Psychoanalytic Writings by Georg Groddeck.* Transl. Gertrud Mander. New York: International Universities Press, Inc., 1977.

Schmidt-Bortenschlager, Sigrid. "Frauen als Opfer-Gesellschaftliche Realität und Literarisches Modell: Zu Ingeborg Bachmanns Erzählband *Simultan*." *Der Dunkle Schatten, dem ich schon seit Anfang folge: Ingeborg Bachmann-Vorschläge zu einer neuen Lektüre des Werkes.* Ed. Hans Höller. Wien: Löcker Verlag, 1982.

Schottelius, Saskia. *Das imaginäre Ich: Subjekt und Identität in*

Ingeborg Bachmanns Roman "Malina" und Jacques Lacans Sprachtheorie. Frankfurt am Main: Peter Lang, 1990.

Seiderer, Ute. *Film als Psychogramm: Bewußtseinsräume und Vorstellungsbilder in Werner Schroeters "Malina."* München: Diskursfilm Verlag Schaudig & Ledig, 1994.

Serbine-Bahrawy, Sabrina de. *The Voice of History: An Exegesis of Selected Short Stories from Ingeborg Bachmann's "Das dreißigste Jahr" and "Simultan" from the Perspective of Austrian History.* New York, Peter Lang, 1989.

Shakespeare, William: *The Merchant of Venice.* New York: Penguin, 1965.

——. *The Tragedy of Hamlet, Prince of Denmark.* New York: Penguin, 1963.

Sheppard, Richard. Ed. *New Ways in Germanistik.* New York, Oxford, München: Berg Publ. Ltd., St. Martin's Press, 1990.

Smith, Paul. *Discerning the Subject.* Minneapolis: University of Minnesota Press, 1988.

Stoll, Andrea. "Grenzerfahrungen der poetischen Existenz. Ingeborg Bachmann 1926–1973. Ein Porträt." Gisela Brinker-Gabler, *Deutsche Literatur von Frauen.* vol. 2, 19. und 20. Jahrhundert. Mänchen: C.H. Beck, 1988.

Stourzh, Gerald. "Der Weg zum Staatsvertrag und zur immerwährenden Neutralität." *Österreich: Die Zweite Republik.* vol. 1. Eds. Erika Weinzierl and Kurt Skalnik. Graz: 1972.

——. *Vom Reich zur Republik: Studien zum Österreichbewusstsein im 20. Jahrhundert.* Wien: Edition Atelier, 1990.

Swiderska, Malgorzata. *Die Unvereinbarkeit des Unvereinbaren. Ingeborg Bachmann als Essayistin, Untersuchungen zur deutschen Literaturgeschichte, 49.* Tübingen: Niemeyer, 1989.

Thiem, Ulrich. Diss. *Die Bildsprache der Lyrik Ingeborg Bachmanns.* Köln: Philosophische Fakultät, 1972.

Thomas, Dylan. *The force that through the green fuse drives the flower, The Poems of Dylan Thomas.* Ed. Daniel Jones.

New York: New Directions, 1971.

Vanderbeke, Birgit. "Kein Recht auf Sprache." *Text und Kritik, Sonderband, Ingeborg Bachmann.* Ed. Heinz Ludwig Arnold. München: Edition Text + Kritik GmbH, 1984.

Weigel, Sigrid. "Ein Ende mit der Schrift. Ein anderer Anfang. Zur Entwicklung von Ingeborg Bachmanns Schreibweise." *Kein Objecktives Urteil– Nur ein Lebendiges.* Eds. Christine Koschel and Inge von Weidenbaum. München: Piper, 1989.

——. "Overcoming Absence: Contemporary German Women's Literature." Transl. Amy Kepple. *New German Critique,* 32, 1984.

Weininger, Otto. *Sex and Character.* London: William Heinemann, 1975.

White, Ann. *Names and Nomenclature in Goethe's "Faust."* Diss., Institute of Germanic Studies, University of London, 1980. Bithell Series of Dissertations, 3. London: 1980.

White, Hayden. *The Content of the Form: Narrative Discourse and Historical Representation.* Baltimore: Johns Hopkins UP, 1987.

Williams, Arthur. Ed. *German Literature at a Time of Change.* Bern: Peter Lang, 1989-1990.

Wittgenstein, Ludwig. *Tractatus logico-philosophicus.* The German text of Ludwig Wittgenstein's *Logisch Philosophische Abhandlung* with a new Transl by D.F. Pears and P.F. McGuinness. New York: The Humanities Press, 1961.

Wolf, Christa. *"Shall I Garnish a Metaphor with an Almond Blossom?* Büchner-Prize Acceptance Speech." Transl. Henry J. Schmidt, *New German Critique,* 23, 1981.

——. "Voraussetzungen einer Erzählung: Kassandra." *Frankfurter Poetik-Vorlesungen.* München: DTV, 1993.

Young, James. *Writing and Rewriting the Holocaust.* Bloomington: Indiana University Press, 1990.

Index

Achberger, Karen, 164
Achmatova, Anna, 110
Adenauer, Konrad, 140
Adorno, Theodor, 30
Aichinger, Ilse, 25, 28, 140
    Aufruf zum Mißtrauen, 28
Anton-Wildgans Prize, 141
Apulia, 116
Arendt, Hannah, 49
Auschwitz, 30, 110
Austria, 24-37, 106, 107, 117,
    139, 189, 190, 202

Bach, Johann Sebastian, 30
Bachmann, Ingeborg
    Advertisement, 148
    After Many Years, 147
    After This Deluge, 181
    *Among Murderers and
        Lunatics* (*Unter Mördern
        und Irren*) also trans. as
        *Among Murderers and
        Madmen,* 24, 32, 199
    At Agrigento 102
    Ausfahrt see *Journey Out*
    *Ballet Pantomime "The
        Idiot,"* 142, 148
    Behind the Wall (*Hinter
        der Wand*), 183
    Black Sun, 155
    Black Waltz, 153
    The Blue Hour (*Die Blaue
        Stunde*), 182

Bohemia Lies by the Sea, 148
Borrowed Time (*Die ge-
    stundete Zeit*), 92, 139,
    140, 145, 147
Brotherhood, 147
The Cicadas (*Die Zikaden*),
    42, 43, 54, 124-126, 134-
    137
Curriculum Vitae, 99, 150
Danke für die Rosen see
    Thank You for the Roses
Darkness in Egypt, 164
Darkness Spoken, 98, 131,
    147
Das Gedicht an den Leser
    (*The Poem for the
    Reader*), 155
Death Styles see *Ways of
    Death*
Deliver Me, My Word!, 100
Der Fall Franza see *Franza's
    Case*
Der gute Gott von Manhattan
    see *The Good God of
    Manhattan*
*Die Aufrufung des großen
    Bären* see *The Invocation
    of the Great Bear*
Die Blaue Stunde see *The
    Blue Hour*
Die Blinden Passagiere see
    The Stowaways
Die gestundete Zeit see

Borrowed Time

*Die Vereinbarkeit des Unver-
einbaren. Ingeborg Bach-
mann als Essayistin,* 60

*Die Wahrheit ist dem
Menschen zumutbar* see
*People can Face the
Truth*

Die wunderliche Musik see
Wondrous Music

Die Zikaden see *The Cicadas*

*Dir entfällt das Wort (The
Word Escapes You)*

Drei Wege zum See, see
Three Paths to the Lake

Early Noon, 100, 141

Ein Geschäft mit Träumen,
139

*Ein Ende mit der Schrift, ein
anderer Anfang: Zur
Entwicklung zu Ingeborg
Bachmanns Schreib-
weise,* 162

Ein Ort für Zufälle, 151

Enigma, 142

Everything, 162, 163, 176,
198

Exile, 132, 181

*Eyes to Wonder (Ihr glück-
lichen Augen),* 11

Fall Down Heart, 146

Flying Blind see *The Stowaways*

Fog Land (Nebelland) also
trans. as *Land of Fog,* 94,
101, 182

*The force that through the
green fuse drives the
flower,* 184

Frankfurter Vorlesungen,
164, 166

*Franza's Case (Der Fall
Franza)* also trans. as *The
Franza Case,* 24, 26, 106,
107, 111, 112, 115, 117,
164, 186

Gomorrah, 124

*The Good God of Manhattan
(Der gute Gott von
Manhattan),* 71, 125,
136, 196

The Great Freight also trans.
as *The Heavy Cargo,*
128, 140

*Great Landscape near
Vienna,* 141, 145, 146

The Heavy Cargo see *The
Great Freight*

*Hill of Shards
(Scherbenhügel),* 181

Hinter der Wand see *Behind
the Wall* 183

Hoofbeat of Night, 147

Hotel de la Paix, 153

How Shall I Name Myself?,
97

*Humanity Can Be Expected
to Bear the Truth* see
*People Can Face the
Truth*

Ihr glücklichen Augen see
Eyes to Wonder

In Apulia, 102

In the Storm of the Roses, 181

Invocation of the Great Bear (*Die Aufrufung des großen Bären*), 91, 139, 146, 148

Journey Out (*Ausfahrt*), 92, 93, 143-148, 152

Jugend in einer österreichischen Stadt, see *Youth in an Austrian Town*

Land of Fog see *Fog Land*

Leave, Thought, 140

Letter in Two Drafts, 101

Literatur als Utopie see *Literature as Utopia*

Literature as Utopia (*Literatur als Utopie*), 25, 148, 149

Love: The Dark Continent, 94, 95, 151, 153, 154

Malina, 2, 4, 5, 6, 7, 8, 9, 11, 14, 16, 17, 18, 26, 35, 106, 107, 110-112, 115, 117, 136, 142, 150, 155, 163, 164-168, 171, 173, 175

March Stars, 98

Message, 146, 184, 185

A Monologue of Prince Myshkin to the Ballet Pantomime The Idiot, 99

Music and Poetry (*Musik und Dichtung*), 186

Musik und Dichtung see *Music and Poetry*

Must One Think?, 94

My Bird, 18, 141

The Native Land, 95, 102, 152

Nebelland see *Fog Land*

Night Flight, 140, 141, 143

No Delicacies, 132, 142, 179, 180, 181

North and South, 101

Of a Land, River and Lakes, 141

Oh Happy Eyes, 76-80, 84, 86

Paris, 98

People Can Face the Truth (*Die Wahrheit ist dem Menschen zumutbar*) also trans. as *Humanity Can Be Expected to Bear the Truth*, 70, 85, 127, 163

Place of Death see *Todesort*

The Princess of Karan, 112

Psalm, 147

Requiem for Fanny Goldmann, 26, 36, 111

Rome at Night, 154

Scherbenhügel see *Hill of Shards*

Das Schreibende Ich see *The Writing Self*

Schlagen, 147

Scream, 146

Settlement, 154

Simultan, 32, 136

Songs from an Island, 100

Songs in Flight, 103, 126-

128, 131-133, 146, 147, 152-155

Songs of Innocence and Experience, 95

Songs on an Island, 131

Spoken and Rumored, 99, 142

A Step towards Gomorrah, 201, 203

The Stowaways (Die blinden Passagiere), 61-67, 72, 73, 74

Stream, 181

Tell Me, Love, 91, 93, 94, 98, 100, 148, 153, 154

Thank You for the Roses (Danke für die Rosen), 27

That Which Is True (Was wahr ist), 181

Theme and Variation, 99

The Thirtieth Year, 123, 132, 135, 162, 168, 188-191, 198, 204

Three Murderers, 164

Three Paths to the Lake (Drei Wege zum See), 6, 76, 77, 86, 167, 171

Todesarten see *Ways of Death*

"Todesarten" Projekt, 9

Todesort (Place of Death), 152

To the Sun, 103, 146

Truly, 150, 181

Twilight, 98

A Type of Loss, 142

Under the Grapevine, 101

Undine Goes (Undine geht), 135, 150, 197, 204

Unter Mördern und Irren see *Among Murderers and Lunatics*

The Voice of History, 24

Die Wahrheit ist dem Menschen zumutbar see *People Can Face the Truth*

Was ich in Rom sah und hörte see *What I Saw and Heard in Rome*

Was wahr ist see *That Which Is True*

The Way Home, 147

Ways of Death (Todesarten) also trans. as *Death Styles,* 36, 64, 95, 97, 106, 108, 110, 112, 164, 171

We go, our hearts in the dust (Wir gehen, die Herzen im Staub), 184

Werke, 19, 132, 139, 148

What I Saw and Heard in Rome (Was ich in Rom sah und hörte), 61

What Shall I Call Myself? (Wie soll ich mich nennen?), 183, 184

What's True, 150

Wie soll ich mich nennen? see *What Shall I Call Myself?*

A Wildermuth, 203

Wir gehen, die Herzen im Staub see *We go, our hearts in the dust*
Wondrous Music (Die wunderliche Musik), 66, 73
Wood and Shavings, 140, 143
The Word Escapes You see *Dir entfällt das Wort*
"Wozu Gedichte," 148
The Writing Self, 147, 161
Youth in an Austrian Town (Jugend in einer österreichischen Stadt), 24, 190, 202
You Words, 150
Die Zikaden see *The Cicadas*
Bartsch, Kurt, 16, 78, 140
Bauer, Ludwig, 48
Baumann, Hans, 111
The Bavarian Film Award, 4
Beethoven, Ludwig van, 30
Bernhard, Thomas, 105, 189
   Heldenplatz, 105
Bettelheim, Bruno, 108
Bienek, Horst, 136
Birkenau, 110
Blake, William, 95
Boa, Elizabeth, 165
Bothner, Susanne, 147
Bottege Oscure, 151
Botz, Gerhard, 105
Boulez, Pierre, 30
Brack, Victor, 117
Brandt, Karl, 115, 116
Brecht, Bertolt, 5, 141, 149

Galilei, Galileo, 5
Broch, Hermann, 25

Carinthia (Kärnten), 106
Celan, Paul, 42, 139, 140, 155, 179, 181
Cixous, Hélène, 36
Conrad, Joseph, 95
   Heart of Darkness, 95
Cuba, 141

Dachau, 113
Defoe, Daniel, 48
   Robinson Crusoe, 47
Derrida, Jacques, 50, 53, 54, 162
   Grammatology, 162
   Heidegger's Ear. Philopolemology, 53
Dollfuß, Engelbert, 25, 27, 29

Eichberg, 115
Eichmann, Adolf, 33, 107
Egypt, 113
England, 145

Falkhauser, Dr., 115
Foucault, Michel, 126
France, 145
Frenkel, Ulrike, 15
Freud, Sigmund, 78, 109, 154
Funke, Horst Günter, 133

German Film Award, 4
Germany, 12, 25-32, 35, 36, 114, 117

Goethe, Johann Wolfgang von, 18, 78, 80, 145
  Deep Night, 79
  Faust, 77
  Iphigenie, 27
  Prometheus, 145
  Selige Sehnsucht, 18
Grafeneck Castle, 115, 116
Groddeck, Georg, 77-81, 83, 85, 86
  Book of the Es, 78
  On Vision, the World of the Eye and Seeing without Eyes, 77, 78
  Psychoanalytic Writings on Psychosomatic Medicine, 77
Group 47 (Gruppe 47), 106, 110, 139, 140
Gruppe 47 see Group 47
Günderode, Karoline von, 19

Hadamar, 115, 116
The Hague, 78
Halverson, Brigitte, 53, 55
Hamburg, 143
Hartheim, 113
Hartung, Rudolf, 135
Heidegger, Martin, 195
Heinrich, Margareta, 11
Henze, Hans Werner, 141
Hiroshima, 30
Hitler, Adolf, 28, 31, 105, 116, 117
Hofmannsthal, Hugo von, 9, 10, 25, 27
  Andreas oder die Vereinigten, 10
  Austrian Idea (Die österreichische Idee), 27
  Die Frau ohne Schatten, 10
  Die österreichische Idee see *Austrian Idea*
Hohenstaufen, 116
Hölderlin, Friedrich, 19, 145, 190
Holeschofsky, Irene, 86
Huppert, Isabelle, 4, 15-17, 19

Irrsee, 115
Israel, 33

Jahresring, 148
Jameson, Frederic, 164
Jelinek, Elfriede, 3, 5-7, 12, 13-14, 17, 19, 164
Jurgensen, Manfred, 147,

Kafka, Franz, 15, 42
  The Metamorphosis, 15
Kaiser, Joachim, 140
Klagenfurt, 32, 105, 117, 139, 166
Kl͏͏͏st, Heinrich von, 19
Klüger, Ruth, 17
Komar, Kathleen, 15, 16
Koschel/Weidenbaum, 9
Kristeva, Julia, 150
Krolow, Karl, 9

Lacan, Jacques, 125-127, 129, 154, 162, 164, 168, 169

Lennox, Sara, 24
Leonhard, Sigrun, 17
Lernet-Holenia, Alexander, 25, 28
Löffler, Sigrid, 9
Lublin, 116
Lynkeus, 140, 146, 155

Mayer, Hans, 9
Mayer, Peter, 142, 198
McAuley, James, 97
Meise, Helga, 68, 72
Milan, 202
Mitscherlich, A., 114
   Concerning Experiments of Female Prisoners. Concerning Later Injuries, 113
   The Death Doctors (Medizin ohne Menschlichkeit), 114
   Medizin ohne Menschlichkeit see *The Death Doctors*
Mörike, Eduard, 48, 49
   Gesang Weylas see *Weyla's Song,* 48
   Weyla's Song (Gesang Weylas), 48
Moscow, 28
Mozart, Wolfgang Amadeus, 30
Musil, Robert, 60, 62, 66, 133
   The Man without Qualities, 60, 62
Mussolini, Benito, 29
Myshkin, 142, 149

de Nerval, Gérard, 150
Neue Deutsche Hefte, 9
Niendorf, 141
Nuremberg, 105, 113-115, 117

Plath, Sylvia, 179
Poland, 110
Prince, Morton, 10
   The Dissociation of Personality, 10

Rank, Otto, 108, 109
   Beyond Psychology, 108
Reclams Filmführer, 4
Reich-Ranicki, Marcel, 9, 76, 86
Richter, Hans Werner, 139, 141
Riefenstahl, Leni, 105
   Triumph of the Will, 105
Rome, 92 116, 192, 197
Roth, Joseph, 25

Salzburg, 84
Sauerland, Karol, 110
Schardt, 9
Schnitzler, Arthur, 25
   Reigen, 153
Schöne Müllerin, 19
Schroeter, Werner, 3-7, 11-19
Schumann, Dr., 115
Schuschnigg, Kurt von, 25, 27
Schwarzer, Alice, 15
   Emma, 15
Seiderer, Ute, 3
Sender Rot-Weiß-Rot, 139
de Serbine-Bahrawy, Lisa, 24-

27, 32, 36
Sexton, Anne, 179
Shakespeare, William, 51
    Hamlet, 52, 53, 54, 55
    The Merchant of Venice, 51
    The Murder of Gonzago, 52
Sicily, 116
Soviet Union, 28
Spiegel, 140
Strauß, Johann, 30
Svandrlik, Rita, 142
Swiderska, Malgorzata, 60, 61
Switzerland, 33

Thomas, Dylan, 184
Trakl, Georg 18
    Grodek, 18

Ungaretti, Giuseppe 139, 152
U.S.A., 30, 33

Venice, 196
Vienna, 2, 26, 27, 29-33, 80,
    81, 105, 110, 140-141, 146,
    197, 200

Vivaldi, Antonio, 30
Völker-Hezel, Barbara, 6
Volksdienst, 115

Wagner, Richard, 18
Waldheim, Kurt, 28
Walcka-Kawalska, Alicja, 110
Warsaw, 111
Webern, Anton, 31
Weigel, Sigrid, 162
Weininger, Otto, 108
    Sex and Character
        (*Geschlecht und
        Charakter*), 108
White, Hayden, 118
Wiesenthal, Simon, 110
Wirsing, Sibylle, 9
Wittgenstein, Ludwig, 18, 188,
    189
Wolf, Christa, 180

Young, James, 107

Die Zeit, 15

Ariadne Press
Studies

Major Figures of
Modern Austrian Literature
Edited by Donald G. Daviau

Major Figures of Austrian Literature
The Interwar Years 1918-1938
Edited by Donald G. Daviau

Major Figures of Turn-of-the-Century
Austrian Literature
Edited by Donald G. Daviau

Austrian Writers and the Anschluss
Understanding the Past –
Overcoming the Past
Edited by Donald G. Daviau

Austria in the Thirties
Culture and Politics
Edited by Kenneth Segar
and John Warren

Austria, 1938 - 1988
Anschluss and Fifty Years
Edited by William E. Wright

Jura Soyfer and His Time
Edited by Donald G. Daviau

Rilke's Duino Elegies
Edited by R.Paulin & P.Hutchinson

Stefan Zweig
An International Bibliography
By Randolph A. Klawiter

Franz Karka
A Writer's Life
By Joachim Unseld

Kafka and Language: In the
Stream of Thoughts and Life
By G. von Natzmer Cooper

Of Reason and Love
The Life and Works of Marie
von Ebner-Eschenbach
By Carl Steiner

Marie von Ebner-Eschenbach
The Victory of a Tenacious Will
By Doris M. Klostermaier

"What People Call Pessimism"
Freud, Schnitzler and the 19th-
Century Controversy at the University
of Vienna Medical School
By Mark Luprecht

Arthur Schnitzler and Politics
By Adrian Clive Roberts

Structures of Disintegration
Narrative Strategies in Elias
Canetti's Die Blendung
By David Darby

Blind Reflections
Gender in Canetti's Die Blendung
By Kristie A. Foell

Robert Musil and the Tradition
of the German Novelle
By Kathleen O'Connor

Implied Dramaturgy
Robert Musil and the Crisis of
Modern Drama
By Christian Rogowsky